M000093493

Sharecropping, Ghetto, Slum

Sharecropping, Ghetto, Slum

A History of Impoverished Blacks in Twentieth-Century America

H. Viscount Nelson Jr.

“Perpetrators may choose not to remember
but the aggrieved never forget”

—H Viscount Nelson Jr.

Copyright © 2015 by H. Viscount Nelson Jr.

Library of Congress Control Number:		2015908791
ISBN:	Hardcover	978-1-5035-7495-3
	Softcover	978-1-5035-7494-6
	eBook	978-1-5035-7493-9

All rights reserved. No part of this book may be reproduced or transmitted in any form or by any means, electronic or mechanical, including photocopying, recording, or by any information storage and retrieval system, without permission in writing from the copyright owner.

Any people depicted in stock imagery provided by Thinkstock are models, and such images are being used for illustrative purposes only.
Certain stock imagery © Thinkstock.

Print information available on the last page.

Rev. date: 07/21/2015

To order additional copies of this book, contact:
Xlibris
1-888-795-4274
www.Xlibris.com
Orders@Xlibris.com

712313

CONTENTS

Preface ix

Acknowledgements xi

Introduction xiii

Chapter 1: Sharecropping and Brutality: Nineteenth-Century Legacies 1

Chapter 2: Jim Crow and the Early Progressive Era 1900–1910 16

Chapter 3: The Late Progressive Era 1910–1920 32

Chapter 4: Travail of the 1920s: An Era of Contradiction 48

Chapter 5: The Great Depression 64

Chapter 6: The World War II Decade 81

Chapter 7: From Ghetto to Slum: Urban Black America at a Crossroad 98

Chapter 8: The Quixotic Revolution of the 1960s 115

Chapter 9: The Regression Decade of the 1970s 133

Chapter 10: Abandonment: The 1980s 150

Chapter 11: Lost and Forlorn: The 1990s 168

Epilogue 185

Notes 193

Bibliography 251

Index 271

Preface

"Our people are peculiar. We are judged by our lower class while others are judged by their upper class."

These insightful words stated during the 1930s by Rev. Richard Robert Wright Jr. spoke to a twentieth-century reality that white Americans held toward the nation's black citizenry. African Americans of higher station resented being judged by the less successful members of the race. After the civil rights movement of the 1960s, class distinctions between African Americans became increasingly significant. With the legal demise of racial discrimination, scores of ambitious blacks who embraced middle-class values took advantage of newly created opportunities to enter mainstream America. Ambitious African Americans who coveted a higher standard of living displayed a quest for higher education, presented evidence of a strong work ethic, and endorsed the concept of deferred gratification. Yet as this nascent black bourgeoisie expanded in size and scope, a significant number of African Americans failed to take advantage of civil rights gains and remained impoverished. A logical question concerning the reason for long-standing African American poverty—white racism versus black ineptness—would be asked to explain the desultory condition of the indigent masses. Intra-racial class concerns that Reverend Wright raised eventually became addressed from a middle-class black perspective. On May 17, 2004, entertainer Bill Cosby shook the foundations of African American society at Constitution Hall in Washington, DC, when he derided lower-class blacks for being woefully irresponsible and the primary reason for their debased condition. Cosby criticized black parents for neglecting child-rearing responsibilities and condemned the African American masses for displaying a lack of interest in education and promoting a culture that had pejorative consequences for black youth. Professor Michael Eric Dyson spoke with equal disdain about intra-racial divisions, but he directed his venom toward Cosby. In an anti-Cosby diatribe entitled *Is Bill Cosby Right? Or Has the Black Middle Class Lost Its Mind?* Dyson excoriated Cosby, and blamed the entertainer for conducting a "Blame-the-Poor Tour." Throughout the book, Dyson vehemently attacked Cosby and accused him of being disingenuous, hypocritical, and making erroneous statements that inappropriately demeaned disadvantaged African Americans.

Bill Cosby could hardly be perceived as the first successful African American to raise questions about the mannerisms, impropriety, and cultural malaise displayed by lower-class blacks. Indeed, one may assume that the majority of accomplished African Americans have difficulty understanding why the so-called black underclass fervently rejects standard middle-class norms. "Reasonable" African Americans, after all, should know that improper diction, anti-intellectualism, perceived slothfulness, and public displays of boisterous, asocial behavior doom the negative purveyors of black culture to marginalization, perpetual penury, and a dismal future.

Cosby and members of the black bourgeoisie and elite would also have queries about the lower-class propensity for hedonism. Rather than practice momentary deprivation to create a base for a propitious future as pronounced in the Protestant ethic, the masses embraced the cliché derived from Ecclesiastes 8:15 that advise people to "eat, drink, and be merry" prior to impending doom. Thus, pride in work and disdain for indolence seem absent and inconsequential for many who comprise the impoverished black masses. An inquiry, therefore, must be raised to explain why a disproportionably large segment of the African American population appears phlegmatic and pessimistic rather than energetic and hopeful. Bill Cosby and Michael Eric Dyson, two obviously successful men, present antithetical opinions on where to place blame for the lowly status of the African American masses. This writer contends that history will prove Cosby and Dyson to be right, wrong, and, regrettably, simplistic.

Bill Cosby, a native Philadelphian, functioned as a catalyst for this book being written. Moreover, Professor Dyson taught in the city's premier institution, the University of Pennsylvania, when he published the anti-Cosby diatribe. Therefore, it would seem appropriate that the City of Brotherly Love would be used occasionally as the locale for evidence that provides enlightenment on the condition of the black masses. Readers will have to ascertain whether the information provided endorses Cosby or Dyson. The reader should also understand that omissions, questionable interpretations, or errors in judgment in regard to this study rest solely with this author rather than with the men who stimulated this discussion.

H. Viscount "Berky" Nelson
Los Angeles, California

Acknowledgements

Scores of people, wittingly or unwittingly, are responsible for ideas contained in *Sharecropping, Ghetto, Slum.* First, I have been inspired by those who worked extremely hard as farmers, janitors, and unskilled laborers of every dimension, who performed backbreaking work to care for themselves and their families. These nameless people, ironically, cause one to wonder why the impoverished who have the opportunity to hold jobs refrain from soliciting employment; historically, a strong work ethic provided dignity and respect for those who were gainfully employed.

Adulation may also be extended to the late, industrious Janet Brown, a white UCLA administrator who inspired students from disadvantaged backgrounds to reach their potential as future leaders. Janet represented those unsung educators who understood the reluctance of those from impoverished origins to become patient, engage in hard work, and understand the benefits derived from deferred gratification. Similar appreciation could be bestowed to the late Chester Earhart, a friend, mentor, and a self-respecting white janitor employed in the public schools of Oxford, Pennsylvania. If Brown and Earhart could be cloned, demonstrate the advantages of intra-racial friendship, and be used to convey the pleasure derived from hard work, life for the underachieving and indolent would improve significantly.

I would also like to thank those who offered constructive criticism on the manuscript. The time and effort spent on reviewing this book by professors Elliott Barkan, Rick Tuttle, John Belalovick, and Cary Wintz has proven invaluable. Suggestions provided by these scholars certainly enhanced the quality of this study, sharpening the analysis and enhancing the writing to make the book more comprehensible. Ms. Doris Najera also deserves special recognition for providing me with invaluable computer support.

Special thanks must be extended to my late relatives who provided excellent examples of the successes and advantages derived from hard work. My great-aunt and uncle Elsie and Lewis Cornish and my great-aunt Sadie Fernanders deserve special mention. I am also beholden to my late father H. Viscount Nelson Sr. who impressed me with the joys derived from performing manual labor. Thanks must also be extended to my late father- and mother-in-law, Mr.

and Mrs. William, and Mildred Ricks, who worked hard and served as positive, loving role models for whom I have the most profound, endearing fondness. The same can be said of my partner, Marcia C. Mills. Marcia has offered comfort, encouragement, and patience so that the laborious tasks of research and writing could be completed. At the time of this writing, I am also most fortunate to have my mother, Leanna Nelson Johnson, who has reached the century mark in age with sound mind and body.

INTRODUCTION

Any scholar seeking to address and explain objectively reasons for the omnipresent and long-standing historical problems encountered by indigent African Americans faces an arduous and daunting task. Unlike all other Americans, the African forbearers entered the New World involuntarily as slaves. From colonial times an immediate line of demarcation, therefore, could be drawn between the experiences of voluntary white immigrants and black slaves. Aside from race, certain aspects of American culture have been aligned against impoverished blacks since the inception of the first white settlers who came to America. European immigrants who voluntarily ventured to the New World contained ADHD[1] traits, exemplified by people who were ambitious, industrious, and intrepid risk takers who made the nation great. The Founding Fathers, imbued with humanism derived from the French Enlightenment, broadened the positive colonial spirit with the adage that all men are created equal. Consequently, those who achieved success rendered attribution to being more industrious than those who failed. Devoid of sensitivity toward the poor, successful people showed disdain toward those individuals ensconced in poverty, a sentiment that still exists in contemporary society. Thus, if the wealthier classes of Americans seem indifferent to the plight of poor people regardless of race, creed, or color, impoverished blacks receive blame personally for ineptitude and incompetence. While the public may believe equal opportunity exists, this study not only intends to refute the claim on equanimity but also demonstrates that the reasons for black poverty are multifaceted.

When reflecting on the black experience in the United States, certain thoughts about the proverbial glass being half full come to mind. In a positive sense, some among a race of people transported from Africa to America in chains and subjected to the most heinous degradation as slaves gained national prominence and acclaim within a few generations after the demise of the "peculiar institution." By the end of the twentieth century, an elite class of scholars, social leaders, athletes, diplomats, politicians, entertainers, and entrepreneurs appeared as an integral part of the nation's political, social,

1 ADHD is an abbreviation for attention deficit/hyperactivity disorder

and economic fabric. But for those blacks unfamiliar with success and progress and mired in a continuous cycle of poverty, the American experience seldom elicited a positive impression. Rather than envisioning the United States as a land where equal opportunity prevailed, low-income, impoverished African Americans only experienced the sordid history of a demeaned and despised race castigated as being inferior and devoid of hope. At best, these most unfortunate blacks could only focus on daily survival and, after death, aspire to a better life in heaven.

Given the American penchant for glorifying the nation's heritage and those who achieved individual success, the poor generally and impoverished African Americans in particular have been ignored. Understandably, political, social, and economic heroes like George Washington, Jane Addams, and John D. Rockefeller among whites, and blacks like Barack Obama, Martin Luther King Jr., and Oprah Winfrey receive and deserve national recognition. But those counted among the unlettered masses—and in this case specifically African Americans—have a story that must be told. US history textbooks contain information about slavery, the peculiar institution, Reconstruction, and the civil rights era. Despite dire conditions and continuous endeavors to survive in a hostile environment longer than any immigrants who came to American shores, scores of African Americans rose from degradation and poverty to attain extraordinary success. Nevertheless, questions must still be raised to explain why a sizeable, underachieving, African American underclass continues to exist in the United States.

While the American propensity for optimism explains why lowly blacks remain overlooked and ignored by pundits, this omission fails to explain adequately the reasons for the increasing void between haves and have-nots in black America. Most whites cling dearly to middle-class values and encompass the Protestant ethic, endorse the concept of deferred gratification, and consequently look forward to a bountiful future. Therefore, successful European Americans would find that a negative, fatalistic view toward life acceptable to a downtrodden, defeated black populous difficult to comprehend. Contrary to Stephan and Abigail Thernstrom's contention in the optimistic tome *America in Black and White* that the majority of African Americans are middle class, a decidedly different perspective exists for those who fail to identify with the black bourgeoisie. Thus, a disproportionate number of African Americans reside in urban slums, experience higher rates of unemployment, and are more likely to be reluctant participants in the prison-industrial complex than any corresponding percentage of low-income white Americans.

When W. E. B. Du Bois avowed in *The Philadelphia Negro* that a "talented tenth" of prominent blacks existed in the United States in 1898, he inadvertently implied that nine of every ten African Americans could be classified, by varyingly degrees, as being something other than members of the black elite.

Since blacks remained on the periphery of middle-class American society throughout most, if not the entire twentieth century, those who comprised the less successful majority more accurately represented black life in the United States. Therefore, we should know far more about the struggling nine-tenths of those who comprise the less than "talented" African American majority than the dazzling achievements recorded by the prominent black elite.

Given the opportunity to achieve middle-class standing in the aftermath of the successful civil rights movement approximately two generations after Du Bois' publication, the size of the black bourgeoisie increased exponentially. Scores of African Americans seized upon the opportunity to become better educated, acquire prestigious jobs, and reside in comfortable neighborhoods. A "talented fifth" emerged. Blacks who acquired fame became renowned throughout the entire United States and gained greater significance than famous predecessors. Acclaimed national heroes, such as Frederick Douglass, Joe Louis, and Walter White, hardly compare with Martin Luther King Jr., Tiger Woods, or Barack Obama, individuals who successfully competed with or surpassed whites in gaining national and international recognition.

But for every prominent contemporary leader, scores of black men and women functioned marginally on the cusp of survival. Disproportionally more blacks, with the possible exception of indigenous Americans and recent immigrants, appear to occupy the lowest rung in American society. Dysfunctional family life, unwed impoverished girls giving birth to babies, anti-intellectualism among teenage boys, a preponderance of drug addiction, endorsement of gangs and criminal elements, scores of incarcerated young men, and disdain for what may be deemed appropriate middle-class values represent the low-income black condition in contemporary society.

The dearth of success evidenced by a significant number of African Americans appears particularly galling given successful civil rights efforts that redressed past grievances attributed to racism. The features contained in the Great Society mandates presented by President Johnson, affirmative action programs initiated by President Nixon, and attempts by President Clinton to address African American concerns suggest that blacks have received attention from American leadership. And yet since 1970, fortunes for many African Americans deteriorated. Accelerated numbers of young black men on probation, parole, or in prison, glorification of a rebellious hip-hop culture, and disdain for academically inclined children castigated for "acting white" places the younger generation of African Americans at extreme peril.

When compared to obstacles faced by African American forbearers, the current generation of black youths seemed blessed. Overt white brutalization toward blacks, characterized by murder and intimidation, no longer exists with absolute impunity. A constant reminder of racial inferiority prevalent in the media or proclaimed by stumping politicians has receded or passed. Black successes figure prominently on television through sports heroes who endorse commercial products, entertainment stars featured on BET, and politicians seeking black endorsement regarding positions in local, state, and federal government. Evidence also abounds demonstrating that African Americans have achieved enormous successes, implying that most underprivileged blacks should derive encouragement from prominent members of the race and thereby strive for individual success.

Despite purported opportunities evident during the second half of the twentieth century, a significant number of low-income African Americans avoided becoming amalgamated into the larger society. A conscious (or unconscious) disregard for mainstream culture may be observed in the dialect and speaking patterns of low-income African American youths. For example, television, as a low-cost entertainment medium, functioned as the primary means through which domestic citizens and foreign-born immigrants hear "proper" English spoken. Virtually all television programs, regardless of content or quality, present people who speak mainstream English. While foreign-language-speaking immigrants used television to enhance their proficiency in English, many black Americans maintained speaking patterns, accents, and word usage that are distinctly unique and invariably incorrect. Indeed, black youths seem to prefer speaking in dialect (identified by the term *Ebonics*) and using language inflections outside the purview of normal discourse. Double negatives, speech laced with profanity, and idiomatic expressions that purposefully and pejoratively differentiated African Americans from the larger American society appeared common among inner-city black youths. Unlike immigrant children intent on learning the language for functional purposes, blacks refused or seemed incapable of "code switching" and using "proper" English. Moreover, black youths chastised peers for using proper diction, studying hard in school, and, thus, "acting white." This desire to maintain black cultural norms inimical to enhancing prospects for middle-class status and gaining economic success requires an explanation.

A significant number of contemporary African Americans reside below the poverty line and demonstrate little inclination to pursue a future based on standard middle-class norms. Dissimilar forms of verbal expression, questionable attitudes toward formal education, unique choices in wearing apparel, and other factors that may be deemed inappropriate enable mainstream Americans to identify disadvantaged blacks. Numerous factors can be identified to explain the long-standing, sordid condition of impoverished African Americans residing in the United States. This endeavor, however, limits the investigation to four identifiable areas that rendered class elevation for low-income African Americans impossible. First, of course, the residual effects of racism must be considered. Racism, with roots dating back to colonial America, placed those of African ancestry at greater disadvantage than other immigrants who migrated to American shores. Second, uncontrollable circumstances having nothing to do with racism undermine prospects for black amelioration. For example, a constantly evolving capitalistic economy rendered certain jobs obsolete, minimizing the need for unskilled wage laborers. A third explanation for the continued existence of an African American underclass may be attributed to an indifferent or self-serving black leadership. Middle-class civil rights advocates maintained bourgeois interests and eschewed toiling for the "undeserving" black masses. Finally, recognizing that low-income blacks, like all Americans, enjoy the right to exercise free will, some counted among the marginalized, underprivileged masses occasionally make erroneous decisions. These mistakes render class elevation impossible and keep less fortunate members of the race mired in poverty.

Few could suggest that prospects for the success of underprivileged, contemporary African Americans are improving. Urban public schools with a preponderance of low-income, inner-city black attendees fail to prepare students for the demands of a postindustrial society. Instead, lessons learned in the streets appear to have greater influence on impressionistic youths than formal classroom settings. Unfortunately, blacks influenced by the repugnant aspects of life and those emulating criminal behavior endorse a lifestyle without redeeming social value. And contrary to the customary American practice of having a male provide for the family, the irresponsibility of many black men perpetuates the continuation of latchkey children residing in a female-headed household.

Currently too many black males shuck, jive, hustle, and live in the present without developing plans that could contribute to a propitious future. Survival skills attained in the streets prove insufficiently transferable to generate wealth legally, stabilize the black family, or create a genuine sense of well-deserved confidence. Posturing demonstrated by vacuous attempts at manhood, a misguided sense of bravado, and unwarranted demands for respect from black peers often contributed to physical confrontation and, occasionally, a violent death. The destructive characteristics and lifestyle omnipresent among African Americans residing in inner-city slums prevents black men from having a positive impact on the black community.

At the risk of being redundant, this work focuses on African Americans who either self-identify as being marginalized or exist in the mind-set of "established Americans" on the periphery of American society. Distinctions attributed to residential neighborhood, a questionable value system, low-income employment, fanciful attire, irreverent language nuances, fatalism, limited ambition, dysfunctional families, and a failure to envision education as a means to achieve upward mobility represent those who characterize the indigent, lower-class masses. Given the harsh experiences of African Americans in the United States, only one, or a combination of these factors, could relegate or mire blacks individually or collectively into the lower class.

Finally, and perhaps most significantly, this study intends to offer an objective discussion on the role played by African American women throughout the course of the century. Often functioning as the single provider for children or the family breadwinner, black women faced enormous obstacles and still enabled their progeny to survive. Functioning under the duality of discrimination based on race and gender, we must explore how these damaging affronts negatively impacted low-income African Americans. We must also ascertain how the child-rearing practices of African American females, influenced by the marginalization of poverty, contributed to the desultory conduct and asocial behavior of low-income black boys and men.

A major difficulty encountered by this author existed in the tendency to be judgmental. At present, thousands of undocumented immigrants come to the United States and find work. While the employment available is arduous and offers little in remuneration, migrants with a strong work effort from Latin America, Asia, the West Indies, and Africa still enter the United States and, against all odds, thrive. The desperation evident in the migrants' country of origins compels newcomers to risk life and limb, keeping in mind that prospects for a better future exist in the United States. Impoverished, native born Americans, however, appear more content than migrants from other countries. Entitlements like Social Security, welfare, food stamps, and potentially Obamacare guaranteed to American citizens eliminate the life-and-death struggle for survival encountered by immigrants. Therefore, low-income blacks, like other Americans, enjoyed options to eschew disagreeable work, knowing that survival was assured. In the streets of Los Angeles native blacks and whites appear more likely to beg than people who live in the United States without documentation.

Throughout the discourse of this book the four aforementioned themes will be used to explain why a significant number of African Americans failed to acquire middle-class standing and remained in poverty. Although racism existed as the primary cause for underachieving African Americans prior to the civil rights movement of the 1960s, limiting factors that kept thousands of African Americans ensconced in poverty during the last half of the twentieth century are varied and complex. Nevertheless, with this new century, a black subculture still exists that abhors bourgeois norms and appears restrictive and self-destructive. Perseverance and industry appear lacking among a black populace unable to think constructively about a propitious future. By focusing initially on the rural South and then to metropolitan areas outside Dixie, this book endeavors to explain why the disadvantaged African American masses failed to achieve success during the twentieth century in a country that became the wealthiest and most powerful nation in the world.

Sharecropping, Ghetto, Slum is hardly a definitive study on disadvantaged African Americans. Instead, this endeavor merely intends to present ideas, raise questions, and reveal answers that explain the trials and tribulations encountered by thousands of disadvantaged African Americans who have failed to attain the American Dream. Some are victims who faced obstacles that proved impossible to transcend. Eager, but unable to find suitable work, many succumbed to the vicissitudes of poverty and generational unemployment attributed to the accident of being born at the wrong place and time to imperfect parents. Others purposely decided to rely on luck or decided to survive without engaging in manual labor by willfully accepting a mundane lifestyle derived from state and federal largess. Collectively, all African Americans have suffered under some degree of racism. And for the downtrodden and angry a seething hatred exists. Historically, the descendants of white perpetrators choose not to remember the past but the aggrieved blacks never forget. Obviously, omissions and faulty reasoning may be found in this interpretive work. The shortcomings and faults in this study are entirely mine.

The is book is dedicated to my belated, loving wife,

Joan Kathleen Ricks Nelson

Chapter 1

Sharecropping and Brutality: Nineteenth-Century Legacies

In many respects, black experiences in the South during the post–Civil War era—the thirty-five years between 1865 and 1900 where the majority of African Americans resided—might have proved more arduous for the African American masses than slavery. As chattel, black people were property, a valued commodity needed to be fed, nursed, housed, and protected. Masters saw value in the most irascible of slaves and would protect and defend their "property" against whites who sought "corrective action" and retribution from a disrespectful bondsman. With the veil of slavery lifted after the Civil War, however, a master's protection disappeared. Thus, the late nineteenth century proved extremely repressive for blacks, as dispirited, insecure, angry, impoverished whites of a defeated South projected their frustration upon manumitted African Americans. This era represented an unfortunate period of time that embittered blacks, undermined prospects for amicable race relations, and established precedents that would have negative consequences for African Americans throughout the twentieth century.

Blacks certainly welcomed freedom and would be disinclined to return to slavery. With the yoke of servile oppression purportedly lifted, blacks savored breathing free air. Freedmen intended to provide for their families, sought economic success, interacted constructively with black peers, and hopefully earned grudging respect from white Southerners. On some occasions blacks even participated in lynch mobs against fellow race members charged with committing capital offenses.[1] This era also marked a time when former slaves and free people of color searched to find meaning in their lives and prepared for a propitious future.[2] Unfortunately, the African American quest for recognition and respect occurred simultaneously with Southern whites' desire to negate any semblance of black dignity and independence. Harassed at every turn and abused when signs of material success occurred, only foolhardy African Americans displayed hostility toward whites and projected a sense of personal pride and confidence.

Only the most progressive white Southerners feared that extremely harsh circumstances awaited recently freed African Americans. With the universal sense of black inferiority maintained by virtually all white Americans, a paternalistic, superior white race decided upon a "virtuous" course of action in regard to recently freed African Americans. White people believed they had the obligation to dominate and control blacks to the benefit of the entire nation. Few would argue with Southern apologist George Fitzhugh who declared that white guidance was necessary to keep blacks from perishing and disappearing from the face of the earth. Fitzhugh also spoke for thoughtful white Southerners when he contended that "a great deal of severe legislation will be required to compel Negroes to labor as much as they should . . ." In addition, a white Union army officer was equally prophetic when he addressed freedmen and said, "You may have a harder time . . . than ever before; it will be the price you pay for your freedom."[3]

Fitzhugh's opinions held veracity for paternalistic white Southerners of that era. White Americans generally believed the Negro to be lazy, being satisfied to perform menial odd jobs to purchase "a little food," enjoy a life of leisure, and, when possible, remain idle.[4] Furthermore, Fitzhugh and others presented the convenient argument that high wages would "spoil" black workers, creating complacency that would be disadvantageous to the Negro. But with equal aplomb, pragmatic whites realized that the lazy Negro would prove inimical to a society dependent upon cheap black labor necessary for preserving customary Southern norms. Decisions proffered to make the freedman useful would have far-reaching consequences that operated to the detriment of African Americans, confining a majority of blacks to a state of continuous penury.

Fitzhugh's thinking became implemented during Reconstruction, when Southerners reinstituted "Black Codes" to control African Americans socially and politically and force freedmen into doing the economic bidding of the Southern white establishment.[5] Without the legal means for blacks to maintain duly authorized rights, the codes proved instrumental in restoring what whites perceived as the proper order for the "Reconstructed South." Several Southern states decided idle blacks—those without written proof of having a job—could be deemed vagrants and, therefore, criminals. These unfortunate freedmen became subjected to vagrancy laws that, as anthropologist Gunnar Myrdal noted, "forced the Negro into situations where he would be under the controlled supervision of his former master or other white men who were ready and willing to exploit his labor."[6] As blacks suffered grievously at the hands of mean-spirited Southern whites, the draconian measures exemplified in the Black Codes caused freedmen to become more threatened by vengeful whites.

During the existence of the peculiar institution, masters bore responsibility for "correcting" slaves. When slavery ended, however, white Southern vigilantes violently coerced blacks by capriciously applying new legal strictures to intimidate and control the African American populace.

In order to establish hegemony over the region after Reconstruction, the devastated, embittered, economically insecure Southern white elite created a nefarious economic wage system known as sharecropping. Recognizing that the overwhelming majority of Southern-bred African Americans remained ignorant and had limited economic options, white landowners and merchants struck a corrupt bargain with the freedmen. Since ambitious blacks sought to acquire land and become independent farmers, whites with means encouraged or forced former slaves to become tenants on white-owned farms and plantations. In return for food, shelter, and farm supplies, blacks (as well as unfortunate, impoverished whites) worked to produce a crop sold at the behest of the landholding creditor. Because the creditors could manipulate the value of the crop to the disadvantage of the sharecropper, black farm laborers remained poor, powerless, and wedded to the land.[7]

With ownership of a crop entirely in the hands of creditors, the sharecropper lacked bargaining power. The value of the harvested crop and the debt accrued for food, clothing, shelter, and farm equipment depended entirely upon the creditors' caprice. By undervaluing a harvest and maintaining high costs for rent and provisions, unprincipled landlords and merchants kept black sharecroppers mired in debt. The freedom and financial independence that African Americans coveted became illusionary. Sharecropping confined generations of African Americans to a life of unmitigated poverty and crushed the hopes of emancipated slaves and their progeny until the Second World War.[8] Evidence of the debased condition of a black man shackled by the grossly unfair economic system appeared as a forlorn Negro who labored incessantly for forty-five years ruefully complained about "beginning with nothing and still having nothing."[9]

Ironically, blacks forced into sharecropping also experienced penury because of an aversion to working collectively. Eager to avoid laboring in gangs that seemed reminiscent of plantation slave crews, black men sought to acquire a sense of autonomy by being their "own boss." Attributes inherent in the independent yeoman farmer permeated the consciousness of black freedmen, as tenants and sharecroppers worked singularly or collectively solely within the nuclear family. An additional rationale for sharecroppers desiring to work alone evolved from the sense that each person could be held accountable for the work produced. Therefore, the individual or family received pay according to personal initiative and productivity rather than dividing profits equally with less industrious workers.[10]

When white landowners and managers recognized the futility in trying to impose work gangs on freedmen, the advantages of having blacks labor within the singular family unit became evident. White men realized that landownership represented economic independence for blacks. Therefore, white agrarian capitalists deftly enticed black men and their families to work farms and plantations, keeping in mind that few would be allowed to become independent landowners. Furthermore, cautious whites feared fledgling black landowners would seek to have a political voice to enhance prospects for social equality. Black landownership, therefore, became anathema to former slave owners intent on maintaining dominance over African Americans in the New South.

Prominent African American leaders like Civil War veteran major Martin Delaney, a physician who studied at the Harvard Medical School, recognized the anxiety black sharecroppers faced during implementation of this unique landlord/tenant relationship. Delaney endorsed the idea of the singular, black tenant family participating in a shared system involving Northern capitalists, Southern landlords, and African American labor.[11] To combat excessive charges avaricious whites imposed on black tenants, Delaney created a Freedman's Cotton Agency to enable profits to accrue to the workers rather than white speculators. Delaney's eagerness to have blacks laboring on farms to participate in this triple alliance, however, proved short lived. Angry white merchants exerted pressure successfully to terminate the agency, resulting in disillusionment for Delaney and continuous poverty for blacks who labored on Southern farmlands. Similar enterprises designed to enable black workers to extricate themselves from poverty and become financially solvent were also undermined by the white power structure of the South.[12]

With the failure of the Delaney plan, domineering white landlords made certain that black tenants would never receive sufficient funds on "settlement day" (when creditors and debtors met to square accounts) to become economically self-sufficient. Illiterate blacks lacked the ability to refute itemized deductions from earnings. But equally significant, blacks who could read and write refrained from challenging the landlord or merchant. Questioning the integrity of white landowners and merchants proved particularly dangerous. Extreme peril, possibly death, awaited blacks who overtly challenged the landlord's accounting system in the New South.[13] In fact, the deaths of Willie Holcombe and Henry Kirkland of North Carolina and Alabama, respectively, occurred during the 1890s because blacks who questioned the veracity of white accounting procedures acted "uppity" and threatened the sharecropping system. Intimidating practices, consequently, caused black sharecroppers to remain mute and accrue greater debt year after year.

In addition to using sharecroppers as a cheap labor force, Southern whites also made certain that the oppressive labor system would keep blacks subservient. White Southerners insisted that proper decorum—unquestioned obedience to former masters and deference rendered to all whites—must be maintained at all costs. Black farmers who demonstrated outward signs of prosperity by painting their home or appearing well-dressed could receive some form of "correction." Beatings, killings, and other illicit actions were applied liberally to keep blacks on the land and in their place. A disgruntled black man from Texas declared, "They still thinks the negro (sic) ought to work for them for nothing and like it. Well, we do, and they make us like it too."[14]

Armed white ruffians took the law into their hands and used "legal procedures" to make certain blacks remained passive and compliant. Sworn officers required to uphold the rule of law not only ignored this responsibility in regard to blacks, but also used the law unfairly to threaten, maim, and kill "offending" African Americans. Any evidence of black success provoked white resentment. Jealous whites destroyed well-kept black homes, stole money, and confiscated the property of financially successful African Americans with impunity. These "lessons" could hardly be forgotten by African Americans residing in the New South.

In addition to the debasement black farm laborers received from callous, avaricious whites, sharecroppers faced another perennial problem—the inconstancy of Mother Nature. Insects, droughts, and other factors that damaged crops rendered prospects for success and independence more arduous. When a crop fell short of expectations, the already-indebted sharecropper became reduced to peonage. Unable to vacate the land until debts were paid, opportunities to obtain a better life became not only dashed but doomed.

Black quests for a better future were also hindered by the favorable treatment accorded impecunious white peers. Poor whites also suffered under the degradation of sharecropping. But unlike blacks, white sharecroppers enjoyed far more leeway in challenging the system. White laborers who questioned the limited financial recompense for annual labor enjoyed far greater latitude in defying landlords than African American counterparts. White tenants also received more money and took greater liberties for services rendered. "Settlin' up" day, and the manner in which the African American sharecroppers responded to the meager pay and increased debt to the landlord, had life-or-death consequences for blacks. White workers, however, could contest the final monetary settlement with relative impunity. Understandably, white landowners preferred passive blacks to less obedient white "croppers." A landowner from Alabama spoke candidly about race and labor when he declared, "Give me Negroes every time. I wouldn't have a low-down white tenant on my place. You can get work out of any Negro if you know how to handle him; but there are some white men who won't work and can't be driven, because they are white."[15] Thus, blacks acquired the unheralded recognition as being the preferable race to be used and abused efficaciously by the white Southern agrarians.

Black farm laborers who attained economic independence proved the exception rather than the rule. But economically successful African Americans also recognized that visible wealth could thrust them into leadership positions that would raise suspicion from white people intent on maintaining control over the black population. Those who acquired land and wealth, therefore, found it expedient to dissociate from the landless, impecunious African American laborers. Only members of the Colored Farmers' Alliance remained steadfast in support of the laboring black masses.[16] Moreover, unlike impoverished, industrious whites who worked hard and attained higher status with universal approval, blacks who endeavored to ameliorate their condition experienced alienation from racial peers. Indeed, mutual intra-racial alienation between moderately wealthy and poor blacks enhanced prospects for a class divide between African Americans.[17] Despite the success of exceptional African Americans, intra-racial solidarity proved difficult, if not impossible, to achieve.

Another appreciable factor that suggested blacks should be treated with greater respect in the agrarian South appeared in high values former slaves ascribed to education. While poor whites rarely displayed a quest for education, desires of black males and females to become literate became legendary. During and after the Civil War, white progressives of the North displayed a profound interest in educating former slaves. Eventually, Northerners and Southerners, blacks and whites, founded hundreds of schools throughout the South to hasten the assimilation of manumitted slaves into the larger American society.[18] One of the noblest undertakings to provide education for all races denied an education occurred in Mississippi. Recently freed slave George Washington Albright initiated the movement to have public education funded by the state. For freedmen previously denied the opportunity to become learned, acquiring an education represented freedom. Equally significant, Albright and other education-oriented black Mississippians demonstrated magnanimity to their previous masters by seeking to educate all children—black and white—in the best interest of the state.[19]

Many blacks throughout the South had a particularly pragmatic reason for seeking literacy, a factor that contributed to greater sense of independence and freedom. Ambitious African American farm workers who could read would know the value of cash crops, accurately discern the costs of food and supplies, and determine whether the landlord and merchants engaged in fair trade. Cunning blacks who understood fair price values could either reach an amiable compromise with the landlord or merchant or clandestinely move away to find more equitable treatment elsewhere. Those fortunate few who worked the grounds of fair-minded white landlords could acquire sufficient wealth to become landowners.

White people appeared particularly offended by blacks who acquired an education and provided evidence of being enlightened. The reasons for white aversion toward educated blacks proved varied and complex. Initially, the long-held racist belief in the innate inferiority of African Americans suggested recently manumitted blacks lacked the capacity to learn. Endeavors to educate the race could be perceived as a waste of time and money. Others offered pragmatic rationales for limiting black access to education. White traditionalists of the planter class believed that by educating African Americans, learned blacks would be disinclined to work the land for paltry wages and no longer function as cheap farm laborers.[20] White supremacists agreed with traditionalists but added that education would cause blacks to demand social and racial equality.

Hard-line Negrophobes sincerely believed that schooling "ruined niggers."[21] These white Redeemers also sensed that educated freedmen, as citizens, could demand political rights, control patronage, attain racial hegemony, and dictate policies to powerless whites. White Southerners also perceived education for blacks as inimical to white survival, and would use every means at their disposal to stifle learning and crush a nascent self-sufficiency for African Americans.[22] Preferring an ignorant black criminal to the educated Negro, these white Southerners profoundly opposed anyone who advocated educating Southern blacks. One observant black Atlanta resident who endorsed the belief that white people embraced convoluted thinking regarding African Americans said, "Not that they feared Negro crime less, but that they fear Negro ambition and success more."[23] Cautious African Americans had reason to fear white Negrophobes; these pragmatic blacks stifled personal ambition and avoided white people to remain out of trouble.

African Americans in the New South who coveted knowledge and demonstrated free thought flirted with death. Practical-thinking black men believed it far better to eschew education and remain ignorant than to exhibit knowledge and remove all doubt about being enlightened. The educated black was perceived by whites as being uppity, a trouble maker, one who did not know proper place, and as a leader who threatened the white Southern version of the status quo. Black educators also became targets for abuse. A particularly demeaning example of intimidation occurred when a black college teacher was chased home at gunpoint by a drunken policeman who resented the sight of a "nigger carrying books and a fountain pen."[24]

Faced with the dilemma of seeking learning that could result in an imminent threat to life and limb, or purposefully remaining ignorant, blacks had to respond carefully.[25] Adults seeking upward mobility through education had to use "mother wit" to show that an educated, skilled Negro would prove advantageous to whites. Sagacious parents residing in the rural South evidently found ways to enable their children to attend school without raising the ire of suspicious whites. Other parents either resided in towns or moved into cities where white people seemed more enlightened and less threatened by Negroes seeking an education.[26] These black Southerners reasoned that an educated African American had a better chance of self-preservation and enjoying a bountiful future than blacks who lived in the rural South and remained illiterate.

African Americans who demanded and acquired more than a mediocre elementary-school education proved far more the exception than the rule. An overwhelming majority of African Americans resided in the rural, agrarian South.[27] Wedded to the land, many black parents recognized the advantage of remaining ignorant and safe and envisioned education as being disadvantageous to the family. Out of necessity, parents realized the need to place children in the fields to work and help the family survive economically. Even if these parents coveted an education for their children, schooling, in regard to survival, appeared as a waste of time and energy. When demanding white employers and landowners threatened to oust tenant families and confiscate all possessions if the entire family failed to work the fields, indifference toward education made sense. Although the percentage of black illiteracy declined significantly between 1870 and 1900 (81.4 in 1870, 70.0 in 1880, 57.1 in 1890, and 44.5 in 1900), the raw numbers of illiterate African Americans aged ten and older slightly increased (2.7 in 1870, 3.2 in 1880, 3.0 in 1890, and 2.8 million in 1900).[28] The black quest for education could hardly be seen as universal.

Considering that between two and three million African Americans remained illiterate between 1870 and 1900, a different perspective should be entertained regarding the significance of education among African Americans. Therefore, given intimidating mandates, schooling seemed counterproductive—a dangerous venture in pursuit of a meaningless, irrelevant task inimical to the black family's welfare. To ensure survival, some parents recognized the advantage of having children—particularly boys—remain ignorant to avoid the wrath of hostile whites. Several additional factors also undermined learning among Southern-born African Americans. Since the South was overwhelmingly rural during the late nineteenth century, many blacks—like white planters—saw little relationship between having a formal education and plowing fields, feeding livestock, and harvesting crops. Book learning had nothing to do with shucking corn, picking cotton, and planting seeds. Parents presumably conveyed these opinions to their children. Other caring parents could also sense that education could heighten frustration among children who had their ambitions thwarted.[29] At best, the black quest for public education appeared uneven. Given the need to survive, education could hardly be envisioned as a priority for the impoverished African American masses in the rural South.

Another phenomenon—peer pressure—also contributed to the varying dilemmas associated with education. In certain communities, any African

American who endeavored to speak "properly" could be deemed "white folksy," a person who betrayed his community and identified with the dominating race. Discerning blacks with reservations about education also had concerns about the information imparted to children. Primers spoke of the superiority of Anglo-Saxon institutions, extolled the virtues of white heroes, endorsed patriotism, and imbued students with information containing a decidedly white Southern bias.[30] A purported minority of "radically" thinking blacks who had misgivings about the curriculum must have feared that the white perspective on educating blacks could have a damaging psychological effect on African American children.

Circumstances also revealed that some blacks virtually had no opportunity to acquire an education. Wealthy whites of the ante-bellum era established private academies and tutors for their children and refrained from paying taxes for public schools. White elites maintained an aversion to paying taxes for public schools after the Civil War, particularly for a race they disdained and intended to control. Moreover, despite efforts of dedicated teachers, few schools existed in close proximity to many rural families, rendering primary, and specifically secondary education (no black high schools existed in the South at that time), difficult, if not impossible, to obtain. Because the white South maintained a consistently negative view toward public education generally, and African American education in particular, the environment in which blacks resided determined the most constructive course of action would be to eschew book learning and survive.[31]

In retrospect, far too many countervailing forces existed to ensure the efficacy of Negro education. Despite the efforts of hundreds of educators, scores of aid societies, and generous philanthropic donations, the resources and educational personnel required to introduce book learning to thousands of recently freed African Americans eager to become literate proved impossible. Far too many forces were in opposition to the creation of a learned black population. First, rural people who worked the land—black and white alike—had little reason to pursue book learning. Second, Southern culture eschewed universal education; few public schools existed in the South. Although a heightened interest in the creation of public schools occurred after the Civil War, rural blacks could hardly envision education as a panacea for upward mobility. Therefore, a sustained interest in acquiring an education among impoverished, rural African Americans during the post-bellum years appears dubious. Neither rural whites nor blacks, logically, would envision education as a priority. Although Tuskegee, Fisk, and other institutions of higher learning became established and scores of primary schools were erected throughout the South, cynical observers would perceive black schools as showpieces rather than significant institutions that would enlighten millions of illiterate, rural African Americans. Finally, most white Southerners made clear that education was not in the best interest of the Negro—an indication that had life-and-death implications for learned African Americans.

Uneducated and ill-informed populaces like the masses of Southern blacks invariably appeared to act irrationally to their personal detriment. The concept that hard work bred success, which existed as the cornerstone of hope for European Americans, however, proved illusionary for the African American masses residing in the South. When blacks received inadequate compensation for services rendered and faced starvation because of their inability to obtain credit, the need to survive remained paramount. Destitute African Americans stole seed, pilfered food, and secretly sold crops on the black market.[32] Despite working long hours tilling land, sewing seeds, and harvesting crops with the expressed hope of becoming independent landowners, as late as 1900 approximately three-fourths of black farmers in the South toiled as sharecroppers or tenants and experienced some kind of debt peonage.[33] Given this environment, few positive results accrued for hard-working, law-abiding African American citizens.

The genesis of black dissolution evidenced by crushed hope and stifled ambition may be traced directly to this lawless, economically depressed era known as the New South. Inconsistent prices associated with the Southern agrarian economy, combined with the questionable role blacks might play in the political, social, and economic life of the post-bellum South, created insecurity among white Southerners. Unfortunately, blacks became pawns in an unfolding drama involving race, class hegemony, and financial gain. The white elite realized the need to mask their domination of poor whites by focusing on perceptions about the inferiority and subhuman nature of the Negro. Poor whites, in turn, had the need to use race to believe themselves superior to blacks. As a people steeped in the prejudice of the era, whites unquestionably believed that African Americans possessed limited brain power, uncontrollable sexual impulses, had a natural disinclination to work, and were prone to commit crimes. With these "truths" deeply embedded in the minds of virtually all Americans, white Southerners possessed a mandate to control blacks in the New South and thereby maintain white domination.[34]

To exercise control of the black masses, the infamous convict/lease system, one of the most heinous practices devised in America, became instituted in the New South. Innocent blacks faced arrests for changing employers without permission, riding freight cars without a ticket, and engaging in boisterous talk.[35] Unscrupulous judges, mayors, and justices of the peace—in concert with white businessmen in need of a cheap, steady, labor supply—levied fines upon unsuspecting black men (and occasionally women). White employers paid the fines and, to recoup their expenditures, worked the "criminals" for months, years, and, in many instances, forced blacks to work until death.[36] Unlike blacks with adventuresome spirits, those who recognized the risks pertaining to Southern travel remained stationary and endeavored to stay outside harm's way. The black masses encountered a no-win situation. Daring, unconventional blacks with wanderlust took chances to improve their status but faced capture, imprisonment, and a bleak future.

Unlike slave masters who valued human property, white businessmen of the New South exhibited little compassion toward leased "convicts." These unfortunate victims labored at the most arduous and dangerous jobs a private businessman, municipality, county, or state had to offer. Convict laborers worked in coal mines, turpentine stores, timber camps, and brick-making factories. Horrendous working conditions caused thousands to die prior to a fine being paid in full or a sentence completed. If a convict died while in custody, no financial liability accrued to the individual or company lessee.[37] Moreover, states like Alabama, Mississippi, Louisiana, Florida, Georgia, Texas, and the Carolinas added millions of dollars to state coffers through the inhumane leasing of African Americans identified as convicts.[38] Thus, by 1900, Southern provincial judges, mayors, justices of the peace, and others with legal authority sentenced blacks to work details in order to produce profits for business establishments and provide cheap labor for state projects.[39] Southern "justice" meted out to blacks certainly caused African Americans to have little regard for the white man's law.[40]

The pernicious convict/lease system and the association of blacks with crime had a deleterious impact on African Americans generally and low-income race members in particular. Virtually all African Americans became subjected to the capricious whims of white people, intimidating the most vulnerable blacks, rendering them to be passive victims devoid of pride and ambition.[41] This late nineteenth-century concept of black criminology established a precedent that continued for decades. As a prelude to the prison-industrial complex, thousands of innocent, indigent, and unlucky African Americans found themselves on the wrong side of the Southern judicial system.

Ironically, those arrested for petty crimes and sentenced to hard labor in the South could be deemed fortunate. Black men accused of disrespecting white women and ignoring the dictates of white men suffered a more ignominious fate. Lynching at the hands of a bloodthirsty white mob became the customary method for intimidating and controlling African Americans. Obviously, being a live "convict" seemed preferable to being the victim of a lynch mob. Nevertheless, the status of blacks facing southern justice proved predictably unfair. In contrast to judicial norms, the presumption of black innocence during this era proved irrelevant. The economic value of the convict/lease system took precedence over justice.

Southerners could hardly be perceived as the only Americans who held African Americans in disrepute as criminals; virtually all white Americans believed blacks operated outside the boundaries of customary law. These views were bolstered by white intellectuals residing in the North who used "scientific methodology" to explain the "waywardness" of the Negro. Social scientists of the day provided a myriad of reasons for high incidences of black crime ranging from a generation of freedom devoid of white control to greater access to public education. These postulations were also attributed to freedoms associated with the urban North, suggesting the South's "control mechanisms" held greater sway in minimizing aberrant black behavior.[42] American social scientist G. Stanley Hall used the 1890 census to prove blacks contained a unique pathology that destined the race to a life of crime. After examining the census, other intellectuals concurred with Hall and offered several reasons for black criminology.[43] While some academics argued that a generation of freedom devoid of white control contributed to black transgressions, others believed that public education caused African Americans to become knowledgeable and more covetous of wealth beyond their means of legal acquisition. Influential German scholar Frederick L. Hoffman essentially provided the "definitive conclusion" about African American criminality when he declared that religion and education not only proved wasteful, but also stimulated crime among the black populace.[44]

Life for African Americans external to the restrictive, unrepentant South hardly resembled a panacea for freedmen. Most Northern blacks resided in cities and practiced a lifestyle alien to the rustic Negro from the South. Philadelphia, Pennsylvania, the nineteenth-century Mecca for Negro life outside Dixie, contained a large but impecunious African American population. Although impressive black elites, including wealthy businessman Steven Smith and the successful Augustin, Jones, and Dorsey catering families resided in the City of Brotherly Love, most African Americans struggled to survive. Owing to omnipresent poverty, black neighborhoods appeared unkempt and represented locales where crime abounded.[45]

African Americans residing in New York City encountered problems similar to black Philadelphians. During the last half of the nineteenth century the African American population remained small and occasionally diminished. By the end of the century, blacks in the Gotham City comprised only 1.9 percent of the population. Moreover, white prejudice confined blacks to living in inferior residential areas where squalor and poverty prevailed.[46] The harshness experienced by impoverished black New Yorkers became particularly onerous and could be observed by the wretched treatment accorded black chimney sweeps. Desperate African American families permitted teenage boys to remove clothes, crawl into narrow crevices, suffer cuts on their entire body, and become covered with soot. Cuts became infected and many young chimney sweeps died prematurely.[47] And in keeping with Northern prejudice, black people experienced the color line in regard to employment. In *How the Other Half Lives,*

Jacob Riis accurately reported, "Trades of which [the Negro] had practical control in his southern home are not open to him here."[48]

Obviously, the difficulty African Americans faced in finding work in the North served as the primary reason for a limited exodus of Southern blacks. Hordes of European immigrants had already filled jobs that became available in the rapidly industrializing North. Equally, if not more disturbing for employment-seeking blacks, European immigrants threatened jobs customarily held by African Americans. For example, in 1884, hotels in New York replaced black help with French, German, and Irish immigrants. Similar difficulties also impacted black Philadelphians where European immigrants displaced Negro workers. In 1899 social scientist W. E. B. Du Bois observed that "foreigners and trades unions have crowded Negroes out on account of race prejudice . . ."[49]

The experiences of African Americans west of the Appalachian Mountains residing in Detroit, Chicago, and the Ohio Valley differed little from their East Coast counterparts. Michigan abolished slavery in 1837, but the residual effect of the peculiar institution remained. Racial prejudice against African Americans existed in the Wolverine State. Detroit, like other Michigan towns and cities, hardly appeared attractive as a prospective destination for freedmen. Black residents of Detroit encountered limited options for housing and found themselves restricted to the older, seedier neighborhoods in the city. The walls of prejudice stymied ambition and fostered gravitation toward underground activities.[50] Between 1870 and 1900, only 2,076 additional blacks trickled into the city, raising the black population to 4,111 persons, comprising a mere 1.9 percent of Detroit's population.[51] Again, the paucity of jobs discouraged black migration from the South to face uncertain employment prospects in Detroit. By the turn of the century, black residents of Detroit failed to find employment in factories controlled by white ethnic groups.[52]

Although Jean Baptiste Point Du Sable, a prosperous fur trader of black ancestry, has been credited for founding Chicago, African Americans nevertheless faced challenges in the Windy City. Negrophobia existed in the Midwest, a factor that became evident in regard to jobs. By the close of the nineteenth century, the bulk of Chicago's black population hailed from border-states and the Upper South where African Americans appeared better prepared to find work in an urban milieu. For blacks seeking employment in lucrative industries, however, the job market remained closed. Most black men and women could only find employment as personal servants or domestics; jobs in industry and commerce remained off-limits. Indeed, approximately two of every three blacks labored in some servile capacity that white workers deemed demeaning.[53]

Midwestern cities never served as refuges for freed people because areas adjacent to the border-states proved inhospitable to African Americans. Prejudice within the Ohio River Valley dissuaded black migration because, as the *Commercial Gazette of Cincinnati* declared in 1899, "The colored line is everywhere."[54] In Evansville, Indiana, white people blamed blacks for fomenting mob violence and justified Southern lynching because of the sexual offenses black men allegedly committed against white women.[55] With unremitting prejudice, inhospitality, and limited prospects for work outside the South, rural Southern blacks remained in Dixie.

Clearly, experiences of the African American masses during the twentieth century would be influenced by blacks rooted in the South who sought economic security and social amelioration in the United States. Several noticeable problems surfaced, however, that placed the black masses at a disadvantage in the quest for equal opportunity. Those who remained in the South faced omnipresent discrimination that curtailed and limited ambition. And yet migrants who moved to more hospital environs in Northern cities appeared to be jumping from the frying pan into the proverbial fire. Devoid of an urban experience desperately needed during a period of industrialization, black travelers from the South encountered difficult odds. First, African Americans had to contend with European immigrants who settled in the industrial North and had the initial opportunity to acquire industrial work. With an employment foothold established, Europeans maintained and protected jobs for fellow foreigners. Second, few blacks found their educational level sufficient to meet the needs of an urban, industrial milieu during a time that required a greater need for literacy.[56] And finally, the reception of black newcomers to Northern cities usually proved hostile. White Northerners showed comparable animus toward African Americans as bigoted counterparts in the South.

Unfortunately, black Southern migrants brought forth another destructive Dixie tradition—a propensity for violence that originated in the South. Since colonial times, white Southerners, regardless of social class, settled personal differences with fists, knives, and guns.[57] Prideful manhood required "satisfaction" from an adversary. Given the pejorative residual effects of a customary violent lifestyle, desperate African Americans observed and emulated this unique brand of Southern culture. Southern norms allowed whites to treat blacks harshly with impunity; therefore, the only recourse blacks had to vent frustration with their lowly position existed by attacking fellow African Americans. Indeed, black-on-black violence presumably increased after the demise of slavery.[58] Since African Americans lost economic value, whites of the New South had little interest in dissuading blacks from engaging in mutual combat.

Given the atrocities whites visited upon African Americans, the white characterization of blacks as violent people seemed ironic. Inhumane acts of cruelty toward blacks approached incredulity. Lynching took on the semblance of a public ritual, one of the most heinous being the murder of Sam Hose, which occurred in Coweta County near Newman, Georgia, in April 1899. For killing a white man in self-defense, Hose was chained, mutilated, and burned to death. Afterward, the lynch mob removed his heart, liver, testicles; crushed his bones into small pieces; and sold his body parts as souvenirs.[59] Because wanton white violence caused blacks to have little respect for law, African American transgressors subjected to incarceration or chain-gang work in the New South became known as "bad niggers" in white law and jurisprudence.[60] But to repressed African Americans, "bad niggers" could be perceived as heroes.

Rather than reporting on the atrocities whites visited upon blacks, the white media stereotyped blacks as being the violent race. While popular magazines and newspapers spoke authoritatively about lowly blacks attacking whites and gleefully reported on intra-racial quarrels resulting in violence, white lawlessness was ignored.[61] Probably the most egregious result of white propaganda regarding the violent nature of African Americans existed when prominent African Americans perceived black violence as normative. Even the formidable, race-conscious Frederick Douglass believed black men had a propensity to engage in excessive lascivious behavior.[62] W. E. B. Du Bois also characterized the masses as being prone to engage in aggressive behavior without giving attribution to the origins of violence in the South. Like other Americans, enlightened African American leaders like Douglass and Du Bois joined opinionated whites who believed the impoverished black masses had a propensity for criminal behavior and violence. Few Americans, moreover, comprehended the social pathologies inherent among desperate people striving to survive on the margins of society. Unfortunately, without the funds to engage lawyers to resolve personal disputes, poor blacks would be inclined to act emotionally and commit wanton acts that provided creditability for detractors who believed African Americans had a propensity to engage in criminal behavior.[63]

On the eve of the new century African Americans would find their race in a disadvantageous position. For a select few, the trek into Southern cities or the urban North garnered hope and enhanced prospects for success. The majority of black people, however, would remain in the agrarian South, impoverished, disillusioned, defeated, and embittered. What became particularly troubling for impoverished African Americans existed in the "damned if you do, damned if you don't" conundrum as blacks functioned as pariahs in American society. Problems associated with the black masses during the early twentieth century may be encapsulated with this paraphrase: "Bound between two cultures, a fading memory and an emerging reality, [blacks were] to remain an enigma for American democracy."[64]

CHAPTER 2

Jim Crow and the Early Progressive Era 1900–1910

At the turn of the century the African American majority residing in the South, and one generation removed from slavery, faced insurmountable odds. No sanctuary from the racism and inequality existed in the United States. In 1896 the Supreme Court's *Plessey v. Ferguson* decision declared that blacks could legally be subjected to segregation, a degrading insult that affected every black man, woman, and child in the United States.[1] To assure that African Americans would remain in a subservient position, white people used the *Plessey* case to institute Jim Crow laws that placed blacks at an economic and social disadvantage. Restrictive suffrage laws virtually eliminated all Southern blacks from enjoying their constitutional right to vote. Sharecropping became firmly entrenched as an institution and remained a scourge that kept most African Americans impoverished. Most African Americans residing in Dixie functioned as servile peons who provided cheap labor for the agrarian property class. Unfortunately, few opportunities existed outside the demeaning South to encourage the large, rustic African American populace to migrate elsewhere.

With the advent of Jim Crow and its application in the Deep South, African Americans faced a unique challenge. First, Jim Crow and white hostility toward African Americans occurred throughout the decade. White mobs attacked blacks in New Orleans (1900); Springfield, Ohio (1904 and 1905); Atlanta and Brownsville, Texas (1906); and Springfield, Illinois, an event which triggered the creation of the NAACP. And second, common folkways and mores inherent in the ante-bellum South never formalized restrictions based on racial segregation. Therefore, when racism based upon legal and legislative mandates occurred at the turn of the century, previous class distinctions that accorded the "better element" greater respect no longer prevailed. Progressive-minded blacks like W. E. B. Du Bois insisted on restoring the rights lost by "proper Negroes" rather than address nefarious practices like sharecropping and the convict/lease system that primarily impacted the disadvantaged black masses.[2] Because most blacks resided in rural areas and were poor, the task at hand focused on acquiring racial dignity in a Jim Crow environment rather than addressing the arduous task of eradicating black poverty.

Of course Jim Crow and the factors designed to maintain white supremacy made intra-racial class distinctions within the African American community irrelevant. Presumably, every sane, conscious black recognized Jim Crow practices as being humiliating and unwarranted. Nevertheless, leaders of each race held specific priorities. White reformers, for example, disdained lynching because of the horrendous stain the nefarious practice imposed on their beloved region. Similarly, since African Americans became the primary object of lynch mobs, virtually all blacks opposed lynching. Black leaders, however, could have somewhat different opinions about segregation. African American professionals who profited from Jim Crow sought to expand and stabilize segregation practices while other members of the black middle class sought to mitigate its effect on their individual life through pragmatic or accommodationist means.[3] One may assume, however, that issues regarding the advantages and disadvantages of Jim Crow segregation remained moot to disadvantaged African Americans who focused on economic survival.

Black angst attributed to poverty became compounded by public acceptance of the culture of inequality, the belief that human failure resulted from personal frailties. Since all United States citizens enjoyed the pronounced platitudes of freedom, equality, and the rights of man, presumably every American enjoyed an equal opportunity to excel. Unfortunately, these maxims seldom applied to African Americans. White Americans overlooked the inequities derived from slavery and racial discrimination that stifled black progress. Hence, failed African Americans became identified as stupid, lazy people who lacked proper morals, exercised poor judgment, and existed primarily to pursue a hedonistic lifestyle. Although racism became a bulwark that mocked the American credo that proclaimed equal opportunity for all, white people ignored the disadvantages that negatively impacted the African American masses.[4]

The evolution of sociology as a social science during the 1890s also placed African Americans in a disadvantageous position. Rather than engaging in objective, groundbreaking research, white intellectuals, such as Lester Ward and Edward A. Ross, accepted and endorsed pejorative norms directed toward blacks. American social scientists, psychologists, and sociologists blamed the lowly classes for their limited station in life. At the turn of the century, Professor Charles A. Ellwood of the University of Missouri contended that "the average Negro is still a savage child of nature" and should not be viewed in a more positive manner.[5] These progressive scholars believed a combination of inadequate personality structures, self-defeating mannerisms, inadequate motivation, and the absence of a paternal role model provided the appropriate formulas for failure. With white political, social, and economic leaders in accord with the academic community about the culture of inequality as it pertained to lowly status of African Americans, prospects for blacks in America seemed doomed.

Scholars demeaned African Americans without discussing the socioeconomic factors related to poverty that caused a disproportionate number of blacks to convey ignorance, engage in asocial behavior, and resort to crime. For contemporary social scientists, poverty and criminology became synonymous with the term "Negro." Frederick L. Hoffman's influential 1896 publication, *Race Traits and Tendencies of the American Negro,* blamed blacks entirely for every negative factor that befell the race.[6] Hoffman even contended that education augmented the black proclivity to engage in crime. To add further credence to the theory that race trumped poverty in regard to crime, Hoffman declared that desolate immigrants were less inclined to engage in criminal activities than equally impoverished blacks.[7] Neither Du Bois nor the Yale-educated black scholar Kelly Miller successfully countered and reversed white opinions that blackness equated to poverty and crime that typified the average American Negro. Even the formidable Du Bois contended that the "immorality, crime, and laziness among Negroes" derived from self-inflicted ills related to slavery.[8]

Journalist Ray Stannard Baker, a contemporary of Du Bois, probably held a more objective view in regard to black crime. Baker realized that cocaine addicts were irresponsible and capable of committing any kind of criminal offense. In response to a spreading cocaine habit in the urban South in 1907, Baker noted, "There are always druggists who will break the law . . . a curse to the Negro [that] has resulted . . . in much crime."[9] Baker believed that insensitive, avaricious people conveniently preyed on indigent blacks who used cocaine as a temporary respite from poverty.

Perhaps the most devastating critique appeared from an African American Civil War veteran William Hannibal Thomas who emerged as the most influential black critic in the United States. Thomas published his infamously famous book, *The American Negro: What He Was, What He Is, and What He May Become,* in 1901. His devastating remarks about members of his own race gave credence to white insensitivity and hostility toward lowly blacks. Basing his "study" on twenty-five years of observations on his race, he not only excoriated all African Americans, but also pointedly criticized the black masses when he said, "The negro [sic] . . . has a mind that never thinks in complex terms; negro intelligence is both superficial and delusive . . ., the negro represents an illiterate race, in which ignorance, cowardice, folly, and idleness are rife; the negro represents an intrinsically inferior type of humanity, and one whose predominant characteristics evince an aptitude for a low order of living . . ."[10] Thomas struck a final blow toward fellow race members by suggesting that black children should be removed from their parents and placed in orphanages in order to be raised by white guardians.[11]

Thomas proclaimed that most blacks were retarded, savages, and amoral, inferior beings incapable of discerning right from wrong.[12] And after concluding that blacks were akin to apes, Thomas received glowing accolades from esteemed white scholars who deemed Thomas's work thorough, objective, and invaluable. A *New York Times* review lauded Thomas and proclaimed, "Mr. Thomas is probably, next to Mr. Booker T. Washington, the best American authority on the Negro question." At the time, Thomas' book received far greater acclaim than Du Bois' classic sociological tome *The Philadelphia Negro* published in1898.[13]

Ironically, an interesting dilemma unfolded as successful blacks created a dilemma for white racists and the black masses. White bigots made a conscious effort to keep all blacks in penury, causing all but the most talented to remain poor and destitute.[14] Individual and family successes recorded in Southern cities like Atlanta, New Orleans, Charleston, Memphis, and Nashville, as well as New York, Philadelphia, Boston and New Haven, however, undermined the myth of Negro inferiority.[15] Yet, a visible black aristocracy suggested that African Americans who failed to succeed and struggled to survive were victims of their own ineptitude. In a perverse sense, enterprising blacks who worked extremely hard and acquired a modicum of wealth minimized prospects for progressive whites directing pity toward the black masses.

The new century also marked a time when the more fortunate African Americans had to decide whether to function separately from the masses or help those "farthest down."[16] During the late nineteenth century most successful blacks resided in aforementioned cities and remained aloof from their less fortunate, bucolic brethren. Established blacks in Philadelphia also eschewed relationships with the urban black masses.[17] Similar intra-racial problems appeared in Detroit, Chicago, Washington, Charleston, Los Angeles, Boston, and other cities during the early twentieth century.[18]

African Americans of means had cause to become the most vociferous critics of the black masses. The proximity of all blacks residing in a restricted ghetto meant that the better classes of African Americans would become the most likely victims of black crime. Poor blacks preyed on their wealthier brethren in order to acquire proper sustenance for food, clothing, and shelter, and to fund whatever entertaining escapes from the drudgery of a mundane existence that could be found.[19] A white backlash provided successful blacks with an additional reason for castigating the masses. As Southern blacks moved North, longtime residents experienced heightened racism from fellow whites. Established blacks believed the behavior of low-income African Americans brought disrepute to the race. A black minister's speech at Cooper Union in 1889 probably represented the thoughts of established black New Yorkers that extended through the second decade of the twentieth century when he said,

> You don't ever see the representative negro [sic] in New York. We get the nigger up here with a cigar in his mouth, with a gold-headed cane and a high silk hat, and it's doubtful if he's got enough money in his pocket to pay the rent.[20]

Although the majority of African Americans were working-class people with common problems attributed to white racism and poverty, the black elite held contempt for the black slackers rather than the widows, orphans, sick, and infirm who also comprised the low-income masses.[21]

During the first decade of the twentieth century, leading magazines, such as *Atlantic Monthly, Century Monthly, Harpers,* and *North American Review,* also lampooned impoverished blacks. These demeaning characterizations further underscored the black bourgeoisie's concern about the damaging impact the African American poor created for their more privileged class.[22] Blacks of property and standing had cause to believe that the masses represented the scourge of the entire race. Given the prospects for racial self-hatred, few among the higher class of African Americans overtly endorsed the thinking of the aforementioned William Hannibal Thomas. White beliefs about the inferiority regarding impoverished blacks, however, became endorsed by academic scholars, popular magazines, and outspoken members of the black elite.

The degradation unfortunate blacks received required a constructive respondent that appeared in the Southern-born Virginian, Booker T. Washington. Since most African Americans at the dawn of the new century resided in the rural South and labored as low-wage sharecroppers or tenants, Washington's personal experience enabled him to speak on behalf of the impoverished black majority.[23] The industrial education Washington espoused at Tuskegee targeted young African Americans, training them to rise from an impecunious status to become more proficient farmers, artisans, and homemakers. Students with sufficient resources, individual industriousness, and good fortune matriculated to Tuskegee and acquired the opportunity to enhance their prospects for a successful future.

Although Washington encouraged hard work and admonished blacks for being "shiftless," his efforts to ameliorate the condition of the rural masses by advocating industriousness proved limited. The heritage of slavery—labor without recompense—remained as a causal factor for blacks shirking work. Moreover, indolence evident among former slaves invariably stifled the ambition of subsequent generations of African Americans. Many among "the poorer class of Negroes" deemed happy-go-lucky felt comfortable working sparingly. Prior to the Atlanta riot, one white employer was heard to say, "I tried to help the Negroes as much as I could. But many of them won't work even when the wages are high . . . when they get a few dollars ahead they go down to the saloons in Atlanta."[24] Ray Stannard Baker voiced a similar observation, noting, rather than work five or six days, the "poorer class of Negroes" truncated their work week to no more than three days, limiting their income and willingly accepting a hand-to-mouth existence.[25] Du Bois attributed black indolence to a lack of training and racial discrimination, and added, "We find the ranks of the laborers among Negroes filled to an unusual extent with disappointed men . . . who lost the incentive to excel . . ."[26] The African Americans with low aspirations and a questionable work ethic—laboring only when hungry—seemed commonplace to ambitious blacks and whites.

Even when Washington reached the height of his power and popularity, stoic blacks believed hard work brought few, if any rewards, to those who toiled. A black Mississippian recognized the plight of the African American masses by recalling, "Their lives did not change materially; they simply got older, grew weary, took sick, and died."[27] Indeed, conditions at this time were so severe that slavery—in many instances—would prove preferable to freedom.[28] During the "Age of Washington," therefore, incidences of white violence and imprisonment directed toward blacks failed to subside.[29]

The questionable work ethic Washington observed within the black masses extended to reaches beyond the South. In Philadelphia, Du Bois found the Negro "willing, honest and good-natured; but . . . also, as a rule, careless, unreliable and unsteady . . . [behavioral norms] expected from a people 'trained to shirk work.'" A white contractor in New York City concurred with Du Bois' observation, declaring, "As a general rule the ordinary coloured [sic] man can't do as much work nor do it as well as the ordinary white man. The result is, I don't take coloured men when I can get white men."[30] Indolence appeared as the norm among poor blacks who had the greatest reason for improving their economic status.

Racial discrimination within unions also stifled the black desire to acquire gainful employment. White workers applied a variety of methods, including violence, to restrict blacks from obtaining jobs in manufacturing, construction, and transportation.[31] Samuel Gompers, president of the American Federation of Labor (AFL), revealed a most insidious and effective method for keeping unemployed blacks destitute. Initially Gompers and the AFL opposed racial exclusion. As late as 1910 Gompers publicly declared, "We seek to build up the labor movement . . ., and we want all the negroes [sic] we can possibly get who will join hands with organized labor." Underneath the façade of inclusion, however, Gompers asserted his true feelings when he informed a reporter that "Caucasians are not going to let their standard of living be destroyed by negroes [sic] . . ."[32] During the turn of the century, racism, obviously, had been deeply embedded in the labor movement.

Education and hard work hardly proved a panacea for the many ills that plagued black Americans. An established but lingering problem impoverished blacks faced existed in the realization of limited opportunities. Impressionistic young boys as well as adult males particularly curtailed ambition to avoid the personal affront of being turned away from a coveted job. One black male from Indianapolis noted, "There are always places for the coloured [sic] man at the bottom 'as unskilled laborers or domestic servants,' but those who endeavored to rise by acquiring an education would be rebuffed." Another aggrieved black man made a similar observation by stating, "What shall we do? Here are our young people educated in the schools, capable of doing good work in many occupations where skill and intelligence are required—and yet with few opportunities opening for them . . . The result is that some of them drop back into idle discouragement—or worse."[33] Negativity personified by acquiescence to known limitations obviously touched black children. For example, a black boy coveting work in New York City endeavored to rise from the door boy to office boy to head bellboy. Even as an adult, employment restrictions suggested that a black male would always remain a boy.[34]

North and South, a sense of resignation permeated disadvantaged African Americans. The psychological damage that accrued from a sense of inferiority impinged on African Americans generally, and low-income blacks in particular. Without high self-esteem, the ability to enjoy human rights, or assert the privileges that accrue with American citizenship, scores of blacks remained poor. These unfortunate realities placed thousands of black people in limbo and limited the prospects for African American success. Indeed, anthropologist Gunnar Myrdal later proclaimed, "It is hard to keep ambition alive and to maintain morale when those for whom you have fondness keep thinking and saying . . . that you are cast by God in an inferior mold."[35]

Evidently the South's penchant for violence had a greater impact on the black masses than the educational reform efforts of Booker T. Washington. Allegedly, the origins of American violence evolved in the South, specifically in Edgefield County, South Carolina. Retaliation to perceived or real slights could mean a fight to the death if an individual or family's honor appeared threatened or demeaned. Honor, as a concept applied throughout the South, meant that men could be a combination of brave, cruel, impetuous, and self-destructive.[36] The Southern honor code also suggested that low-income African Americans—like white counterparts—would have a predisposition to engage in violent acts and commit crimes.

On the eve of the 1906 Atlanta riot, scores of working-class African Americans from rural areas migrated into the city. The uncouth mannerisms of the newcomers who frequented gambling dens, appeared ostentatiously idle, and used firearms throughout the dead of night disturbed the tranquility enjoyed by the black elite. Working-class whites who migrated from the hinterlands and the established white citizenry also became disturbed by the overt opposition to white hegemony. The more blacks became subjected to discrimination in the Jim Crow South, the more impoverished African

Americans displayed a greater need to operate outside the prescribed law. Desperate and destitute African Americans stole vegetables to survive and, if caught, would be subjected to receive legal prosecution. Blacks who committed the same offense as whites, however, received far greater punishment. For public intoxication, contemporary journalist Ray Stannard Baker reported that a white man could escape with a reprimand, be sometimes fined three dollars and costs, but the black man received a ten- to fifteen-dollar fine and be sent to the chain gang.[37] Trumped-up charges ascribed to vagrancy and other so-called minor offenses also led to months of labor on the chain gang. Equally significant, some bold blacks challenged the authority of the racist criminal justice system, resisted arrests, and even used guns and knives to ambush police officers.[38] Blacks had good cause to be offended. The white perception of black criminality supported by "the worthless Negro" stereotype promoted by Atlanta newspapers and white paranoia about the rapist inclinations of black men contributed to the Atlanta riot of 1906.[39]

The Atlanta Riot merely served as the most public example of the white willingness to use violence and coercion to maintain dominance over African Americans. Because blacks experienced arrest for the most trivial offenses, the convict/lease system imposed by an unrepentant South continued its usefulness as a heinous and contemptible method for acquiring cheap labor. In 1903 the state of Mississippi emulated Kentucky's harsh application of the law and sentenced blacks who stole poultry to five years in prison.[37] That same year, however, the federal government dismissed all charges and fines against perpetrators who successfully retained blacks in peonage.[40] Given the need to find workers for road building in the South, blacks became suitable victims of Southern justice working on chain gangs. In addition to providing the labor for road construction, black convict laborers continued enhancing state coffers. In 1906, Georgia alone amassed a profit of $354,853.55 through the convict lease system.[41] An indifferent federal government, combined with callous state and business leaders, allowed thousands of poor blacks to labor and suffer in obscurity.[42]

Of course more serious charges resulted in long-term stays in prison. African Americans found unequal treatment in legal matters toward their race particularly galling. The word of a Southern white consistently took precedent over that of an African American regardless of the black person's stature or innocence.[43] Recognizing that the law proved deferential to whites at the expense of blacks, African Americans carefully avoided bringing legal matters about white people before the courts. Consequently, blacks had few qualms operating outside the law regardless of the righteousness of their cause.

Reasons for black disrespect for the law became strikingly clear from Shirley Bragg, a white man who served as president of the Board of Inspectors of

Convicts in Alabama in 1906. When commenting on the convict/lease system, Bragg was moved to say, "The demand for labor and fees has become so great that most of them now go to the mines where many of them are unfit for such labor . . . Consequently they pass from this earth." In conclusion, Bragg declared the mines "nurseries of death."[44] Given the chicanery in seizing black men and the significantly unjust judicial system that unfairly condemned blacks to serve on labor details, African Americans had no cause for respecting for Southern laws.

Devoid of sufficient opportunities to succeed, penniless blacks needed to find a means for survival. African Americans judiciously made efforts to avoid white wrath. But realizing that black transgressions toward whites had dangerous implications, unsavory elements of the race recognized that theft and the brutalization of fellow African Americans could occur with impunity. Therefore, some destitute blacks turned on each other.[45] Since whites of the South ignored black-on-black violence and crime, a criminal element could exist and thrive uninterrupted among the African American masses. Thus, as young black people understood that education and ambition produced only frustration and disappointment, and that returning vengeance on white perpetrators could only lead to annihilation, destitute blacks turned on each other. The lawlessness evident in the South at large, combined with the absence of justice accorded blacks, invariably contributed to some deviant behavior that led to intra-racial violence among impoverished African Americans.[46]

Intra-racial violence within the black South stemmed from the inability to acquire justice or resolve disputes through the courts.[47] Even if African Americans could be made whole through the legal system, systemic poverty precluded Southern blacks from hiring lawyers. Another factor that caused blacks to resolve intra-racial disputes by resorting to violence may be attributed to ignorance. At the turn of the century very few blacks had more than a rudimentary education. Only a small minority possessed sufficient knowledge of the legal system to use the law advantageously, and most of these blacks resided in the North.[48]

Some southern black youths of the early twentieth century developed a surly attitude. They refused to be whipped, eschewed sharecropping, and embarked upon a life of thievery to meet economic needs.[49] Educator and future Baptist minister Dr. Richard R. Wright Jr., recalling the fate of a male childhood friend sentenced to serve in the chain gang back in Augusta, Georgia, noted that the boy appeared proud of his notoriety and enhanced standing in the community and declared, "Some of the boys talked about him as though he were a hero."[50]

While young African Americans found violence more conducive to meeting Southern norms than acquiring an education, white Southerners employed a variety of methods to limit black enlightenment and maintain the Southern status quo. Some insecure whites feared that educated, accomplished black males could seduce white women; violence against black men of achievement existed as a convenient deterrent.[51] Others—specifically those who owned cotton plantations—displayed heightened resentment toward paying taxes to fund public schools generally and black schools in particular. As the popularity for state-funded schools increased, white people became increasingly resentful of money being used to educate African Americans. Rather than abide by the separate but equal clause in the *Plessey v. Ferguson* case, whites in power slashed the salaries of black teachers and reduced the number of months African American children could attend school. This disparity broadened a socioeconomic gulf between blacks and whites, gave credence to the false belief that blacks could not learn, and placed African Americans at a learning deficit far into the twentieth century.[52]

Black education became a political and economic issue for Southern whites. James K. Vardaman, running in 1903 for governor of Mississippi, said, "The only effect of Negro education is to spoil a good field hand and make an insolent cook."[53] This kind of rhetoric appealed to the average Southern white voters who elected hate-mongers like Vardaman to the governor's office and eventually the United States Senate. In the Southern hinterlands, few, if any black, schools existed. White planters recognized that by educating African Americans, prospects for continuing blacks as a cheap labor system would be diminished.[54] Southern whites established an unfortunate harbinger for the future in regard to black education. The sagacious W. E. B. Du Bois observed what "the white South feared more than Negro dishonesty, ignorance, and incompetency (sic) . . . was Negro honesty, knowledge, and efficiency."[55] Even a somewhat progressive city like Atlanta rendered public education inaccessible for scores of African American children. Despite the efforts of black leaders to build a segregated high school in 1903 and 1910, their efforts failed. [The Booker T. Washington High School, the first erected in the city of Atlanta, opened as late as 1924.] Segregated black public schools at best only accommodated half the children of school age. Those unable to attend schools, unfortunately, acquired an education in the streets.[56] An investigative report noted that "illiterate Negroes . . . furnish more of the criminals than those who read or write . . . ." Nevertheless, the feeling prevailed among influential whites that education spoiled the Negro.[57] Thus, white beliefs that the entire black race was inferior meant that Negrophobes could confidently argue that blacks should remain uneducated.

Cautious African Americans failed to bolster black intellectuals' quest for education. In addition to fearing retribution from whites who hated educated Negroes, many blacks recognized that few jobs awaited African Americans who possessed more than a cursory education. Fearing the frustration educated children seemed likely to experience--difficulty in finding gainful employment--some parents purposely limited their progeny's access to schools.[59] Therefore, many blacks appeared in concert with white Southerners who feared "overeducating" African Americans would prove dangerous.[60] A blunt, working-class white man revealed the sentiment of all the "genuine Southern people," saying that when the Negro "remains the hewer of wood and carrier of water . . . everything is all right, but when ambition, prompted by real education, causes the Negro to grow restless and . . . bestir himself to get out of that servile condition . . . there will be trouble."[61] To the chagrin of African Americans who recognized the advantages of acquiring an education, for financial reasons, safety precautions, the lack of opportunity, or purposeful indolence, the masses, to the detriment of the entire race, saw advantages in remaining unlearned.

For the fortunate few capable of gaining access to industrial schools like Hampton and Tuskegee, a propitious future seemed possible. The extended arm of industrial schools, however, touched only a fraction of blacks in need of training and moral support. Usually the travail of lowly black Southerners appeared through the continuation of sharecropping and other forms of harsh, menial work performed without adequate compensation.

Although impoverished African Americans struggled to survive in the South during the turn of the century, black life in the urban North could hardly be deemed ideal. In the new century, long established blacks still encountered difficulties attributed to white greed, discrimination, and prejudice. Avaricious landlords charged blacks exorbitantly high fees to live in cheap, back-alley houses or tenements. Rented rooms were overcrowded and improperly ventilated, subjecting residents to unsanitary conditions that contributed to disease and enormously high death rates. The impoverished black populations' susceptibility to illness also stemmed from employment in the most health-adverse occupations, insufficient rest, and improper diets.[62] Black infant mortality rates also proved exorbitantly high because of the insalubrious environment, insufficient nourishment attributed to poverty, and absentee working mothers who had difficulty caring for their children.[63] The high cost for electricity, water, and heating fuel required in an intemperate climate limited prospects for economic amelioration. Therefore, recent black migrants from the South who moved North vacated one impoverished environment and entered another.

Using hedonistic pursuits to deaden the omnipresence of poverty, low-income blacks in Northern cities found amusement through gambling, drinking, excursions, balls, and "cake walks."[64] Gambling and drinking caused the indulgent to maintain dissolution, rendering prospects for escaping a sordid life impossible. Meanwhile, formal education could hardly be equated with amusement for low-income African Americans. In keeping with the time, few Americans went beyond the sixth grade in public school. And in all fairness to impoverished African Americans, people living a hand-to-mouth existence faced more pressing problems than acquiring a rudimentary education. Food, clothing, and shelter took precedent over mastering the As, Bs, and Cs. Du Bois spoke from the perspective of the black elite when he declared, "It cannot be said that Negroes have fully grasped their great school advantages . . . by keeping their younger children regularly in school, and from this remissness much harm has sprung."[65] Du Bois, however, concluded his assessment regarding the education of black Philadelphians by noting that only one in a thousand attended college because of issues far more pressing than attending school. The great sage recognized that poverty rendered education difficult, if not irrelevant.

Given the problems African Americans seeking to earn a decent living faced, life for the black family proved exceedingly difficult. Without earning sufficient income for marriage, people bonded out of wedlock. But even with this understanding, common-law marriage proved no panacea for the challenge in acquiring rent and obtaining funds for a proper diet. Without a satisfactory home life, prospects for long-term relationships diminished, sexual promiscuity flourished, and family stability eroded. For low-income African Americans, problems appeared omnipresent and difficult to transcend.

Like Southern whites who ignored transgressions imposed on blacks that contributed to crime, Northern white people also perceived African Americans as being a criminal class. Rather than focus on the many contributing factors related to poverty that contributed to lawlessness, white people focused on the disproportionate number of black criminals. In the *Philadelphia Negro,* Du Bois spoke of the "submerged tenth," the loafers, gamblers, prostitutes, lazy individuals, and professional criminals who engaged in every kind of illicit activity.[66] New York City also contained a disproportionately large criminal element. In *The Black North,* W. E. B. Du Bois proclaimed that of the sixty thousand blacks who resided in "Gotham City" at the turn of the century, an unsuccessful sub stratum—some fifteen thousand souls—comprised "God's poor, the devil's poor, and the poor devils" contained the "vicious and criminal classes." People with extreme needs—even individuals intent on remaining honest—would drift in and out of crime. He also noted, "The morality and education of this black world is naturally below that of the white world . . . and functioned as the core of the negro (sic) problem."[67] In mid-July 1903, The *New York Times* declared, "There are in New York thousands of utterly worthless Negro desperadoes . . . gamblers when they have money and thieves when they have none, moral lepers and more dangerous than wild animals."[68] In addition to the *Times,* other contemporary observers believed lowly blacks engaged in delimiting practices like crime and indolence that limited the success of downtrodden African Americans.[69] Even the sympathetic Mary White Ovington recognized that omnipresent poverty had a deleterious impact on black communities. She found that "crimes are committed by black neighbor against black neighbor."[70]

Impoverished blacks in Detroit and Chicago hardly fared better than counterparts elsewhere. Viewed with hostility by native-born Americans and immigrants from Europe who envisioned local blacks as economic competitors, life proved arduous for blacks trying to make a living in industrial cities. Insulted and constantly wary of the unprovoked attack, life for poor but law-abiding African Americans within an urban context proved difficult. The lowest strata of blacks residing in Detroit occupied the worst housing in the city and contained paupers and marginal criminals who committed crimes in order to survive.[71] Blacks residing in Chicago also suffered from the ignominy of Jim Crow and received hostility from the police and the courts. The segregated vice district existed in the Black Belt, providing the police the opportunity for harassing black saloon keepers and those who frequented their establishments.[72]

A few progressive blacks and whites exhibited sufficient concern to develop mutual assistance programs. As bucolic folk migrated to nearby towns and cities, those more familiar with an urban environment recognized the need to train newcomers to become dependable employees as domestic servants, laborers, and participants in other forms of menial work that enhanced prospects for survival. New York City became the initial locale for altruistic progressives concerned about the condition of black women recently removed from the South. White reformer Frances Kellor, along with former slave Victoria Earle Matthews, believed that something must be provided to aid black female migrants' adjustment to urban life.[73] In 1905 Kellor established the Inter-Municipal Committee on Household Research and organized an organization to protect black women in Philadelphia and New York.[74] Between 1905 and 1909, Kellor, Fred R. Moore (a close associate of Booker T. Washington), Mary White Ovington, and others formed Associations for the Protection of Colored Women in many cities throughout the nation.

Cities like Philadelphia and Detroit followed New York's reformist lead. In 1903, John Emlen, a white Philadelphia Quaker, founded the Armstrong Association, a precursor to the Urban League that provided industrial training for African Americans. Distinguished African American leaders in Detroit founded the Refugee and Rescue Mission Home in 1906. And in 1909 this leadership elite established the Christian Industrial Club that aided black girls and women recently removed from the South.[75] Yet despite the efforts of Kellor, Emlen, the black churches, and other urban reformers intent on assisting migrants and preparing them for life in industrialized cities, the task proved overwhelming. One dedicated reformer succinctly declared, "One thing is quite apparent to our committees, and that is that colored people are settling here about too fast, faster than they can be assimilated and adjusted to surrounding conditions."[76]

Most progressive white reformers, however, joined industrialists in currying favor with European immigrants rather than impoverished blacks. Despite linguistic differences and alien cultures, Italians, Czechs, Romanians, Russians, and other Europeans avoided the ignominy of being black and negatively stereotyped. For example, in Chicago, white social workers established sixty-eight settlement houses to administer to the spiritual and social needs to impoverished immigrants, but not one comparable establishment existed in the black community.[77] Even the charitable Andrew Carnegie, the magnanimous magnate who contributed thousands of dollars to Booker T. Washington's beloved Tuskegee Institute—an institution that trained blacks to be efficient workers—hired European laborers rather than blacks in his steel mills. Consequently, African Americans remained confined to lowly jobs as domestics, personal servants, and menial laborers. Supervisory and higher-paying jobs remained closed to members of the race.[78]

Indeed, white European immigrants acted as a deterrent for indigent blacks eager to leave the South. Because most blacks remained mired in the South as the region's cheap labor force, immigrants from Europe ventured to United States shores en masse to work in the burgeoning factories of industrial America. East Coast cities like New York—with hundreds of thousands of immigrants entering the city and nation through Ellis Island—and Philadelphia became prime locales settled by European immigrants.[79] European immigrants also ventured into the Ohio Valley, where blacks residing in Cincinnati and Pittsburgh who sought work found themselves at a disadvantage because white industrialists preferred to hire foreign-born European workers. Unlike immigrants, blacks retained the ignominious stereotypes of being indolent, irresponsible, indifferent, and inclined toward criminality. Even in hinterland cities black men discovered that work became difficult to acquire because of the white European influx.[80]

European immigrants also gained access to unions, institutions that restricted blacks from membership. In1900 virtually all unions involved with the rubber, steel, railroads, boilermakers, machinists, and plumbers had excluded African Americans. Equally disturbing, black laborers became subjected to the capricious whims of anti-labor industrialists. When European and native-born union members demonstrated against low pay and dire working by resorting to strikes, industrial management used black laborers as strike breakers. By angering unionists and remaining pawns of the industrialists, prospects for black upward mobility remained limited. This unfortunate trend continued throughout the first decades of the century. Outside the meat-packing industry in Chicago where blacks found work in smelly stockyards and slaughterhouses, African American men could not find adequate employment. During an era when President Theodore Roosevelt "busted" trusts, blacks remained so distant from the affairs of white people that trust busting proved irrelevant.

Although some enterprising African Americans found ways to elevate their economic standing by practicing frugality, using mother wit advantageously, or through sheer luck of gaining employment under a beneficent boss or fair-minded company, most languished in dead-end jobs. Although low-level, menial employment invariably avoided being impacted by the vicissitudes of an inconsistent economy, black workers hardly enjoyed job security. When necessary, desperate whites affected by a downturn in the economy endeavored to supplant African American workers. African Americans engaged in service industries like barbering and catering, jobs that provided opportunities for upward mobility by servicing a white clientele, gradually succumbed to white encroachment. Accepting lower-paying, menial jobs or moving to find better job opportunities became the only available options.

Gender discrimination existed as another impediment to the advancement of African Americans. Because black women appeared less threatening to white men and did not compete against European immigrants for jobs, African American females in the North found work. With the exception of Chicago and Philadelphia, black females outnumbered males within the urban milieu. The gender imbalance hardly augured well for the race. Entangling social relationships, the absence of males to serve as positive role models, ill treatment of women, the inability for females to find a suitable mate, and other associated factors made the industrial North less than ideal. With more black women than men living in Northern cities, females had the responsibility for taking care of themselves as well as the local family or relatives in the South.[81] Black women worked longer hours than European females. Black women, moreover, were denied the opportunity to become employed in the better-paying, more attractive jobs. Prior to 1910, black females never worked in factories or performed clerical duties. Other than working as low-income hotel maids, domestics, and food service employees, the only available jobs existed in the exacting, unhealthy steam laundries.[82] When black women assumed the role of family providers and suffered from racism and sexism, desperate African Americans suffered.

In the first decade of the new century, most African Americans were impoverished and suffered grievously from racial animosity, repression, and the indignities associated with Jim Crow. Few prominent whites spoke with equanimity and sensitivity toward disadvantaged blacks. Most white people treated African Americans with disdain and only coveted blacks as an inexpensive labor force. In addition to the unfair sharecropping system, judicial malfeasance, and infamous convict/lease programs, events unfolded that served as constant reminders of the race's lowly position.

Nevertheless, regardless of gender or socioeconomic class, blacks learned that the adage to "hang together or hang separately" rang true. Perhaps the most significant positive feature the masses could glean from this horrendous era would be the semblance of black intra-racial accord. Some among the black elite, of course, desired to remain aloof from the indigent masses. But the one-drop theory and the negativism applied to all of African ancestry meant that every African American, regardless of class or color, experienced racism. Therefore, members of the higher classes, including those of mixed blood like Booker T. Washington, W. E. B. Du Bois, and the mulatto John Hope who would head Morehouse College, embraced their African heritage and sought to ameliorate the black masses' condition.

Impoverished African Americans had cause to view the new century with a sense of foreboding. Although virtually all African American leaders maintained a profound sense of race consciousness, black amelioration proved limited. Booker T. Washington endeavored to enhance black prospects for success by engaging in a range of altruistic endeavors designed to benefit sharecroppers as well as incipient businessmen. Other members of the black elite founded self-help organizations to diminish the burden of race that impinged upon all African Americans. And W. E. B. Du Bois organized the fledgling Niagara movement with the purpose of demanding rights for all black people. Still, white animus toward blacks undermined the noblest African American efforts to ameliorate the lowly condition of their race. With the exception of a few white philanthropists, most white leaders demonstrated little concern for black uplift and remained content to allow the African American masses to remain destitute.

Slightly one generation removed from slavery, scores of ambitious blacks would have their future dashed by circumstances beyond their control. Omnipresent racism rendered racial uplift impossible. Demands for cheap labor on Southern farms caused white landowners and merchants to refrain from treating blacks fairly. Moreover, sable sharecroppers had no means for legal redress; the white man's word remained inviolate, preventing blacks from obtaining economic justice. In the North, European immigrants cornered factory jobs, minimizing possibilities for black men to find work. The only jobs available for African American men and women remained confined to menial and service work that offered little pay and no benefits. Only largess from beneficent whites provided lowly blacks with prospects for upward mobility. In short, the black masses had no control over their destiny. At best blacks could try to retain a sense of humanity and suffer the burden of neo-slavery stoically and, at worse, engage in inimical actions that resulted in prison, the chain gang, or death. Limited job opportunities and common poverty in the urban North provided no sanctuary for wretched African Americans. The omnipresent forces of economic, physical, psychological, and political intimidation resulted in understandable apathy. Coping methods evidenced in church sermons that spoke of salvation, or escapism found in temporary respites from alcohol, appeared as the only options available to impoverished African Americans.

Chapter 3

The Late Progressive Era 1910–1920

Despite being an era known for progressive reform, the second decade of the twentieth century hardly proved propitious for impecunious African Americans. Evidence of the dichotomy between reform and indifference toward the Negro appeared in the progressive-minded New South. While early twentieth-century Southern reformers attacked the monopolistic practices of regional railroads, took action against high insurance rates charged by companies located in the Northeast, and fought against the exorbitant charges applied by big oil and its subsidies, these same leaders held little regard for blacks.[1] In 1910 more than 93 percent of all African Americans resided in the South, most of who toiled on farms as sharecroppers and rent farmers. Most of these unfortunate laborers earned less than seventy-nine dollars annually.[2] Because landlords intended to make profits at the expense of black laborers, tenants were grossly underpaid; and sharecroppers, regardless of industry and effort to raise a bountiful crop, remained in debt. Southern whites had no guilty conscience in regard to mistreating the Negro. And with extreme irony, Southerners perceived the legalization of racial segregation as evidence of reform, providing a sense of order to the white South.[3] Southern white politicians appeared particularly interested in bringing progressive reforms to the South. Governors Napoleon Bonaparte Broward of Florida, Hoke Smith of Georgia, William Goebel of Kentucky, and Braxton Bragg Comer of Alabama projected a sincere and profound interest in helping farmers in their respective states. Although Northern progressive reformers ignored the plight of rural Americans, Southerners in the United States Congress—as well as others with rural constituencies—succeeded in passing legislation favorable to Southern farmers. The Smith-Lever Act of 1914 provided federal grant-in-aid subsidies for agricultural education and the Smith-Hughes Act of 1917 offered federal assistance for vocational education. Southerners also succeeded in having the Virginia-born Negrophobe President Woodrow Wilson pass legislation designed to reduce the interest in farm loans. Consequently, the Federal Farm Loan Act of 1916 provided credit to farmers at low interest rates. Since most blacks rented, rather than owned land, and suffered enormously from economic discrimination, few benefited from federal largess.[4]

To the chagrin of disadvantaged blacks, most Southern governors acquired power largely by "out niggering" an opponent, claiming to have the best ideas for keeping African Americans downtrodden. With the success of a white politician contingent upon who could voice the most insidious means for keeping the "Negro in his place," lowly blacks continued suffering from white racism.

After 1910, Southern white leaders initiated deliberate efforts to deny public education for black children. Despite the *Plessey v. Ferguson* ruling that declared black and white institutions could be separate but equal, the high court's dictum was ignored. Lily-white Southern governments increased funding for white schools but refrained from providing comparable educational opportunities for African Americans. Although every Southern state developed uniform educational standards that required every rural county to contain at least one schoolhouse, no secondary school beyond eighth grade existed for blacks residing in the rural South. Many Southern counties failed to provide funds for black schools, and where schools existed, the teacher-to-pupil ratio could be as high as 1 to 125.[5] Indeed, as late as 1915, Mississippi, Alabama, Louisiana, and Georgia collectively only had six public secondary schools for African American children. White landlords recognized black children represented cheap labor and demanded that young blacks work rather than study. Parents seeking to enroll children in rural schools for nine months faced a daunting, if not impossible, task. But even urban areas of the Old Confederacy failed to offer two years of high school education for African Americans.[6] In spite of a windfall of $100,000,000 spent on public education in 1914, the Southern Educational Board terminated the South's educational reform programs for black students. The African American quest for equality in education had been sacrificed to maintain white hegemony.[7]

Despite the restrictive educational system African Americans encountered from recalcitrant white Southerners, external forces remained at work to provide educational opportunities for rural blacks. Philanthropic contributions from Northern industrialists geared to benefiting the entire South forced Southern whites to allow some funding for Negro schools. As early as 1882, the Peabody Education and the John F. Slater Funds had been established to educate black children. With a $1,000,000 pledge from the Rockefeller family, the General Education Board became established in 1902 to acquire information and publicize the wretched educational situation encountered by impoverished Southerners. In 1907 the Anna T. Jeanes Fund became added to the list of philanthropic foundations. And by 1912 and 1913, the Julius Rosenwald Fund and Rockefeller Foundation, respectively, made enormous contributions to provide educational opportunities for blacks residing in the South.[8]

Booker T. Washington's association with merchant mogul Julius Rosenwald proved exceedingly beneficial for Southern, rural African Americans. In 1913 Washington, the "Wizard of Tuskegee," obviously encouraged Rosenwald to establish the first black Rosenwald primary school in Macon County, Alabama, near the Wizard's beloved industrial institution. African Americans raised $132 to purchase the land and contributed an additional $132 in labor to construct the building. Beneficent white citizens added $360 and the Rosenwald Fund contributed $300 to finalize the project at a cost of $924.[9] Fortunately for blacks, the state and county agreed to maintain the school and incorporated the newly created facility into the public school system. The Macon County School proved a precursor to future successful endeavors.[10] By October 1917, Rosenwald provided $40,000,000 additional funds for Southern education with a significant amount being directed toward Negro schools. But even when some sections of the South increased revenue for black schools, the concessions occurred for agricultural training to keep sable workers on land to continue providing cheap labor for white landowners.[11]

Another windfall that positively impacted rustic African Americans appeared through the county training school movement. Through the General Education and Slater Funds, rural high schools for black students became established throughout the South. The Slater Fund focused exclusively on creating schools and providing a means to support the education of Negroes. To accomplish this goal, Slater benefactors provided money to colleges that would train secondary schoolteachers to educate black students in the rural South.[12]

Educators known as "Jeanes teachers" also contributed to the enhancement of education in the rural South. Funds derived from the aforementioned Anna T. Jeans Foundation and Slater Fund enabled instructors with industrial training to travel throughout Southern counties, lending their skills to help rural teachers. These itinerate educators visited newly established schools, and with the compliance and assistance of special superintendents, provided enormous learning opportunities for rural African Americans. Equally important, the women who toured the South as "Jeanes teachers" cultivated interests in the importance of education to the black populace, made the school curriculum relevant to students, and contributed to the general enhancement of rural communities.[13] With this kind of encouragement even the most recalcitrant rural Negroes opposed to education had cause to support efforts to enlighten their race.

Black Southerners' thirst for education existed among black counterparts residing in Northern cities. African American adults eagerly attended evening schools. Black children flocked to elementary and secondary schools eager to acquire knowledge denied them in the South. In Chicago, for example, the percentage of African American children attending school exceeded percentages for foreign-born whites and eventually rivaled or matched attendance of native-born Caucasians.[14] Regardless of the locale—North or South, rural or urban, wealthy or poor—and despite severe obstacles during the second decade of the twentieth century, African Americans collectively placed a high premium on education.[15] The NAACP and National Urban League also engaged in ameliorative activities designed to help African Americans acquire a functional education. While the NAACP used legal recourses to provide educational opportunities for all African Americans, George Hayes of the Urban League focused primarily on job procurement, using educational instruction and training to help migrants find work.[16] The task proved arduous because extensive assistance was required to aid disadvantaged blacks. This task demanded personnel and resources far beyond the capabilities of the most sincere progressives and progressive black institutions. Despite efforts black institutions made to help African Americans acquire education, a gnawing problem remained. Educated blacks were not guaranteed work.[17]

Aside from promoting incipient primary schools in the rural South and educational opportunities and the reform efforts of the NAACP and Urban League, other aspects of life for downtrodden blacks during the second decade of the twentieth century hardly appeared promising. In 1910 the life expectancy for black females and males was 38 and 34 years respectively as opposed to 51.8 and 48.4 for the larger white populace.[18] The following year American newspapers reported that a lynching occurred once every six days in the United States. Black ghettos became sanctioned by law. White primaries came into existence, schools still remained inadequate and insufficient, and racial discrimination prevailed.[19] Moreover, nearly 90 percent of the African American population languished in the South, the most backward, racist region in the United States.

Many Southern blacks became confined to segregated rural villages. Compounds of unkempt cabins or shacks dotted the landscape. Poverty caused the villages to convey a seedy appearance owing both to the impecunious nature of the residents and the fear that a painted dwelling or manicured lawn would create the wrath of hostile whites. When opportunities beckoned, younger folk ventured from home and moved to larger towns on the periphery of white communities. Here, the common appearance of poverty continued. White residential areas had paved roads, electric lights, running water, and sewers. But in segregated black communities, white municipal authorities chose not to extend the expected norms of the average American lifestyle to Southern

African Americans.[20] Prior to World War I, Southern blacks remained outside the pale of social, economic, and human development. For every reform effort designed to ameliorate life for Southern whites, the Southern white "reformers" intentionally limited prospects for African Americans.

Southern blacks suffered psychologically from the strain of omnipresent discrimination. From the most basic salutation and courtesy, where white people refrained from using "Mr.," "Mrs.," or "Miss" toward African Americans to other demeaning Southern norms, blacks endured constant insults without redress. Relentless ill treatment at the hands of white racists instilled blacks with a sense of inferiority; only the most resourceful, self-contained African American could refrain from engaging in some manifestation of self-hatred.

Even the economy conspired against disadvantaged blacks as the South experienced a depression in cotton prices. Half of all tenant farmers worked in the Cotton Belt as sharecroppers. This system of exploitation had a negative impact upon the entire region. The wasteful labor system resulted in depleted and exhausted soils, inferior crop yields, unkempt houses and yards, poor roads, and decaying bridges.[21] The initial problem with cotton originated in the Old South with the infestation of the boll weevil in 1910. Therefore, when the price of cotton plunged dramatically in 1913, tenants generally, and black tenants in particular, were pushed off the land and suffered grievously.[22]

In the final analysis, throughout the decade Southern whites would rather kill every "uppity" Negro they encountered than compromise on the concept of white supremacy. Virtually every action in which blacks engaged seemed threatening to insecure whites.[23] White men and women feared blacks who refused to honor the old customs of slaves and pay proper deference to the Caucasian race. Keeping blacks in their so-called place became an obsession. Prior to America's entry into World War I, a prominent white South Carolinian spoke for himself and fellow sons and daughters of Dixie and for many white Northerners when he wrote, "Truth is the people of the South—and of the United States—have no idea of conceding to the negroes (sic) the full rights of American freedmen in this year of our Lord 1917."[24]

While white supremacy offended African Americans, this concept became an imperative for white Southerners. Poor whites believed skin color existed as the only advantage they had in life and defended that advantage at all costs. Yet even the better sort of white people retained the same prejudicial views as their impecunious cousins. Neither class of white people appeared capable of recognizing that successful, hard-working blacks would function within the legal norms of the South and contribute to the region's economic well-being. White Southerners also failed to understand why the younger generation of African Americans refused to perform tasks for white people without proper recompense. A mournful white complained, "The negro (sic) youth will no longer cheerfully spend half a day doing a white man's small jobs for a ham bone or a drink of whiskey."[25] Impoverished black youths' disinclination to provide cheap labor would continue throughout the remainder of the century.

Southern reprisals for any semblance of black achievement and independence proved exceedingly harsh, stifling ambition and minimizing the incentive to achieve success. All white classes engaged in methods to keep blacks down. And to maintain white supremacy, Southern whites systematically disfranchised black men, imposed rigid patterns of racial segregation, and sustained extraordinary levels of violence and brutality.[26]

Since the entire machinery of Southern justice was devoted to controlling African American labor by keeping blacks in a servile state, white people controlled African American life. The courts granted immunity to white people charged with committing crimes against black men and women. A general maxim remained true that declared that if a Negro kills a white man, most likely the Negro be lynched or hung. But if the situation were reversed, the white man faced no reprisals and would be exonerated by the courts.[27] Understandably, blacks least capable of contesting oppression resented white authority and continued a sustained hostility toward the American judicial system.

Low-income blacks probably became even more inclined to stay out of harm's way in relation to white people. As often as possible poor blacks realized they could become "sport" for bloodthirsty whites. Any pretense made to approach, address, or accidentally brush against a white woman could result in a violent death. And while the unkempt, simian-featured, demonic black male had been constantly perceived as the person most interested in deflowering innocent white Southern women, the actual number of blacks even accused of committing rape or other sexual assaults proved miniscule.[28] Rape functioned as a figment of the imagination of whites rather than being a remotely common practice perpetrated by "fiendish" African Americans.

Other factors militated against low-income African Americans. In 1915 and 1916 a boll weevil infestation ruined the Southern cotton crops in Louisiana, Mississippi, Florida, Georgia, and Alabama, forcing blacks out of work. Heavy rains also had a deleterious impact on the Southern economy, destroying other crops upon which black farmers depended for their livelihood. Moreover, the rise of absentee ownership, as planters moved into towns, contributed to mismanagement and furthered the decline of a plantation economy. A shrinking economy that severely impacted black tenants and sharecroppers provided African Americans with additional incentive to leave the South.[29] And finally, some blacks became victims of "white capping," a nefarious practice in the rural South where fearful whites suffering in a down economy forced blacks off the land.[30] For scores of desperate African Americans, emigration North appeared as the only viable option.

The outbreak of war in Europe in August 1914 provided African Americans with the greatest opportunity the race enjoyed since Emancipation. European combatants required soldiers and restricted customary immigration to the United States. Meanwhile, American industrialists sold military necessities to all belligerent powers and garnered enormous profits. But when the United States entered the war in April 1917 and began drafting young men for the military, corporate America experienced a profound labor shortage. The railroad industry became the first corporate entity to recognize the need to augment its workforce. After contemplating the hiring of Mexican workers and white hobos, the *New Republic* boldly declared in 1916 that "the Negro gets a chance to work only when there is no one else."[31] The experiment by desperate Northern industrialists to hire black men and eventually black women to work en masse outside the South commenced.

In addition to the war, other factors caused the black masses to leave the region of their birth. Drought, torrential rains, and flooding—combined with the aforementioned boll weevil that flourished under wet conditions—ruined the cotton industry for at least two years. Other low-income African Americans had customary reasons for leaving the South—low pay, bad treatment, woefully inadequate schools, and various forms of discrimination and oppression. [32] Opportunity, however, far more than the challenges wrought by mother nature and racial animus, caused venturesome African Americans to brave the unknowns of the urban milieu far from the familiarity of the rural South. Jobs provided in railroad yards, steel mills, garment industries, food-processing plants, and other industries lured blacks to cities in the North, Midwest, and Far West.[33]

An exodus from the South between 1916 and 1919 resulted in 400,000 to 500,000 African Americans leaving the South. As the tide of migrants swept North, they broke in a huge wave beginning in Chester, Pennsylvania, in the East; St. Louis in the Midwest; and Los Angeles in the Far West. The crest of the wave broke in Detroit, Chicago, and Philadelphia.[34] Other cities experiencing an influx of black migrants included New York, Boston, and Pittsburgh. Unskilled laborers comprised the largest percentage of the black migration. These workers sought common labor and found jobs as longshoremen, stevedores, freight handlers, miners, and as "gandy dancers" (railroad men). Women with comparable low-level skills worked as domestics, cooks, laundry workers, baby nurses, and house maids.[35] Black men removed from the South experienced daily wages that increased from $0.76 to $4.00. Although wages for female domestics, by comparison, proved modest, black women enjoyed a daily pay increase from $0.75 to $2.50.[36] Black migrants expanded urban ghettos that contained hordes of the untrained, quasi-literate, but hopeful migrants who represented the majority of African American populace.[37]

Eyewitness journalist Ray Stannard Baker revealed that the migrants comprised discontented tenant farmers who fled the misery imposed by white landlords and black youths unwilling to accept Southern mores that required

African American deference to white people. Although ambitious middle-class blacks also moved North, the migration became characterized primarily by those who represented the lower strata of African American society.[38] In keeping with the large numbers of impoverished blacks who migrated into cities, established blacks of property and standing predictably resented the "shiftless, dissolute, and immoral newcomers who moved into their neighborhoods."[39]

Despite new opportunities to acquire work in mills and factories, Northern prejudices remained.[40] Unskilled Southern migrant laborers were assigned the most demanding, dangerous, lower-paying jobs. Even migrants who possessed skills were consistently forced to accept jobs lower than acquired levels of experience and expertise. They learned that discrimination rather than competition kept them out of skilled trades. As late as 1917 only 1 of 2,800 skilled black workers in New York City obtained work in their chosen occupation.[41] Similar problems occurred in Chicago. Blacks seeking work only found menial jobs disdained by European immigrants available.[42] Given the paucity of job opportunities in skilled trades, the North proved no more hospitable for low-income African Americans than the South. And though black migrants enjoyed greater prospects for being treated as self-respecting men and women, only the strongest, most resolute migrants could transcend omnipresent problems attributed to poverty and racism and remain optimistic and confident.

Another dilemma that brought confusion to the African American masses existed in the Washington-Du Bois controversy that presented two diametrically opposite positions toward black economic amelioration. Washington, among others, subscribed to the capitalist position—the "Gospel of Wealth" that advocated individualism and endorsement for the industrial elite—and eschewed support for labor unions. Furthermore, African Americans had a natural bias toward unions because of the overt discrimination unions displayed toward black workers. Therefore, African Americans traditionally became strike breakers and maintained a strong animus toward organized labor.[43]

Du Bois and the NAACP, conversely, envisioned a marriage between unions and African Americans. Perceiving anti-union bias as an "old attitude," Du Bois recommended that African Americans should find common ground with the union movement. Recognizing that most blacks were of the working class, endeavors to enter unions appeared as the only logical approach toward achieving economic amelioration. Subscribing to the socialist tendencies of economic progressives, Du Bois, the NAACP, and other progressives on the left never believed that the economic salvation of blacks existed in the laissez-faire, trickle-down theory espoused by the business elite.[44]

Although the newly created National Urban League initially aligned with business interests, it too would support efforts to acquire jobs for African

Americans. As early as 1913, league members met with prominent leaders in the AFL to facilitate black entrance into the union. Despite noble efforts of the Urban League, few black workers received the opportunity to join skilled unions and enjoy the advantages of union membership. Lily-white policies adopted by both union heads and the rank and file prevented low-income African Americans from obtaining apprenticeships or enabling artisans to work at a familiar craft. Anti-union sentiment held by most black leaders failed to create intra-racial accord for the black laboring class. At best, African American leadership's views toward unions proved ambivalent and inconsistent.[45] Even if black leaders and organizations reached a consensus on supporting unions, racial discrimination closed union membership to African Americans. Despite noble efforts, the National Urban League failed to find a solution to the impasse between white unions and black workers. Black leaders could do little to enhance economic prospects for the lower-class members of their race.

Exclusion from unions and better-paying jobs kept the African American masses poor regardless of Southern or Northern birth. Both regions kept blacks relegated to underpaid menial positions and confined African Americans to the lowest echelon of the American economy.

Given the challenges that migrants faced in the North, southern black leaders, specifically ministers, endeavored to keep low-income laborers in the South. Spokespersons that eschewed migration and encouraged black workers to remain in Dixie, however, were often perceived as being ignorant of black aspirations, self-serving people who profited from black laborers, or appeared dismissive of Southern racism. Booker T. Washington himself functioned as the most renowned black advocate to recommend that African Americans should remain in the South.[46] Yet despite Washington's Herculean efforts to enable blacks to rise from serfdom to acquire middle-class standing, life for indigent African Americans hardly improved. Understandably, the African American majority would be inclined to view some established black leaders with skepticism.

Unions alone could hardly be blamed entirely for the misfortunes of black migrants. Ironically, some black churches in the North also operated as a detriment to the black masses. Black churches, historically existed as the mainstay of African American society. The church provided a primary outlet for human emotions, served as the key to black social life, and provided comfort to those seeking escape from the harshness of American society. With the increase of Southern migrants to Northern cities, the increased size of urban congregations enabled the wealth in churches to increase exponentially. Unfortunately the adage "strength in numbers" failed to apply in regard to migrants. Although the number of black churches in New York City increased fivefold between 1900 and 1920, the religious community had prominent naysayers who abhorred the spending practices of church hierarchies. NAACP executive secretary James Weldon Johnson proved to be a particularly harsh critic of black churches. Johnson complained that churches drained off money to erect fine edifices rather than engage in efforts to improve hospital care, focus on providing agreeable homes for the elderly, or bolster other agencies that administered to the needs of low-income African Americans.[47] While certain ministers focused on "hell and damnation" and increased church coffers, the needs of the poor remained unaddressed.

Cities where African Americans resided also failed the black masses. Few recreational centers and parks existed that catered to the black populace. In 1913, George Edmund Hayes, a Columbia-trained sociologist and a man responsible for creating the National Urban League, observed that in New York City, "playgrounds in Negro neighborhoods are so rare as to excite curiosity . . . ."[48] That same year Chicago's Juvenile Protection Association reported that when altruistic blacks endeavored to help their downtrodden brethren, insufficient resources were offered by city managers to reduce or eliminate aberrant juvenile behavior. [49] A comforting institution like Chicago's famous Hull House did not exist for African Americans. Moreover, leading altruistic black institutions lacked sufficient means to mitigate the many challenges encountered by disadvantaged African Americans who ventured into northern cities.

With a rustic background, accompanied by the demonic nature of street life, the morality of black newcomers became suspect. The initial problem, ironically, evolved from the unique circumstances associated with the employment of black females. Even prior to the Great War, black women secured jobs easier than black men. Nevertheless, despite job opportunities enhanced by the World War, women still encountered difficulties. This problem held true specifically for women with children. A disproportionate number of black females heading households worked long, irregular hours, enabling children to wander aimlessly in the streets without proper supervision. Children and young adolescents, therefore, lacked direction and invariably created mayhem. Youthful newcomers would remonstrate, display ignorance, become pariahs in their newly adopted communities, and establish an infamous reputation for all newly arrived migrants.[50] With inadequate recreational facilities for children, parents working long hours to meet the heightened costs of urban living, and pressures exacted from residing in overcrowded, increasingly dilapidated housing established a precedent for the disastrous experiences of black urbanites far into the twentieth century.

In many respects, low-income African Americans became more influenced by street culture than by formal institutions. The established black population revealed an unvarnished hostility toward "street corner" men and migrants from the South deemed responsible for turning respectable neighborhoods into ghettos.[51] Young, rebellious, and testing the boundaries of liberation in the liberal North, the newcomers displayed boisterous behavior, wore gaudy-suggestive clothing, used inappropriate language, and engaged in "suggestive" activities that offended genteel African Americans. By acting in an untoward manner, the black masses became a marginalized populace in the urban North. Confined to living with Southern newcomers in the cramped ghetto, the established black bourgeoisie recognized few redeeming qualities in Southern black culture.[52] The Urban League in Chicago even prepared a seven-point manifesto designed to acquaint newcomers about the proper decorum, apparel, sanitation, and maintenance of property expected from new residents.[53] Given the large migrant population that entered Chicago and rendered living conditions difficult, the manifesto seemed warranted.[54] Although many white people migrated from the South to the North, their lack of visibility and ability to move easily into white neighborhoods failed to create an anti-migrant backlash comparable to African Americans. The multi-headed hydra that encompassed racism existed in regard to the lowly African American and contributed to the Red Summer, highlighted by Chicago's bloody race riot of 1919.[55]

Societal thinking of that era ascribed black crime to race rather than to poverty. Despite the enlightening pronouncements of social scientists who perceived crime as a direct result of poverty, most people seemed inclined to condemn low-income blacks for unsavory conduct and behavior. Even a perceptive and sensitive reformer like Du Bois blamed low-income blacks for a lack of moral turpitude and good judgment. Excessive drinking, loose sexual morals, and other perceptions associated with irresponsible behavior became difficult stereotypes for the black masses to overcome. Meanwhile, few blamed blacks' debased condition on the enormous challenges impoverished African Americans encountered. White landlords charged exorbitant rents to enable blacks to live in subdivided apartments, forcing blacks desperate for living accommodations to reside in unsavory, overcrowded African American neighborhoods.[56] One may presume, therefore, that people who realize the unfairness of life would have less cause to abide by accepted middle-class norms.

Since escaping poverty became difficult, if not impossible, for alienated and destitute blacks, some found that crime became equated to survival by any means necessary.[57] Enterprising blacks opened gambling facilities, speakeasies, and dens of prostitution. Individual blacks committed offenses that ranged from pick pocketing to violence.[58] Without the ability to obtain "respectable" jobs and experiencing daily reminders about the wretched living conditions encountered in low-income neighborhoods, those who had an inclination or a propensity for wrongdoing found an abundance of opportunities to go astray in the city.[59]

During the Progressive Era, middle-class African Americans invariably became the most vociferous critics of the black migrants. The proximity of all blacks residing in the ghetto meant that the higher classes of African Americans would become the most likely victims of black-on-black crime.[60] Again impoverished blacks preyed on their wealthier brethren in order to acquire enough sustenance for food, clothing, and shelter, and to fund entertaining escapes from the drudgery of a mundane existence. But middle-class blacks had an additional reason for castigating black migrants. Although established blacks made every effort to display proper decorum and refinement before white counterparts, they believed that aberrant behavior attributed to the Southern rubes cast aspersions on the entire race. To the black establishment "low-life" Negroes continued undermining noble efforts to garner white respect and contributed to a backlash from white peers.

As blacks moved North, the white South conveyed an ambivalent attitude toward African American flight. White Southerners who resented the "new Negro," an individual perceived as being more self-respecting and arrogant than the "darkeys" of old, were heartened by the black exodus. On the other hand, landlords in Georgia and Alabama dependent upon tenant farming became concerned about losing a high percentage of prime-age workers. As economic pragmatists, white men with considerable property tried to prevent "these rude, insolent, aggressive, obstinate, worthless workers from leaving them."[61] Only progressive white Southerners came to realize the South had to pay fair wages and treat blacks honorably to keep the necessary laboring force at home. For aggrieved African Americans, however, higher wages and the promise of fair treatment failed to compensate for the historical disrespect Southern whites accorded blacks. The migration north continued.[62]

Destitute blacks who headed to the "promised land" because of the Great War ventured into an unhealthy environment.[63] Sickness proved pervasive, as unkempt Southerners had little knowledge about the significance of hygienic practices necessary to lessen the spread of disease. Outdoor privies proved commonplace in the overcrowded ghetto, and those fortunate enough to rent apartments with flush toilets had little knowledge about their use and maintenance. Bathtubs appeared as an oddity, and the concept of privacy proved irrelevant. Additionally, the need for sunlight, fresh air, recreation, proper medical care, and suitable clothing seemed illusive and unessential to people struggling to survive in the impersonal city.[64]

The insalubrious health conditions inherent in ghettos caused impoverished African Americans to face severe health risks. Deaths attributed to tuberculosis, pneumonia, and diarrhea historically had been two to three times higher for blacks than whites. And when Spanish influenza reached epidemic levels in 1918, blacks, like whites, suffered grievously. Although the African American death rates attributed directly to flu surprisingly proved lower than for whites, a significant disparity in health-care facilities related to segregation placed blacks at a disadvantage. In Baltimore, Maryland, for example, the only black health facility that housed African Americans became overwhelmed, forcing the hospital to send away scores of extremely ill patients.[65]

Those who migrated North could hardly be held accountable entirely for the ever-increasing, unsavory conditions of the urban ghetto. White housing restrictions confined black newcomers to African American neighborhoods, causing the already impoverished communities to become even more seedy and inhospitable. While European immigrants who acquired sufficient wealth could move unfettered to a more desirable neighborhood, enterprising blacks did not enjoy the same privilege. In Chicago an estimated ten thousand black migrants poured into the city each month and crowded into already occupied apartments. Slum lords, meanwhile, continued the practice of charging exorbitant rates while simultaneously neglecting maintenance on overly strained housing complexes. Officials in the Windy City also contributed to migrants' misery by curtailing the use of municipal services that included police protection, proper street lighting, and making provisions for sanitation.[66]

In virtually every city migrants entered during the second decade, white municipal leaders institutionalized segregation. Heightened Jim Crow ordinances occurred in border-state cities as well as the urban North. Although the Supreme Court declared residential segregation unconstitutional in the *Buchanan v. Warley* case of 1917 that originated in Louisville, Kentucky, the court's dictum remained ignored. Southern and border states maintained segregation at will and Northern cities found the means to restrict African Americans by intimidation and through restrictive housing covenants and tenants' associations.[67] Even the most industrious, ambitious, established African Americans remained confined to the ghetto.

Ironically, ghettos contained endearing qualities embraced by low-income African Americans. Despite the unsavory aspects of ghetto life, an undeniable sense of comfort and familiarity existed for residents comfortable living among their "own kind." Outside the ghetto, blacks became subjected to white caprice, overt hostility, and embarrassment. Therefore, Southern-born migrants consciously decided that the ills inherent in ghetto life—including paying higher prices for inferior merchandise and residing in cramped qualities—seemed preferable to risking a loss of newly found dignity to disrespectful whites.[68]

While opportunities evolved for African Americans during the Great War, related events created additional challenges for blacks. African Americans who served in the armed services acquired experiences and developed a heightened desire to enjoy all the benefits of American citizenship. Blacks from both the rural South and urban ghettos acquired a sense of self-pride when adorning a military uniform and, when serving abroad, experienced a sense of freedom and hero worship never previously received in America. Reactionary whites in the army, however, feared blacks accustomed to servile positions who served in the military would demand full American citizenship. Even before black troops returned from Europe, the military used discriminatory tactics to diminish the significance of African Americans. Consequently, blacks who served in the Great War returned to the United States seething with anger at the treatment they received abroad from white Americans in the military.

Domestically, the race problem became national in scope, as whites sought to retain hegemony over African Americans. In the South, violence reined as white mobs in Mississippi, Georgia, Arkansas, Florida, and Alabama continued murdering blacks.[69] Northerners also participated in violent acts against African Americans. Although some cities like New York's Harlem, Chicago, St. Louis, Des Moines, Buffalo, Cincinnati, Cleveland, Columbus, and Kansas City allowed victory parades for returning black veterans, white citizens in other cities, namely Omaha, Nebraska, and Duluth, Minnesota, elected to suppress a burgeoning race consciousness by engaging in violence.

White resentment toward blacks became manifested in race riots. The initial racial confrontation occurred on July 1, 1917, in East St. Louis, Illinois. Whites resented low-income blacks being hired in a factory that received government contracts. Angry mobs stabbed, clubbed, and hanged black victims. Even an innocent two-year-old child was shot and thrown into a burning building.[70] At least 39 blacks comprising laborers from the South died in the attacks. The East St. Louis riot, however, represented a departure from previous confrontations. This time blacks fought back in defense and killed five white vigilantes.

The greatest concentration of postwar violence, however, occurred in Chicago, Illinois. Given the large numbers of impoverished Southern blacks who ventured North, the Windy City fittingly became the locale of the most vicious race riot of the era. Between 1910 and 1920, the black population doubled (primarily between 1915 and 1917), increasing from 109,458 to 233,908 respectively.[71] In response to the race riots of 1917 in East St. Louis, Illinois, the *Chicago Tribune* urged Southern blacks to remain in the South, asserting that the migration was a huge mistake.[72] The *Tribune's* request, however, failed to deter blacks from venturing into the city. Eventually, tensions continued to mount as a myriad of issues caused violence to explode. The initial reason for white hostility in Chicago could be traced somewhat to Southern migrants alien to the folkways and mores of a Northern city. These Southern newcomers caused long-established, middle-class African Americans to seek housing outside the black ghetto. White home owners' associations, athletic clubs, and vicious hoodlums made no distinction between upper- and lower-class blacks and resented all African Americans. Law-abiding middle-class blacks who either worked in white areas or lived on the periphery of the Black Belt became targets of white hostility. Labor disputes between blacks and whites also contributed to racial confrontations in the Windy City. Blacks customarily used as strikebreakers abhorred unions that operated as white-dominated organizations that segregated and ridiculed blacks and excluded the race from membership. When the meat packers' union insisted that African Americans join or refrain from working, skeptical blacks refused. Animosity resulted, leading to threats that also contributed to the Chicago riot of 1919.[73]

The Chicago riot revealed low-income blacks faced a daunting future. While blacks did not form gangs and venture into white neighborhoods, Black Belt residents defended their community and, when possible, took out vengeance on white people. Because Southern migrants moved to Chicago in search of a better life, enjoyed economic opportunities, and experienced social justice previously unknown, these newcomers proved willing to die for the right to exist in peace. Black veterans also appeared amenable to using their military training to defend hard-earned rights as American citizens. Most blacks fighting and dying in the Chicago confrontation were young, poor, and restless males, a leaderless throng unwilling to be intimidated by hostile whites.[74] Hostile whites contributed to intra-class solidarity among African Americans.

For desperate, impoverished African Americans, the second decade of the twentieth century marked an interesting departure from a mundane and lowly existence. This difference occurred because blacks became useful to the advocates of capital and labor simultaneously. In the South, white landlords and merchants desired to keep black tenants on the land to harvest crops. At the same time, industrialists in major cities lured blacks North, promising jobs with higher wages and a better future. Regardless of region, size of community, or aspirations of impoverished African Americans, low income blacks played only a minor role in determining their destiny. Finding gainful employment in areas where racism proved less limiting provided the best possibility for a propitious future. Unfortunately, racial discrimination meant that only the most industrious and fortunate could extricate themselves from the poverty that characterized life for most African Americans.

Despite the economic and social obstacles and omnipresent violence that impacted African Americans throughout the nation, the decade ended with greater promise for the race than any period since the Civil War. A "New Negro" had evolved. The North existed as a beacon encouraging blacks to escape virulent Southern racism. New job opportunities, coupled with worldly experiences acquired through military service, fostered the notion that low-income blacks could eventually enjoy the same rights as other Americans. Meanwhile, business leaders of the white South dependent on the cheap black labor force failed to find satisfactory ways to keep thousands of African

American laborers in Dixie.[75] Better prospects for low-income farm laborers created an exodus from the South.

The second decade of the twentieth century also represented a time when African Americans accustomed to passivity became more assertive. While many aspects of slavery remained consciously or unconsciously in the minds of many blacks, the winds of change became increasingly evident. Black farm boys out of the rural South were conscripted to fight against the nondemocratic Germans in Europe. And for the first time in their life, scores of black men received accolades from white people—the men and women of France. The appreciation of respect provided lowly, oppressed African Americans with a sense of dignity.

Although African Americans generally, and the black masses in particular, made significant progress since the demise of slavery, vestiges of the peculiar institution remained. The majority of African Americans remained in the South. Sharecropping continued, confining thousands of blacks to farms where they lived a penurious existence. Black residents in Atlanta, New Orleans, and other cities hardly fared better than their bucolic cousins. Racism stifled ambition, for as one disgruntled Southern black said, "It weren't no use in climbin' too fast, weren't no use in climbin' slow neither, if they was goin' to take everything you worked for when you get too high."[76] Southern black urbanites experienced debilitating racism that limited job opportunities, rendering access to middle-class status impossible. In the North and Midwest, African American migrants remained poor and wretched, experiencing horrendous living conditions that contributed to physical discomfort and mental depravity.

Despite efforts of altruistic progressives associated with the fledging NAACP and National Urban League, hostile whites at the local, state, and national levels remained dedicated to keeping African Americans impoverished and subservient. And while the Great Migration enabled thousands of Southern black peons to leave the debilitating South, their exodus contributed to heightened intra-racial differences in Northern and Midwestern cities. Although established black citizens in Philadelphia, known as Old Philadelphians or OPs, welcomed business opportunities provided by newcomers who frequented black-owned establishments, these same people became leading proponents that harbored resentment toward Southern migrants and other blacks deemed below their station.[77] This schism would have deleterious consequences for low-income blacks. Bedeviled by circumstances beyond their control, impoverished African Americans would face enormous challenges and difficulties throughout the century.

Chapter 4

Travail of the 1920s: An Era of Contradiction

Although black life during the 1920s suggested a sense of euphoria for African Americans because of the Harlem Renaissance and excitement created during the Jazz Age, most blacks fell on hard times. Heightened racism and race riots during and after the Great War soured relations between blacks and whites. Intolerance, prejudice, and fear, far more than flamboyance and gaiety, represented life for the African American masses during the Roaring Twenties. The Republican administrations of Warren G. Harding and Calvin Coolidge proved decidedly indifferent to African Americans. Neither president initiated programs nor aggressively supported legislation that mitigated the harsh treatment accorded African Americans. Although African American leaders cared about the welfare of their disadvantaged brethren and tried desperately to aid "the man farthest down," significant, measurable results from energies black leadership expended would prove limited. Reactionary white people used virtually every means at their disposal to stifle black ambition and retain hegemony over African Americans. Despite economic opportunities derived from migration attributed to the Great War, most blacks still resided in the South and remained poor.[1] These collective developments occurred in a decade that proved disadvantageous to impoverished African Americans.

Within two years after the World War I Armistice of 1918, the South experienced a severe depression. Overwhelmingly agrarian, Southerners relied upon cotton production as the cash crop responsible for keeping the region solvent. When the price of cotton fell from forty cents a pound in the summer of 1920 to fourteen cents within six months, cotton maintained an unevenly low price level throughout the decade. Southerners obviously encountered severe economic difficulties; landlords and tenants suffered collectively.[2] White Southerners became surlier in response to economic pressures, and impoverished African Americans, correspondingly, suffered accordingly for being powerless and black. Black educator Nathan B. Young recognized that blacks in Alabama, Georgia, Florida, Louisiana, and Mississippi remained slaves in the racist confines of the Solid South. Eyewitness William Pickens held similar views regarding black life in Arkansas but astutely noted that poor whites served as tools for their wealthier counterparts by keeping Southern labor cheap. Blacks residing in Georgia also suffered grievously from the racism that confined African Americans to the land, limited access to education, and imposed unjust laws that made the Peach State a living hell on earth for those of African ancestry.[3]

Increasingly restive because of the weakened Southern economy, the white South insisted on retaining economic and social control over blacks throughout the 1920s. A reassertion of Southern values by white oligarchs and followers who believed in omnipresent white racial dominance occurred. White supremacy became manifested in a conservative value structure that included one-party politics, conservative moral and social values, anti-liberal manifestations, fundamentalist religious practices, opposition to academic freedom, and local control. But for African Americans, the glue that fostered adhesiveness on all matters that comprised the Solid South was related specifically to maintaining supremacy over the Negro.[4]

Evidence of white economic fears could be observed through the atrocities committed against a fledgling black organization in 1919 known as the Progressive Farmers and Household Union of America. Under the leadership of Robert L. Hill, blacks in Phillips County, Arkansas, intended to improve their debased condition by forming a union. In response, fearful whites attacked African Americans, arrested 1,000 black men, murdered 25, and sentenced 12 to death. Although accused of starting the riot, Hill fortunately escaped to Kansas for sanctuary. Hill's condition as a freeman immediately appeared bleak because of "Judases" within his race. Flattered by being appointed to the Arkansas Governor's Advisory Board, prominent black Arkansans like AME Bishop J. M. Connor, and college presidents J. M. Cox and Joseph A. Booker of Philander Smith and Arkansas Baptist Church respectively expressed confidence in their state's judicial system. Speaking on behalf of the Governor's Advisory Board, the "toadies" urged the white Kansas governor Henry Justin Allen to return Hill to Phillips County to stand trial.[5] Fortunately, Governor Allen displayed more charity and sensitivity toward Hill than the Negro Board members and allowed the fugitive to remain safe in Kansas and avoid certain death in Arkansas. Governor Allen's treatment of Hill proved fair and fortuitous. A few months after Hill remained safely ensconced in Kansas, Grant Smith, a black man extradited from Michigan to Kentucky, died within twenty-four hours of his arrival in the presumably more progressive Bluegrass State.[6]

Economic anxiety evident among powerful whites continued to the disadvantage of African Americans in regard to legal and extralegal practices in the South. Although the harshness of Southern penal institutions became tempered by professed adherence to legal sensibilities, more prisoners became pressed into service during the 1920s than in any previous decade. In 1929, one of every nineteen black men twelve and over in Alabama had been captured and impressed into involuntary service. That same year similar practices occurred in Mississippi. Two sheriffs earned between $20,000 and $30,000 each for seizing black laborers and selling the "felons" to white planters.[7]

Nevertheless, unfair incarceration appeared preferable to the extralegal white Southern bloodlust that continued to remain high in regard to African Americans. At least 315 African Americans died at the hands of Southern white mobs.[8] Several of these intemperate acts seemed particularly brutal. On May 6, 1922, three innocent African American men were tortured and burned at the stake in the town square of Kirvin, Texas, for the grisly murder of a white woman committed by two white men. And in 1927, a white mob in Little Rock, Arkansas, murdered John Carter, an eighteen-year-old boy, for allegedly killing an eleven-year-old white girl. After removing Carter from the city jail, vicious white men burned him alive and dragged his body through the streets. One thousand blacks immediately left the city.[9] Lawless activities reinforced the concept that low-income blacks had the option of remaining in the South passively as sharecroppers and laborers or move to more hospitable environs in the North, Midwest, or Far West.

Without prospects for finding work, most blacks decided to suffer the ignominies of racism and remain in the South. Despite problems evident in the depressed South of the early 1920s, the masses elected to contend with the devil they knew rather than face the unknown in less familiar environs. Although industrial recruiters still ventured South to secure laborers, the peacetime economy resulted in the reduction of jobs and a diminutive workforce. Without favorable prospects for work, the black exodus from the South continued but slowed to a crawl. Most Southern African Americans remained south of the Mason-Dixon Line.[10]

For those African American men who remained in the rural South, migration to a regional city like Nashville, Tennessee, appeared as a judicious decision. Fewer opportunities existed in the Tennessee hinterlands for blacks than for whites. Between 1890 and 1930 the black population in rural Tennessee declined by 38 percent. Black men restricted from joining trade unions found employment in "practically all of the unskilled labor of Nashville." The best option for black males of Tennessee was to leave the South entirely.[11]

The experiences of African American women thrust into the role of breadwinners as skilled and unskilled workers, however, proved most significant in making demographic moves to leave the state. Between 1920 and 1930 black females represented the greatest rate of migration from the hinterlands of middle Tennessee.[12] These women faced enormous challenges that seemed prescient in regard to black employment. The best jobs black women could muster as independent seamstresses and washerwomen, unfortunately, became phased out during the 1920s. The introduction of washing machines attributed to the rise of commercial laundries after World War I rendered employment of washerwomen obsolete. Likewise, factory-produced clothing caused black female employment as dressmakers, milliners, tailors, and seamstresses to decline as well.[13] Without opportunities leave domestic service, learn new trades, or acquire work in factories and offices, black women faced a limited job future.

The problems confronting and the treatment of African Americans in Tennessee paled in comparison to blacks who resided in communities adjacent to the Mississippi River. In 1927 a massive flood occurred in Meadville, Louisiana that destroyed the cotton crop and severely impacted landlords, tenants, and sharecroppers residing in the Mississippi Delta region. The widespread devastation caused the Red Cross to visit the area to provide food and clothing, offer shelter to black victims, and relocate displaced individuals to refugee camps. The planters accepted the Red Cross overture on one condition—the rescue organization must pledge to return black tenants to the original plantation. To enforce the agreement, the National Guard, under the direction of the Red Cross, prohibited black refugees from leaving the camp. In times past, a disaster that destroyed a crop automatically canceled the contract between landlords and laborers. This time, however, procedures were different. White landlords mandated that sharecroppers must return to plantations even though tenant housing was untenable or destroyed.

Destitute Southern blacks answered to capricious whites and received Red Cross largess only if vouched for by a white person willing to speak on their behalf.[14] Gus Smith, a man with a tubercular wife and a daughter with severe rheumatism, traveled back and forth between Louisiana to Mississippi to find work for himself and hospital services for his spouse. Because he failed to return to the plantation where white managers controlled largess, Smith received little assistance and his wife faced certain death.[15]

Evidently for their psychological well-being, anxious Southern whites needed to have life-and-death control over African Americans. Although the Melville flood rendered blacks and whites alike destitute, a commission of prominent local white citizens made certain the entire federal appropriation would be allotted to white people. Southern white leaders held sway. A Red Cross caseworker canvassed Melville and verified that blacks had not received rations in more than two months. Obviously an equal distribution of goods and services would not be tolerated by local white authorities. Given the horrendous circumstances African Americans experienced, whenever possible, blacks eagerly left the South despite white Southerners' attempts to stave off emigration.[16]

Collusion between Southern planters and the Red Cross created other difficulties for destitute blacks. Black refugees who returned to the plantation discovered that food was rationed and disseminated by the Red Cross. Unfortunately for the sharecroppers, the flood-damaged food contained worms that created a widespread pellagra epidemic. Therefore, only the most ambitious black tenants escaped the plight of continuous penury by using stealth, deliberate determination, and, probably most significantly, luck to survive.

Migrants' misgivings about leaving the South and moving to the North or Midwest may also be attributed to the second rise of the Ku Klux Klan that established klaverns throughout the nation. Resuscitated in 1915 by Georgian Joseph Simmons in response to the exciting but infamous film *Birth of a Nation*, the new Knights of the Ku Klux Klan became a political and social force throughout the United States during the 1920s.[17] The resurgent Klan directed animus primarily toward Catholics and Jews. Few African Americans, however, could assume that Klansmen exorcized racism from customary views and practices directed toward blacks. Low-income African Americans certainly had justifiable reasons to be fearful of the Klan.

The arrival of the Klan in Northern cities like Chicago, Detroit, and Indianapolis logically created apprehension for African Americans. These cities experienced an enormous increase of black migration, fostering a white backlash and an augmented Klan membership. Klan resurgence in Detroit could be related specifically to the influx of Southern blacks to the Motor City.[18] Since many Klansmen comprised working-class whites—-natural competitors of low-income blacks—urban America proved less hospitable to African Americans than the black influx might have warranted.

Impecunious blacks and whites shared many common characteristics that represented the culture of poverty. Members of both races understandably displayed a profound need to maintain dignity and self-respect. William Pickens recognized that avaricious, rich white landowners in Arkansas effectively used racism to maintain a divide between poor blacks and whites. Low-income black and white men reacted negatively in a similar fashion to their impoverished status. Married men who found themselves incapable of being family providers refused to perform household chores, engaged in wife beating, abused children, and drowned disappointment in alcohol.[19] Nevertheless, racial differences still prevailed to the advantage of low-income whites. Blacks labored ignominiously as tenants on the southeastern flatlands as debt-ridden sharecroppers. Poor whites residing in the northern highlands, meanwhile, blamed blacks for their wretched condition and loss of pride. While poor whites practiced racism toward African Americans to enjoy a sense of superiority, impoverished blacks were incapable of taking retaliatory measures against white people. Blacks could only experience dignity by leaving Arkansas.[20]

As African Americans living a hard scrapple existence continued moving to the new "promised land," they moved into malformed ghettos that reeled from previous migrations. As the Great Migration of the previous decade continued into the 1920s, black enclaves increased in size and scope with negative consequences for the African American populace. White housing restrictions continued as the primary reason for congestion in black neighborhoods. Though the Supreme Court declared municipal segregation ordinances unconstitutional in the *Buchanan v. Warley* case of 1917, conniving whites introduced housing covenants that ignored the law and continued restrictive policies far into the twentieth century.

Enterprising realtors recognized that finding housing for black migrants could be lucrative and engaged in block-busting techniques to induce panic selling among white homeowners. Although the expanded ghetto created a bonanza for realtors, established black urbanites resented the nefarious practices that proved inimical to African Americans. An investigator for a black newspaper in Philadelphia summarized the seething resentment of price gouging that impacted all African Americans by reporting that a white realtor said, "If . . . the real estate agencies decided to sell to 'niggers' . . . they would charge four or five hundred dollars more because 'niggers' ought to be made to pay for the privilege of living in a decent, respectable neighborhood."[21]

The negative response toward migrants became continuously intensified by real or imagined perceptions of blacks engaged in crimes. At the turn of the century, corrupt businessmen and politicians tolerated vice in black communities. As the Great Migration augmented the physical deterioration of African American neighborhoods and Prohibition enhanced prospects for breaking the law, black people and crime became synonymous. Although the white power structure condoned or encouraged crime to flourish in black communities, the rhetoric of influential leaders—black and white—invariably blamed African Americans for urban crime.[22]

While some African American spokespersons berated race members for having criminal tendencies, astute black reformers attributed black crime to racism. Discriminatory attitudes of the police, unfairness inherent in the criminal justice system, and understandable anger toward white people provided convenient and justifiable rationalizations for black crime.[23] During the 1920s, vice districts still remained, and the sensuality projected on blacks during the Harlem Renaissance hardly caused the connection between sin, vice, sex, and blacks to abate in the minds of white people. Increased migration occurred concomitantly with augmented vice relocated to low-income black communities, causing many poor, innocent blacks to be caught in the maelstrom and disproportionably become subjected to arrests.[24]

Although progressive-thinking blacks recognized that a relationship existed between social pathologies regarding poverty, racism, and black criminality, white people still believed that black crime resulted from inherent black racial, moral, and cultural norms. For example during the 1920s, researchers found that the increase in juvenile delinquency attributed to black migration could also be associated with the retrenchment of recreational facilities. The "discretion" used by the police and the courts that resulted in arrests and incarceration was applied to the disadvantage of black juveniles without constructive outlets. Institutional racism displayed by the indifference of municipal leaders toward black recreational needs continued to prove inimical to African American youths.[25]

Avaricious, indifferent landlords continued contributing to the malaise in black communities by crowding more and more tenants into limited space and enabling despicable housing conditions to become worse. Even when migration had a marginal effect on the local populace, housing in segregated back communities remained horrendous. Residential conditions for blacks in Indianapolis, Indiana, represented the unfortunate norm as African Americans paid high rents for inferior accommodations. One observer noted, "The death rate among Negroes remains high but [white] real estate men refuse to provide sanitary and desirable dwelling places due to what seems to be a covert understanding that conditions must not be made too attractive or more Negroes would immigrate here . . . ."[26] Similar difficulties existed in ghettos located in Texas. Black communities lacked modern conveniences—electric lights and adequate water supply, sanitary conditions, paved streets, and rapid transit facilities.[27]

Middle-class African Americans outside "Dixie" abhorred heightening evidence of Jim Crow and continued holding deep reservations about the influx of newcomers from the South. The black bourgeoisie endeavored to remain aloof and refrained from mingling with migrants. Snubs generated by established African Americans instilled the lower class with a perpetual sense of inferiority, self-loathing, and resentment toward established residents. Class differentiation attributed to Jim Crow gained momentum in African American neighborhoods.[28]

Although the black bourgeoisie opposed the migrants and the increased inter-racial hostility the newcomers generated, all black socioeconomic classes benefited from residing in African American communities. For the black bourgeoisie, the ghetto provided a means for economic security, as segregation enabled small black businesses to exist and prosper. But black urban enclaves also provided functional support for the masses. For migrants, the segregated black community offered protection and a shield from a white society in which they could not compete or sustain themselves emotionally, linguistically, or culturally. Moreover, low-income blacks faced uncertainty when encountering white people. Forrester B. Washington of the National Urban League and an observer of low-income blacks stated, "It must be borne in mind that the Negro is slow in responding to opportunities for cooperation [with non-blacks] because of past treatment. He is suspicious of anything offered by the white man. This is particularly true of Negroes coming from the South."[29] Evidently, underprivileged blacks had accepted the notion of inferiority. Thus, being confined to a black ghetto would not seem extraordinary or discomforting.[30]

The ghetto also appeared impervious to the masses in regard to limitations based on race. As the NAACP attacked Jim Crow practices that confined blacks to restricted black communities, the mission of this civil rights organization had little, if any, meaning for economically disadvantaged African Americans. Consequently the NAACP became identified during the 1920s more as a conservative, gradualist organization like the old Tuskegee Machine, Hampton Institute, and the Urban League than as an organization functioning on behalf of the black masses.[31] Furthermore, the black intelligentsia seized upon the cultural aspects of ghetto life for artistic and personal satisfaction personified in the Harlem Renaissance. The masses remained untouched by the aura conveyed by whites who went "slumming" and the black cognoscenti who gave expression to the "seedy allure" of black life. For the masses, the black ghetto allowed for a means of coping and survival, representing a fitting example to the adage that "misery seeks company."

The comfortable residential ghettos, however, failed to protect the masses from deeply embedded racism that continuously prevented black males from finding suitable work. Cities in border-states proved particularly notorious in practicing racial discrimination. As an example, industrial plants in Baltimore, Maryland, desperately needed laborers. Unrelenting biases against employing African Americans still existed. Sociologist Charles S. Johnson of Fisk University enumerated ten reasons why certain industries excluded Negroes from occupying decent, well-paying jobs. The fear of losing white workers and the aversion of bringing black men in contact with white women conceivably became paramount to the lack of training of African Americans and unsatisfactory work experiences with black laborers.[32] Obviously these concerns never applied to European immigrants who spoke languages other than English.

Female migrants adjusted to life in the ghettos of the 1920s with greater ease than black men. Again, a familiar pattern regarding employment emerged. Unlike men, women more easily found and held jobs, enjoyed a higher earning capacity than male counterparts, and served as the stabilizing force of the family. Because black males were prohibited to play the role of men in America's patriarchal society, the black matriarchy became a natural means for surviving harsh conditions that challenged African Americans during the 1920s.[33] A black matriarchy rooted in slavery continued among low-income African Americans.

Despite contentious factors related to class and gender that caused intra-racial division, blacks continuously experienced racial discrimination and had reason to coalesce. Because white racists mistreated African Americans, the NAACP used the courts to defend every black socioeconomic class during the 1920s.[34] But in addition to the NAACP, the newly formed National Bar Association (NBA) also became involved in civil rights activities and acted on behalf of all African Americans. Founded in 1925 in Des Moines, Iowa, the NBA contacted African American attorneys throughout the nation with the intention of extending legal assistance for every black citizen regardless of color, class, or creed. The NBA proposed that African American attorneys report, investigate, and defend blacks adversely affected by judicial improprieties. NBA lawyers also devoted specific attention to indigent blacks. Wherever a racial problem occurred that negatively impacted low-income African Americans, an NBA member would be expected to act on behalf of a black client.

With employment remaining a priority for low-income blacks, the significance of the National Urban League (NUL) increased. Because a postwar depression impinged severely and disproportionably on African Americans—rendering thousands of blacks jobless—the NUL understood job procurement became paramount. Heightened racism evidenced through anti-black violence, virulent prejudice, and segregation underscored the traditional employment slogan—"last hired, first fired"—in regard to African Americans. In the aftermath of the race riots in East St. Louis and Chicago, NUL leaders believed that the founding of Urban League chapters throughout the nation could mitigate or prevent racial confrontations. Furthermore, the NUL remained committed to an additional calling—to provide "for social service among Negroes." Obviously African Americans required multiple levels of assistance.[35]

Recognizing difficulties unemployed African Americans faced throughout the nation, the League discerned that white workers in the North had an equal, if not greater, aversion to black employees as Southern white counterparts. Almost all local unions excluded black workers, rendering the opportunity to enter the skilled or semiskilled trades virtually impossible. In response to this dilemma, league directors again endeavored to make African American workers attractive to both industrialists and labor unions. Sensitive to the needs of each faction, the NUL desired to encourage industrialists to employ blacks during normal hiring practices and refrain from using the African Americans as strikebreakers. Correspondingly, the NUL encouraged unions to affiliate black workers and thereby eliminate the likelihood that African American scabs would undermine union strikes. The league also recognized that during an economic recession, black migrants should not be concentrated in employment centers like Detroit. Rather, the league understood that black workers must be disseminated to all cities and areas where jobs existed.

League officials recognized that racial conflict stemmed from white fear and black frustration. Although racism and the desire for racial superiority propelled whites to engage in violence, multiple factors caused increased tension and anger to erupt among African Americans. Blacks residing in East St. Louis abhorred inhumane working conditions. Wretched housing conditions in Chicago inflamed African Americans. And in Washington, DC, the demeaning status attributed to racial segregation fostered black resentment. Therefore, the NUL intended to enlist the support of responsible civic leaders to mitigate tensions and create a more salubrious environment for African American workers.[36]

Because the labor movement historically discriminated against African Americans in disputes between capital and labor, black churches, fraternities, and social organizations understandably disliked unions. Any black organization seeking accord with unions risked credibility within the established African American community. During the Pullman strike of 1925, however, the anti-union bias changed, as the NUL and NAACP sided with labor. Although A. Philip Randolph founded the Brotherhood of Sleeping Car Porters, the first black union that same year and garnered expected support, the Urban League necessarily walked a fine line. The NUL depended upon industrial capitalists to employ black workers and feared antagonizing prospective employers that might hire African Americans.

Further potential problems surfaced when the Urban League supported the creation of the Negro Labor Congress, a communist-backed organization founded in 1925 that could only augment industrialists' concerns about NUL motives.[37] In addition to industrialists' fears, African Americans also abhorred communism. Conservative leaders believed NUL support for the Negro Labor Congress placed the race in the untenable position of being perceived as anti-American. For blacks seeking equality in the larger American society, flirting with communism undermined the black bourgeoisie's desire to acquire civil rights for the entire race.

In order to improve black laborers' opportunities for securing employment in 1927, the Urban League revamped the Booker T. Washington concept of industrial training by developing a "Negro in Industry Week." After enlisting the help of national organizations comprising the YMCA, YWCA, National Negro Business League, black churches, Greek letter and social organizations, the NUL intended to disseminate training programs for black workers throughout the United States. By extending black knowledge of trades, increasing black proficiency, and enlightening employers about black skills, the NUL hoped to find regular employment for African American workers.

The National Urban League also sought to enlist Congressional support for a Negro Industrial Commission. Introduced in 1921 and again in 1923, the NUL proposed the adoption of a legislative bill designed to help African Americans. The nonpartisan commission would investigate the social and economic condition of African Americans, make proper recommendations for improvement, and apply suitable remedies. Moreover, the NUL hoped the legislation would provide funding for the proposed activities. The bill never acquired a congressional hearing and stifled the NUL's good intentions. Again, low-income blacks were deterred from competing for laboring jobs.[38]

Although an institution dedicated to mitigating the harshness of ghetto life, the NUL never completely altered the thinking engrained in black migrants from the rural South. Impoverished African Americans moved North in quest of greater economic and social opportunities. Yet many migrants failed to discard a diffident behavioral pattern developed over generations of black/white relationships. Southern conditioning taught blacks that personal security required them to be disheveled, differential, and satisfied with their lowly condition. Blacks with Southern roots also learned that the proud, self-respecting Negro encountered problems. Thus, certain migrants believed that ambition did not directly correlate to happiness. While the lowly station and slovenly appearance of African Americans met with approval from Southern whites who occasionally provided succor, these practices had little bearing on blacks residing in low-income neighborhoods outside the South. Pejorative Southern mannerisms would be deemed off-putting, repulsive, and an indication of slovenliness and ignorance.[39] Subsequently, African Americans deeply embedded with Southern cultural norms seldom met or received beneficence from whites or established black professionals. Disgusted by the lack of vision within migrant families, Reverend James N. Scott, District Superintendent of the Delaware Conference, provided his observations about urban migrant families when he said, "Forty-six houses in the block house 123 families, 715 men, women, and children. Between three and four families live in one house. The families average $250 spent for rent per week and $400 spent for alcohol."[40]

The individual who best represented migrants and the disadvantaged black community, ironically, was an immigrant from Jamaica named Marcus Garvey. Garvey migrated to the United States in 1915 to meet Booker T. Washington, the foremost African American leader who spoke for the black masses. Although Washington died before the meeting occurred, an undaunted Garvey decided to champion the cause for black amelioration. Relying on countrymen from the West Indies for support, Garvey launched his career as a race leader in New York City's Harlem. Aware of Harlem's significance as the hub and cultural center for the African American intelligentsia, and with a background in publishing, Garvey proceeded to become a participant in the New Negro movement by founding a newspaper entitled *The Negro World*. Garvey published thousands of editions of the excellently edited newspaper and introduced readers to his fledgling organization known as the Universal Negro Improvement Association (UNIA). Interested readers from the United States, the Americas, Europe, and Africa soon learned about Garvey and his vision regarding people of the African Diaspora. Although Garvey led the UNIA from New York City, his message had far-reaching implications that addressed and excoriated colonialism. But for African Americans, Garvey represented something far more significant than as an opponent of colonialism. The alienated and ignored black masses perceived Garvey as a dedicated leader.

As a dark-complexioned, simian-featured man far from the Anglo-Saxon perspective of beauty, Garvey spoke with articulate passion about the positive attributes of being black with Negroid features in white America. In racist white and color-conscious black America, Garvey's eloquence and prideful utterances provided balm on the wounds of a black majority encumbered by a sense of inferiority. As the first prominent "dusky" leader of the late nineteenth and early twentieth centuries (Douglass, Washington, and Du Bois would be classified as mulattos), Garvey struck an interesting cord among Southern black migrants, West Indian immigrants, working-class African Americans, and even some counted among the black bourgeoisie. Because of the uplifting rhetoric espoused from the dais at Liberty Hall and the flair reminiscent of country preachers speaking to parishioners accustomed to the liturgical mien of Holy Rollers, Southern migrants embraced Garvey as one of their own. These same people also lauded Garvey for injecting them with a sense of pride absent in their heritage as slaves, sharecroppers, and second-class citizens.

Prideful, independent-minded West Indians, black Southern migrants, and local Harlem residents flocked to hear Garvey's broad messages that transcended skin complexion, dialect, and nationality. In addition to pride and self-respect, Garvey offered devotees the opportunity to purchase stock options in the Black Star Line, a business venture designed to transport goods to the Caribbean and other ports on the Seven Seas. Furthermore, Garvey advocated a Back to Africa movement, an emotional promotion that instilled the African American masses with unrealized racial pride. Garvey also appealed to the masses personally, encouraging fellow race members to support black businesses and institutions.

Unfortunately, Garvey participated in divisive intra-racial hatred. He publicly excoriated light-skinned African Americans, accusing them as being integrationists who disdained darker members of the race. Garvey seemed unaware that white Americans, unlike Jamaicans, eschewed determining class status by shades of color. Because everyone with Negro blood—even the fairest and most accomplished black professionals—could be deemed inferior and subjected to discrimination, Garvey's injection of color consciousness raised the ire of Du Bois and other fair-skinned leaders. Nevertheless, Garvey's concern about the significance of color in the black community could hardly be overstated when a ditty composed by Lorraine Chambers, a Philadelphia poet influenced by the Harlem Renaissance, read,

> I might have married her some day
> This lovely Nina Clark
> But this one thing stands in the way—
> Her skin, which God made dark.[41]

Blacks who followed Garvey appeared indifferent to his origins. Garvey benefited from being foreign born. Credibility gained from being different and worldly enabled Garvey to attract a broad array of supporters. Although a devotee of Washington's self-help maxim, Garvey offered a perspective that exceeded the limitations associated with industrial education. By adding 1920s optimism exemplified by the potential for generating wealth through the Black Star Line, Garvey represented the interests of lowly African Americans far more than any contemporary black leader of the era.

Although being a foreign national held initial advantages for Garvey, his lack of familiarity with United States customs and practices proved problematic. Had Garvey demonstrated better business acumen, confined his message to uplift—demonstrated in the motto "Up You Mighty Race"—and refrained from playing the color card against mulatto opponents, Garvey and UNIA might have continued unabated. Instead, Garvey created a maelstrom within established black circles who worked assiduously to have him silenced. The vituperation between Garvey and his critics proved all-encompassing and devastating for the little Jamaican. Attacks against Garvey came from both A. Philip Randolph who represented the left and W. E. B. Du Bois of the more staid and traditional black leadership cadre. Intra-racial animosity of the 1920s proved more inimical to ameliorating the condition of the black masses than the more publicly renowned dispute between Washington and Du Bois.

Encouraged by anti-Garvey factions, the federal government charged Garvey with mail fraud and had him arrested, incarcerated, and deported. These events struck a fatal blow to nascent black capitalism designed to benefit the African American masses. Because Garvey lacked the expertise to channel his enthusiasm, develop ideas, and create a positive reality for thousands of African Americans, the masses would be continuously devoid of hope for a propitious future.

Garvey proved a unique spokesman for the black masses. No black man since Booker T. Washington approximated Garvey's ability to galvanize the masses to strive for financial security within a race-conscious construct. Unlike Washington, however, Garvey publicly created a movement based on racial pride. Hence, Garvey and the UNIA proved the most significant phenomena that combined Southern migration with Black Nationalism and class equanimity. Garvey also instilled the masses with a strong affiliation with Africa by advocating a return to the motherland. While other colonizationists like Bishop Henry M. Turner represented the black intelligentsia and viewed emigration as a proper position to be taken by the race in response to American racism, Garveyism truly represented a movement of, for, and by the masses with only a few scattered supporters from the black bourgeoisie.[42]

Consciously or unconsciously, Marcus Garvey initiated, contributed to, or became part of the era with many names—the Jazz Age, New Negro movement, and the Harlem Renaissance. These terms reflected a period when white people become captivated with negritude, a unique muse that recognized the significance of black culture. But equally, if not more important, the earthier or perceived base aspects of negritude—the masses—became romanticized, appreciated, and extolled. Even the seamier impression of black life—the debased, sensual, love-obsessed, orgiastic perception of Africa and its progeny—garnered interest from both white benefactors and the cognoscenti that comprised the black bourgeoisie. Through poetry, prose, dance, music, theatrics, fine art, and Garveyism, the black masses acquired recognition and fanciful respect.

Garveyism and the New Negro movement also evolved and matured during an era when white racial animosity toward African Americans was intense. Blacks suffered grievously at the hands of mobs from Rosewood, Florida, to Tulsa, Oklahoma, and in cities throughout the North and Midwest. In response to racial atrocities, blacks engaged in both protests and prideful art forms deemed representative of black underclass thought. Claude McKay, a fellow Jamaican with Garvey, revealed pride in blackness. But McKay also responded angrily to the treatment white people accorded African Americans in heralded poems like "If We Must Die" (1919) and "The Lynching" (1922). McKay also wrote about the streetwalkers of Harlem, cabaret dancers and urban workers with sensitivity and understanding.[43]

Langston Hughes's poetry, along with Alain Locke's compilation of literary and artistic masterpieces presented in *The New Negro*, revealed the range of black emotions in the highest literary art form to capture the essence of impoverished black life. Thus, Hughes, objective and dramatic, spoke of the Negro masses.[44] In a book of poetry entitled *The Weary Blues* (1926) and in *Fine Clothes to the Jew* (1927), Hughes presented a pessimistic but stoic image. His characters proved varied and interesting. Laughter, sorrow, and, to an extended degree, cynicism appeared through lyrical sketches on the silent, complex, yet unaddressed aspects of black life. And it was Locke's anthology, *The New Negro*, that painted the broadest brush that encapsulated every aspect of black culture during the decade. Locke's aristocratic persona—a Harvard graduate who became the nation's first black Rhodes Scholar—prevented him from paying proper respects to Garvey and his movement. Nevertheless, Locke's work reflected the era magnificently. Thus, black group awareness, race consciousness, disillusionment, revolt, spiritualism, and a common purpose through the eyes of sable intellectuals evoked feelings that represented the common, earthier members of the race.[45]

The energy, euphoria, and racial pride generated by black intellectuals in New York City masked the timidity of African American leaders elsewhere. One observer noted, "Where Negroes have no economic status and where their living has depended largely upon personal service jobs . . . there is a lack of positive, aggressive leadership.[46] George W. Lee said, "'Self-styled' Negro leaders contentedly 'left well-enough alone,' at best, and at worst, grasped the white man's point of view when he handed . . . a platter of gold."[47] Thus, fearless, unselfish leadership rarely existed outside the safe confines of New York City.

Unlike prior eras, the 1920s marked the first and only time that the trials and tribulations of common black folk received proper expression. The many musicians and bands that gave voice to this Jazz Age added further vibrancy to the role of a black underclass. Although composer Duke Ellington, singer/dancer Florence Mills, the multitalented Paul Robeson, and impresario Roland Hayes could be classified as musical prodigies with an elite pedigree, others like Bill "Bojangles" Robinson and the numerous jazz artists like Louis Armstrong, singer and actress Ethel Waters, and blues singer Bessie Smith hailed from common stock. Conceivably, the true condition of low-income blacks could be explained by a critic of blacks residing in Indiana who said, "He has cast off the slothfulness of the Delta Negro; lost the backwardness of the Alabama Negro; thrown away the submissive demeanor of the Louisiana plantation—yet lacks the pioneer spirit of the Kansan . . . ."[48] This assessment presented a contradiction to the spirited black grandeur of the Harlem Renaissance of the 1920s.

Perhaps even greater significance may be realized that the cognoscenti of the Harlem Renaissance failed to reach the impoverished masses. The South proved notorious in restricting black access to education. In Tennessee, for example, the Volunteer State only spent nine dollars annually to educate a black child as opposed to twenty-four dollars for a white student. Virginia contained only seven public high schools for blacks, and only four offered a satisfactory and challenging curriculum.[49] Understandably, less than two-thirds of eligible black youths in Virginia enrolled in school. But even in a less prejudiced state like Minnesota, apathy existed within the lower strata of African American society. Eyewitness Roy Wilkins bristled at the indifference toward education and lamented, "Colored students and parents more often than not take advantage of the law which permits the withdrawal of students after they have finished the eighth grade or reach the age of sixteen. Hundreds drop out at the conclusion of the grade school curriculum . . . ."[50] Although the future NAACP director's race consciousness may have far exceeded that of both the masses and black leadership in the Gopher State, his observations possibly spoke to the contentedness of the masses and backwater leadership rather than the intellectuals of Harlem.

Despite the racial pride and frivolity displayed during the Jazz Age, for the black masses the decade represented an era of continuous poverty and overt racism. Prior to the Black Tuesday crash in October 1929, most African Americans had already experienced economic difficulty. That same year cotton production dropped from forty-three to twenty-three million acres, a problem that severely impacted the South, the region where most African Americans resided. Since three of every four black farmers acquired 40 percent of their income from growing cotton, the economy for blacks had already reached a depressed state.[51] Prospects for African Americans residing in the North proved similarly bleak. Black service workers experienced layoffs, and those with jobs faced the likelihood of being replaced by unemployed whites.[52] Anna Arnold Hedgeman, a ranking African American official employed by the Jersey City, New Jersey YWCA noted that Jersey City's poor and working-class black women needed greater pay and workplace safety rather than "uplift." Hedgeman concluded, "The North and the South [held a] basic philosophy. In the South the weapon was a meat ax; in the North, a stiletto. Both are lethal weapons."[53]

Literary pundits perceived the 1920s as a romantic era that glorified the African homeland and African American culture. African American teachers specifically benefited from the imposed segregation because of heightened prospects for work and becoming leaders in the black community. Southern black children, however, suffered from the indifference white administrators held toward educating school-aged youngsters. Dedicated black teachers and white philanthropists who funded black normal schools could not transcend meager budgets and disenfranchisement that rendered proper instruction and the full rights of citizenship impossible.[54] The African American masses knew pathos, struggle, and pain rather than artistic genius and success.

Chapter 5

The Great Depression

The Great Depression caused African Americans to focus primarily and directly on survival. With the nation experiencing the most severe economic crisis in history, blacks engaged in a myriad of activities to assure a continued existence. Some remained pessimistic and fatalistic, caring only about individual sustainability. Some depended on the federal government and relied upon leadership in Washington, DC for succor. Some sought escape coveting religious salvation and fantasizing about a better life in heaven. And some acted altruistically to provide assistance to extremely disadvantaged blacks. Regardless of strategies for survival, life for impoverished African Americans in rural settings, hamlets, and metropolises during the 1930s would prove extremely challenging and difficult.

People customarily believe the Great Depression commenced with the stock market crash in October 1929, but for many African Americans "hard times originated in the winter of 1928. T. Arnold Hill, director of the National Urban League, noted that in the South, "white men are driving trucks and express wagons . . ., repairing streets, doing the scavenger work, delivering ice on their backs where formerly Negroes delivered and white men collected deliveries, serving as waiters and bellmen in hotels and doing other tasks which were once regarded only fit for Negroes."[1] Hill also stated that the job transformation also extended to the North, as whites replaced blacks as elevator operators, doormen, house servants, and hotel workers.

The rugged individualism and laissez-faire philosophy extolled by President Hoover and his administration failed to provide the comforting rhetoric or necessary activity to address the needs and concerns of Americans generally and African Americans in particular. In order to allay human suffering, recoup financial losses, and restore the national economy, local, state, and the federal governments needed to work collectively to address omnipresent poverty. But since the inept Hoover administration failed to comprehend the depths of the Depression, blacks—representing the most destitute, impoverished Americans—received the least consideration in regard to employment, unemployment benefits, or other forms of assistance. In 1931, Hill of the Urban League declared, "At no time in the history of the Negro since slavery has his economic and social outlook seemed so discouraging."[2]

The economic collapse impacted blacks so severely that some former slaves reminisced about the halcyon days of their youth. Millie Evans, a former slave born in North Carolina in 1849, declared, "I git so lonesome when I think 'bout times we used to have. 'Twas better living back yonder than now."[3] Evans continued her recollections by concluding, "I can't 'member everything I done in them days, but we didn't have to worry 'bout nothing . . . . We had such a good time . . . ."[4] Millie Evans hardly proved the only ex-slave with misgivings about their contemporary status who held positive recollections about slavery. Another former slave reminisced, "Our miss Sallie was the sweetest best thing in the world! She was so good and kind to everybody, and she loved her slaves, too . . . . If all slaves had belonged to white folks like ours, there wouldn't been any freedom wanted."[5]

Former slaves had cause to look favorably upon the past. During the 1930s white people displayed disinterest in jobless African Americans and resented blacks who were gainfully employed.[6] Blacks who held jobs in certain communities, in fact, became the objects of white wrath. African American newspapers informed readers of the random violence that occurred when blacks held jobs considered far above their station. The *Chicago Defender* and *Pittsburgh Courier* reported that in Louisiana and Mississippi, blacks who worked as railroad firemen were killed by white vigilantes who sought to prevent African Americans from holding respectable jobs. The black press speculated that jobless white union firemen were directly or indirectly responsible for the murder of nine and wounding of scores of black workers. Although blacks hired counsel and detectives to find the perpetrators of the heinous acts, no successful arrest or prosecution of the willful assassins occurred.[7] The views of former slaves who reminisced about a favorable past had merit. Slaves existed as a valued commodity at that time rather than as economic competitors singled out for attack by insecure, jobless whites.

The 1932 presidential election enabled downtrodden African Americans who voted for the Democrats to look forward to the future, join other disillusioned citizens, and sweep Franklin Delano Roosevelt into the White House. The Roosevelt administration, however, faced a significant challenge in regard to mitigating the harsh life experienced by destitute African Americans. Since nine of eleven million, or approximately 80 percent of African Americans in 1930 resided in the South and were severely impoverished, the Great Depression represented the most severe challenge African Americans experienced since the Civil War.[8]

If the new administration intended to assist downtrodden blacks, it faced an enormous challenge. More than half the African American population resided in rural areas, and 40 percent engaged in some kind of agricultural work. Moreover, racism, combined with the dearth of job opportunities during the economic downturn, rendered at least 70 percent of black agrarians who labored as field hands, tenants, and sharecroppers impoverished. The average black earned only 73 percent of the wages paid white peers.[9] And for those unfortunate blacks who resided in the Black Belt, life became even more severe. In the best of years, black laborers cleared fifty to sixty dollars annually, remained in perpetual debt, and failed to escape imposed bondage.[10] Although black laborers suffered grievously from the limited income derived through sharecropping, their plight seemed insignificant when compared with tenant farmers thrown off the land. Black laborers in the cotton-producing region of the South were particularly impacted as federal mandates to produce less cotton reduced the need for farm laborers. Elderly tenants and families headed by females specifically proved vulnerable to eviction and reduction in status. The black population in the cotton-producing South would be in decline.

Although Roosevelt and his New Deal instilled average Americans with positivism and a means for redressing the economic disaster that impacted the nation, the altruistic policies failed to reach blacks who represented those farthest down. In fact, Roosevelt's policies had been instituted primarily to save the middle class—the group deemed the lifeblood of the United States of America. Recovery programs in agriculture—specifically the Agricultural Adjustment Act (AAA)—focused essentially on protecting land-owning farmers by keeping farm prices sufficiently high by providing government subsidies to farm owners. High prices stabilized and, occasionally, increased farmers' income. Equally important, New Dealers intended to make certain that farmers had sufficient funds to make necessary purchases like new agricultural machinery to sustain agricultural productivity. Through acreage and production control, the federal government dispersed benefits to farmers who allowed their crops to be regulated. These farmers either destroyed crops or allowed their land to remain fallow. Similar options were rarely available for black farm employees who labored as sharecroppers.[11]

Life for blacks who worked in the cotton-producing South suffered a particularly harsh existence because of New Deal agricultural policies. During the Depression an excellent picker at best could only earn a dollar for every four hundred pounds of cotton picked.[12] New Dealers never entertained subsidizing cotton laborers because white landowners opposed any government subsidies that provided an independent source of income for black tenants. Between 1934 and 1935, black sharecroppers received only one-ninth of the government's benefit payments. With racist white Southerners in control of key congressional offices and the Roosevelt administration dependent on Southern support to pass New Deal legislation, black farmers became irrelevant to Washington bureaucrats, were expendable, and suffered grievously with the advent of agricultural machinery.[13] Blacks who failed to migrate from the region during the 1930s would either move into adjacent towns and cities in search of odd jobs or remain on the land and find seasonal employment in weeding and harvesting.[14]

Because few African Americans in the South owned land, the black masses functioned at the bottom of the agricultural ladder and existed outside the federal government's largess. Government officials were unconcerned that acreage reduction could displace thousands of black tenant farmers, sharecroppers, and hired hands.[15] When the AAA failed to require a fair distribution of subsidized federal money, blacks fell upon the "tender mercy" of white landlords who invariably failed to share federal payments with tenants.[16] Consequently, during the Great Depression most Southern blacks experienced abject poverty, lived a hard scrapple existence, and subsisted primarily through the beneficence of white landowners.

The New Deal's Farm Credit Administration (FCA) also proved detrimental to Africans. The FCA often refused to extend credit to African American tenants or landowners to lighten their economic burdens. Moreover, blacks who toiled on plantations as tenants were prohibited from selling the crops independently on the free market. Landlords still seized the harvest and sold crops at the highest price while paying tenants a pittance of a crop's value. Even when blacks acquired the opportunity to obtain an FCA loan, white landlords found ways to hold the money, charge interest on the loan, and make additional profits at the black farmer's expense.[17] The cruel and pernicious practices of insensitive white Southerners left a pejorative, indelible imprint on the well-being of African Americans long into the twentieth century.

Lax New Deal policies regarding social security had an additional deleterious impact on low-income African Americans. When the Roosevelt administration created the Social Security Act in 1935, recalcitrant Southern congressmen feared government assistance programs would increase wages for rural black workers. Therefore, white legislators prevented a large contingent of African Americans from the pensions, disability, unemployment compensation, assistance to dependent children, and succor for the aged inherent in the original Social Security Act.[18] Essentially, blacks devoid of means would be excluded from benefiting from assistance offered in the New Deal's welfare programs.

New Deal policies were in accord with the American majority that encouraged the federal government to focus on impoverished whites rather than blacks. Popular novels like Erskine Caldwell's *Tobacco Road* and John Steinbeck's *The Grapes of Wrath* created sympathy for the white tenant farmer to the exclusion of blacks. The editors of *Fortune Magazine*, moreover, instructed reporters to focus on poor whites rather than blacks.[19] Unfortunately, struggling African Americans had no creative novelists or popular magazines that captured the general public's sympathy for the plight of impoverished members of their race.

The degradation of African Americans in the South could be observed through the trials and tribulations of rural families. In his classic study *Growing Up in the Black Belt,* sociologist Charles S. Johnson identified a myriad of problems African Americans experienced. Johnson found that the devastating economic and cultural malaise inherent in the rustic South impacted education, housing, religion, and recreation, the entire fabric of black life.[20] Years of neglect attributed to poverty and racism created debilitating scars that severely impinged upon virtually all African Americans rooted in the South.

Black poverty in the rural South during the Depression devastated black families. The typical black tenant family comprised two parents and six children. The family resided in a ramshackle two-room house with sparse, broken utensils and furniture with no discernable keepsakes of value. Parents were incapable of helping their children progress. The father worked constantly from Monday morning to Saturday night and had little opportunity for social intercourse with his children. Despite the years of toil, the family had no money. In fact, one-third of the rural African American families could not provide reliable information about their income.[21] The only salvation black sharecroppers envisioned appeared through parents who encouraged their children to secretly steal away from the plantation and escape to the North. This kind of parental guidance, however, created risks. A disgruntled landlord who learned of a proposed flight could evict the entire family from the plantation.[22]

An additional by-product of rural poverty within African American families existed in the observations children made about parenting. Reminiscent of slavery, people perceived that black women enjoyed a higher status than black men. And while black women held a dominant role in the family, the black men, correspondingly, occupied an ignominious position often characterized by dependence, irresponsibility, and irrelevance. A man deserting his family, therefore, became the norm rather than the exception, leaving black children with a distorted image of family life.[23] Indifference toward the father became manifested as a significant example of an impoverished child's experience during the Depression era. When fathers deserted the family, children appeared unemotional, understanding that the mother or relatives—aunts, uncles, grandparents, or occasionally a stepfather—would ensure their survival.[24]

Problems regarding poverty and parenting also stifled the social and intellectual growth of black children. In order for a rural black family to survive, children worked year-round to sow, maintain, and harvest crops. Parents in the most severe circumstances considered formal education irrelevant. By the end of the decade only 5 percent of black adults in the South boasted a high school diploma.[25] Understandably, impecunious parents forced older children to quit school so that a meager family existence could be maintained.[26]

For many African Americans residing outside the South, the Great Depression had existed for some time. E. Washington Rhodes, editor of the *Philadelphia Tribune*, never mentioned the stock market crash that occurred on Black Tuesday, October 29, 1929. In fact, Rhodes never mentioned the Great Depression until the December 4, 1930, edition of the newspaper, nearly fourteen months after the October crash.[27] Rhodes's omission regarding the October 1929 date made sense. In 1929 more than three hundred thousand black industrial workers had already experienced unemployment, severely impacting African American families in the North and Midwest. By the end of 1932 the economic conditions of African Americans worsened considerably. Joblessness among blacks proved 30 to 60 percent higher in 106 American cities than for whites.[28] In addition to the lack of welfare assistance accorded for Southern black farmers, help also failed to trickle down to black industrial workers.[29] By the time of Roosevelt's inauguration in 1933, virtually every African American family suffered.

While the black majority residing in the South never entertained joining unions, black progressives in industrial cities perceived union membership for the small black workforce as an interesting possibility. First, these black leaders had to wean their conservative brethren—Negro ministers specifically—away from a dependence on the largess of white businesses. Given the reality that big business had been largely responsible for creating the Great Depression, prospects for having the working class join a fledgling Congress of Industrial Organization (CIO) seemed propitious. Because the CIO recognized that steel and automobile manufacturing and meat packing contained a significant workforce, and knew that blacks had been conveniently used as strikebreakers, the union had cause to incorporate African Americans into the organization. Unfortunately for the black working class, the CIO mimicked the AFL by failing to act on the promises for incorporating blacks into the union.[30]

Prior to the establishment of the CIO in 1935, black leaders had already approached American Federation of Labor president William Green to garner support for incorporating skilled blacks into his union. Green appeared amenable to the overture. When the National Negro Labor Conference convened in January 1930, President Green lauded the efforts of the conference sponsor, the Brotherhood of Sleeping Car Porters, and declared, "Trade Union membership is open to all Negroes. The majority of trade unions accept Negroes as members." Green then added, "Negro workers may apply for charters direct from the American Federation of Labor."[31] Robert Vann of the *Pittsburgh Courier* and T. Arnold Hill of the National Urban League seemed satisfied with the prospect of having African Americans in the AFL and praised Green for his encouraging comments.

Skepticism about Green, however, surfaced even during the formation of the conference. Hill reminded Green about the previous reluctance of the AFL to bridge the racial divide. The Urban League leader also wanted Green to encourage white unionists to become mutually supportive of blacks in the collective sense of helping all laborers.[32] Hill and other black leaders certainly recognized that President Green's pronouncements lacked substance and appeared insincere. Other than placing the onus of joining unions upon blacks, Green neglected to demand that white-dominated unions incorporate blacks into their ranks. Black leaders knew that while African Americans were encouraged to organize unions, white unionists harbored few inclinations to accept black colleagues into international, national, or local chapters.[33] Customarily, blacks remained mired in "Negro jobs" and were denied seniority, passed over for promotions, and excluded from participating in union activities.

Blacks also realized that resolutions passed by the American Federation failed to protect black workers. While the AFL could hardly be expected to resolve the nation's white animus toward blacks, the Union was perceived as being guilty of negligence. Moreover, the AFL demonstrated a lack of vision in failing to promote accord between black and white laborers and lied about its dedication to bring African Americans into the labor organization.[34] Blacks who acquired employment outside the jurisdiction of the AFL in semiskilled trades involving coal and iron mining, furnace and smelting, steel and tin rolling mills, as well as saw and planning mills encountered an unexpected problem. These workers not only failed to acquire union recognition but also faced expulsion from work when management and union leaders reached an accord in regard to strikes. Similar difficulties also befell black unskilled workers. Those who had jobs during the 1920s were replaced by white workers during the Great Depression.

As late as October 1934, William Green continued his call for blacks to join unions. As previously, Green placed the entire onus for unionization on blacks rather than whites. Whether Green presented a sincere personal desire to augment the AFL with black unionists seems less relevant than facts revealing that a disproportionate number of blacks than whites appeared on welfare rolls. A disgruntled but progressive and sympathetic white man from St. Louis, Missouri, publicly excoriated Green for being disingenuous when espousing the cause of interracial unionism by saying, "Surely you are aware of the inability of highly qualified Negro carpenters, masons, etc., to get jobs . . . . Here is one of the most glaring instances of race discrimination . . . ."[35] These chastising words from an objective white man undoubtedly represented the thinking of skeptical African Americans in regard to labor unions.

William Green and the American Federation of Labor hardly appeared as the most significant challenge facing the black worker. The federal government also seemed to be working counter to the interest of the African American working class who toiled inside or outside "Dixie." As the "last hired and first fired," in industrial jobs, black Americans had justifiable cause to harbor grave concerns about the race's survival. President Franklin Delano Roosevelt's New Deal pledged to assist all citizens of the United States. For the black masses, however, the New Deal proved more helpful to the AFL than to the struggling Negro devoid of union membership.[36]

Dire circumstances caused blacks to search for scapegoats, an unfortunate situation when frustration morphed into internalized self-hatred. African American children as well as adults manifested internationalized negativity in a variety of ways, and the most blatant causes for divisiveness existed in distinctions related to skin color and class that originated with slavery. Those with lighter complexions, the proverbial "house Negroes," enjoyed higher status than darker-hued brethren who toiled in the fields. Unfortunately, the multitudes with darker coloring in the South internalized their debased condition through self-hatred, establishing an unfortunate malaise that continued in ensuing decades.

From the rural South and locales as varied as Philadelphia and Los Angeles, the deplorable aspects of color consciousness still pervaded African American society. Dark Negroes still despised their complexions because of the opprobrium received from whites and light-skinned African Americans. Economic opportunities also became more feasible for blacks with fair complexions. Ebony women specifically suffered from color discrimination, being relegated to lower-paying jobs at best and, at worse, experienced unemployment and homelessness.[37] Like white counterparts, blacks also practiced class and gender discrimination. But for African Americans, skin color provided another dimension that contributed to black-on-black self-hatred.

The humiliation derived from skin color extended from adults to children. Boys and girls interviewed in the rural South of the 1930s identified dark Negroes as being ugly. Charles S. Johnson reported, "One young girl declared that she hated both her parents and herself because she was black and because the children 'laughed at her.'"[38] Johnson's research revealed that black skin consistently held a negative connotation involving appearance and class. Although Johnson concluded that in the rural South color had less impact on class distinctions because so many dark men worked hard to excel, in the minds of African Americans "duskiness" was still related to poverty.[39]

Color and class distinctions that symbolized self-hatred could hardly be confined to the rural South. Sociologist E. Franklin Frazier found similar problematic affronts existed in border regions that comprised Washington, DC, and Louisville, Kentucky. Observations of children regarding color and class proved telling, believing that teachers favored lighter-skinned, higher-class students than those of darker hue and low-income status. When describing her teacher, a thirteen-year-old girl in Washington, DC, stated, "I hate her.

When she gives plays she only puts the real light children in them with long pretty hair. She always lets them go on her errands, too. An'she don't never let no dark children do nothing. Or, if she does have to use 'em in a play, she always gives 'em the shortest, backwardest parts." A lower-class black child in Louisville offered a similar opinion about her teacher, declaring, "There was a short, light teacher . . . who was partial to position and color. If your people were big, she gave you a good grade. You could get a good grade too if you were light." And then she commented on a tall, dark-skinned male teacher she hated by noting, "He was partial to position. All he wanted to know was, 'Who are your people?'"[40] This conditioning within schools containing black teachers and students caused African Americans of light complexion to dislike those of darker hue; and ebony-skinned blacks from lower-class families, in turn, resented the "snooty" mulattos.[41]

Another factor Charles S. Johnson discovered that had negative repercussions for the African American masses (possibly related to associating poverty to a dark complexion) appeared in what may be deemed a purposeful rejection of middle-class norms. Consciously or unconsciously lower-class African Americans eschewed middle-class socialization regarding marriage, marital relations, illegitimacy, divorce, child rearing, religion, love, and death. Further evidence of emotional distress and self-hatred occurred when those emanating from impoverished households badgered and demeaned the few children whose families came from more fortunate circumstances. A concerned mother whose daughter came under attack succinctly explained the situation, stating, "The trouble is Sadie looks a little better than most these children and we own our place and they're just jealous of her. You know a jealous nigger is a dangerous thing."[42] Furthermore, those who purposely functioned outside middle-class folkways and mores seemed to revel in being outcasts—gamblers, prostitutes, gangsters—representing all the manifestations of the "bad nigger."[43] When abject poverty contributed to internalized hatred, those operating outside the norms of mainstream society could act viciously and would be willing to fight and kill anyone who offered a personal affront. Even among the most disadvantaged, dispossessed, and dishonored, a code of chivalry and honor existed.[44]

One of the worst legacies of the Great Depression that kept blacks mired in poverty through future generations continued occurring because of the race's limited access to education. Initially prospects for disadvantaged Southern blacks to acquire an education looked promising. During the first years of the Depression, New Deal agencies spent millions of federal dollars on rural Southern schools. Southern white leaders knew that impoverished, segregated black schools should be given greater consideration in the disbursement of educational funds. Racism, coupled with harsh economic conditions, however, caused powerful whites in local, state, or federal governments to ignore the educational needs of African Americans. Rural black schools that served two-thirds of the African American populace, therefore, received little consideration. In 1933, for example, two hundred counties with blacks comprising at least 12.5 percent of the population contained no African American high schools.[45] Of more than $263 million in federal money earmarked for schools, the Public Works Administration only provided $5 million for black school projects. As late as October 1936, black schools in Louisiana, Arkansas, Florida, Georgia, Kentucky, or South Carolina received no money.[46] With thousands of Depression era black children denied access to schools, a dangerous precedent had been established that made education immaterial to an unschooled, impoverished black populace.

Because of the paucity of jobs during the Great Depression, in Northern cities like Philadelphia, free evening schools operated by the Board of Education kept unemployed but active minds busy. In addition to enhancing reading and writing skills, student enrollees took classes in home economics, cooking, waiting, homemaking, home nursing, millinery, and art work.[47] Most students sought to use the training to improve prospects for finding work. More than 30 percent of all evening school students in Philadelphia were black. The economic downturn, however, suggested that few black students appeared likely to acquire jobs by attending night school.[48]

Black interest in education in other regions outside the South also seemed promising. In border states, for example, children offered positive remarks about education and discussed the efficacy of attending segregated, as opposed to, integrated schools.[49] Despite deplorable conditions attributed to fiscal neglect, overcrowding, and self-hatred determined by color and class, scores of African American children remained in school. Without prospects for work, black children had no other alternative than to continue attending classes.

And yet the anti-intellectualism inherent in the South dominated the thinking of scores of black children who perceived education as being unnecessary. The overarching racism evident in the rural South, for example, acted as a disincentive to study, even for black youth raised in families with some means. By both circumstance and choice, many black Southern youths made the decision to ignore education with the rationalization that "there isn't much use of working hard in school. What's it going to mean to you down here [the South]?"[50] An additional problem for African American youths existed in their belief that the best jobs blacks could acquire were limited to service work as cooks or chauffeurs—jobs that did not require an education. Even poor but hard-driving adults who wanted their children to obtain an education succumbed to disappointment. Invariably, many children quit school prior to graduation.[51]

During the 1930s low-income black children established a pattern that had far-reaching consequences. Poor children tended to remain poor into adulthood because of limitations constantly evident in the lives of impoverished African Americans. Eyewitness investigator Charles S. Johnson cogently and succinctly described a critical reality when he observed,

> The youth from lower-class families have . . . difficulty . . . in moving into the next highest group. The hopelessness of their status contributes to a type of free living that acknowledges little responsibility to accepted standards. Education is used by the lower classes less as a means of escape than as a means of handling some urgent practical problems . . . . With less opportunity for recognition through education, money, or status, the youth of these families may seek their self-assurance in free sexual activity, in a reputation for physical prowess or for being a bad man, and in other forms of asocial behavior.[52]

Johnson's comments proved exceedingly prescient. He recognized an unfortunate trend that had far-ranging results. Boys dropped out of school because of the quest for money, while girls, though similarly disillusioned, remained in school longer but faced a difficult life devoid of hope and happiness.

The lowly condition of the Southern African American masses may, in part, be placed directly on the dearth of money and quality of educators in black schools. The *Plessey v. Ferguson* "separate but equal" mandate never materialized. Black educators and schools remained severely underfunded. Moreover, of the estimated six thousand teachers needed to fill existing vacancies in black schools, only two thousand graduated from teacher training institutions. Equally significant, two-thirds of the black instructors in the South had less than a high school education and the remaining third had less than two years of college. Funding cuts during the Great Depression in the segregated South meant that black schools would be economically depressed: "The entire educational establishment [was] controlled and run by the white people and mainly for the white people."[53]

The residual impact of deplorable Southern schools left an insidious, indelible, and continuous imprint on African Americans. The dearth of education became particularly evident when Charles S. Johnson performed Intelligence Quotient (IQ) tests on black boys and girls in eight rural Southern counties. Johnson surveyed counties in North Carolina, Tennessee, Mississippi, Georgia, and Alabama. The average age for boys (15.14) and girls (15.08) suggested that the grade average normally should be higher (for boys, 7.32, and girls, 7.63) than reported. But given the limited funding for instruction, the horrendous physical condition of school buildings, and the inferior education of African American teachers, black children could never perform at grade level.

The most startling results from Johnson's research appeared in data derived from intelligence quotient testing. Johnson reported that boys comprised an average IQ score of 77.47 and girls, 79.60. Of course IQ testing could hardly be deemed an exact science that accurately measured intelligence or predicted prospects for success.[54] The tests nevertheless proved a correlation existed between environment and registered scores. Thus, black children raised in an impoverished, stilted environment who lacked proper stimulation for learning scored lower on IQ tests than more privileged white students.[55]

The results of Johnson's IQ tests contributed to another and equally compelling conclusion that cast aspersions on African American children. While test results may be derived in part by environment, heredity also had a significant impact on a child's intellect. During the 1930s most parents of the children surveyed worked as sharecroppers or farm tenants with limited exposure to education. This restricted their knowledge base and presumably impinged negatively on intellectual prowess and development. Therefore, parents with limited "learned" intelligence, revealing low IQ results through no fault of their own, produced and raised children in a less-than-stimulating environment. Consequently, as low IQ males and females reached maturity and produced children, their progeny had a greater propensity for having learning deficiencies and being academically inept. As intellectually challenged Southern migrants moved into Northern ghettos, the disadvantages that accrued from centuries of abuse would be disseminated wherever African Americans resided. Rustic blacks beset with limitations attributed to heredity, poverty, and lack of opportunity more than likely had their children placed in classrooms with other uninspired students from similar backgrounds.[56] Thousands of black children suffered from being confined to woefully inadequate public schools throughout the nation that inhibited learning. Educational shortcomings indigenous to the South would eventually be national in scope and hamper prospects for future generations of African Americans.[57]

Poverty, however, probably existed as the quintessential factor that limited black intelligence and prospects for success. Urgent needs encompassing paying the rent, placing food on the table, and paying for necessities like heating fuel, medicine and child care took precedent over brain-stimulating activities. Other debilitating aspects of behavior, evidenced by higher rates of obesity, acting as less attentive parents, ignoring preventative health care, alcoholism, succumbing to drugs, and making poor financial decisions caused impoverished blacks to think differently from more fortunate African Americans. Low-income blacks consequently appeared to be irresponsible and stupid. But people constantly in survival mode had no reason to engage in brain stimulation by solving crossword puzzles or discussing the merits of being a sonneteer. The intelligent quotients of destitute African Americans understandably remained low.[58]

Although the life experiences of impoverished African American urbanites could be slightly better than the mundane existence of their rural counterparts, disadvantaged blacks in cities faced new, internal pressures required for survival. Unlike the camaraderie that seemed commonplace in the countryside, the need to survive mean streets of the inner city dictated that people look after personal interests first. Understanding the need for self-reliance, black newspapers ranging from the *Philadelphia Tribune* to the *California Eagle* promoted individual initiative and excoriated low-income blacks for not being more aggressive in seeking work. Black editors accused the masses of preferring the breadline to finding gainful employment that would result in a living wage.[59]

Impoverished urban blacks faced an equally debilitating problem in regard to housing. In fact, housing policies instituted by the New Deal—specifically the Home Owners Loan Corporation—established redlining practices that enabled realtors to prohibit inner-city blacks from obtaining mortgages.[60] New Deal administrators also limited black access to Federal Housing Association loans, making it difficult, if not impossible, for African Americans to purchase and acquire equity in a house. Blacks, therefore, were excluded from obtaining property, the primary means by which white citizens established a nest egg for subsequent generations.

Unfortunately for the masses, the Depression Decade stifled the altruistic, race-conscious direction previously forged by African American leaders and intellectuals.[61] Regardless of the long-standing issues that required attention or the problems that surfaced because of the economic downturn, middle-class blacks also thought primarily about self-preservation. When New Deal legislation fostered employment programs, the black bourgeoisie thought initially about finding suitable jobs for themselves.[62] Given the tenor of the times, those seeking to survive omnipresent racism and poverty had reason to use New Deal policies to ensure personal survival. But as the black bourgeoisie acted out of self–interest, race leaders created an even greater divide between the haves and have-nots in the African American community. The black bourgeoisie now seemed less inclined to identify with or assist the masses.

Leading African American citizens in Atlanta specifically used the New Deal to achieve security at the expense of the impoverished blacks. The black bourgeoisie not only failed to intercede on behalf of the masses but, through purposefulness and guile, also seized largess intended for desperate African Americans.[63] When New Deal bureaucrats decided to clear slums and provide low-income black people in Atlanta with decent housing, African American leaders decided who among the respectable poor would occupy newly created low-income dwellings. Usually, the majority of new residents comprised members of the black middle class.[64]

The objectives of traditional black leaders in Atlanta seemed comparable with the African American bourgeoisie in Philadelphia who also used the New Deal to promote personal interests. In the City of Brotherly Love, African American leaders worked assiduously to place blacks in prestigious positions as judges, social workers, and teachers, and in respectable jobs that included store clerks and police officers. Unfortunately for the black masses, many among Philadelphia's long-established black aristocracy—the Old Philadelphians—demonstrated little concern about the plight of indigent African Americans. Recognizing that the majority of black people forced to go on the dole originally came from the South, OPs believed that those who received welfare cast aspersions on the entire race generally and African American elites in particular.[65] Rather than demand a more equitable distribution of welfare money, Philadelphia's black establishment demanded that New Dealers use influence to place more black teachers in public schools and increase the number of WPA investigators.[66]

Black leadership's focus on protecting its class rather than focusing on aiding the masses stemmed primarily from the stifling effect of residing in the low-income ghetto. In virtually every city in the nation—from Boston to Atlanta, and New York to Los Angeles, Detroit, St. Louis, and Chicago—the African American population found itself confined to live in wretched black enclaves. Most blacks were exceedingly poor, comprising long-time residents as well as newcomers from the hinterlands of the South. While the commonality of race provided a modicum of comfort and security, to insecure but proud residents, the grime, disheveled-ramshackle homes, stench from overflowing privies, and constant reminders of poverty hardly instilled pride in home and hearth. Black professionals lived adjacent to or across the street from less fortunate African Americans who worked as common laborers or survived as pimps, prostitutes, and thieves. When crimes occurred, the perpetrators—and victims, including physicians, teachers, ministers, and other professionals—engaged in the game of survival.

The so-called better classes of African Americans particularly suffered from being constantly reminded that their race was bedraggled, inferior, and maladroit when compared with the larger white society. Even the most prideful, sturdy, and confident blacks would have misgivings about the Negro race and exude, on occasion, some aspect of self-hatred projected on fellow African Americans.[67] Therefore, racial amelioration referred primarily to individuals comprising the higher African American classes rather than the black masses.

Although many counted among the black bourgeoisie sought personal solace from the harsh reality of ghetto life, some progressive blacks believed that the masses required assistance. Recognizing that Roosevelt's New Deal and the federal government could not be relied upon to relieve the plight of downtrodden African Americans, race conscious African Americans joined or created progressive organizations. The newly established National Negro Congress (NNC) and the Communist Party of the United States of America (CPUSA) endeavored to secure peace and justice for the African American masses.

White and black radicals who embraced communism as a foil to capitalism envisioned impoverished African Americans as promising recruits for the Communist Party. Since the majority of blacks still resided in the South, the CPUSA made initial attempts there to galvanize support. In 1932 the Communist Party competed in the presidential election, selecting James W. Ford, a black man, as the vice presidential candidate. In its platform, the CPUSA declared, "The Negro people, always hounded, persecuted, disfranchised, and discriminated against in capitalist America, are, during this period of crisis, oppressed as never before. They are the first to be fired when layoffs take place. They are discriminated against when charity rations are handed out to the unemployed."[68] Given the tenor of the times, the communist platform appeared accurate and seemed capable of eliciting a favorable response from desperate African Americans. The party also advocated the establishment of a forty-ninth state in the Black Belt that would provide a safe haven for African Americans.[69]

Two events provided the CPUSA with an opportunity to make inroads with the black masses. The first involved a celebrated case involving the plight of the Scottsboro Boys. When nine African American youths riding a freight train were accused of raping two white women on March 15, 1931, a white posse near Scottsboro, Alabama, seized the boys and threatened them with death. The NAACP initially intended to defend the boys, but the International Labor Defense (ILD), a subsidiary of the Communist Party, convinced the defendants to rely on the ILD for exoneration. The case became an international cause célèbre and gained national attention for the CPUSA. Although evidence revealed the boys were innocent, recalcitrant Southern juries ignored facts and demands to release the young men. Therefore, in 1935, the ILD, in cooperation with the NAACP, American Civil Liberties Union, the League for International Democracy, and the Episcopal Federation for Social Service formed the Scottsboro Defense Committee and worked assiduously to gain freedom for the innocent victims of Southern justice.[70] This celebrated case caused the NAACP to move toward the left in response to CPUSA's vigorous defense of indigent blacks. The Communist Party proved instrumental in momentarily moving traditionally conservative black leaders into making greater efforts to help low-income African Americans.

Drama involving Angelo Herndon proved nearly as dramatic as the injustice accorded the Scottsboro Boys. Herndon, a young man of nineteen years from Cincinnati, Ohio, had been arrested in 1933 for leading a hunger march in Atlanta. Herndon sought to force county commissioners to provide greater assistance for needy African Americans. After distributing leaflets demanding equal relief assistance for impoverished blacks, Herndon was arrested and charged for inciting an insurrection. The court convicted Herndon and sentenced him to twenty years on the chain gang. Fortunately, the legal efforts of the black Harvard-educated attorney and communist Benjamin J. Davis Jr. helped Herndon eventually gain freedom in 1937.[71]

The Scottsboro Boys and Herndon incidents stimulated progressive black leaders sufficiently to create an organization designed to assist the black masses. Early in 1936, black intellectuals met at Howard University in Washington, DC, and founded the aforementioned National Negro Congress, the most all-encompassing, supportive black-mass-oriented group to exist in the annals of African American history. The NNC represented a coalition of labor, fraternal, civic, and religious groups charged with the mission of alleviating the black majority from difficulties caused by the Great Depression.

Leaders from the NAACP, the Communist Party and a myriad of additional organizations sent delegates to the first NNC convention that convened in Chicago on February 14, 1936. Conventioneers from twenty-seven states—ranging from Alabama to Wisconsin, and the District of Columbia to California—attended the initial conference, including some of the most prominent African Americans in the nation. Representatives from Chicago included Oscar Brown Sr., A. C. McNeal, and Thyra Edwards of the Chicago NAACP. Other conferees attending were the Urban League's Lester Granger and A. Philip Randolph, who headed the Brotherhood of Sleeping Car Porters from New York City; Snow F. Grigsby, head of the Detroit NAACP; and prominent attorney Louis Redding of Wilmington, Delaware. Ohio sent the distinguished Dr. Richard Robert Wright Jr. and Bishop Reverdy C. Ransome of Wilberforce University. Scores of Philadelphians also attended, including newspaperman Joseph V. Baker and Wayne L. Hopkins of the National Urban League. Former Philadelphian, Rhodes Scholar, and professor at Howard University Alain Locke attended from Washington, DC, as did Dr. Ralph Bunche, Dean Kelly Miller, and activist-educator Mary Church Terrell.[72]

The Congress proposed seven objectives to mitigate African American suffering. With the exception of Objective 7, which pertained to opposing war and fascism, all concerns addressed the needs of impoverished African Americans. The right of Negroes to hold jobs at decent wages; relief, security, and insurance for every needy Negro family; aid to the Negro farm population comprising tenants and sharecroppers; opposition to lynching and mob violence; equal opportunities for Negro youth; and equality for Negro women galvanized support from virtually all 817 delegates who attended the conference.[73] The Chicago Congress proved an enormous success and culminated the meeting by electing A. Philip Randolph and John P. Davis president and executive secretary respectively. The conferees agreed to gather in Philadelphia the following year.

In 1937 the NNC reconvened in Philadelphia. Headed by Arthur Huff Fauset, novelist Jesse Fauset's brother and regional vice president of the congress, the NNC presented an array of pertinent topics that addressed a myriad of issues. Sessions on youths, trade unions, civil liberties, government workers, unemployment, education, housing, health, women, the church, culture, and farms lured delegates into meeting rooms.[74] Philadelphia organizers also presented gala programs at the Metropolitan Opera House and heard speakers address the concerns of low-income African Americans. Walter White of the NAACP and Patrick Kennedy, a white man who served as the lieutenant governor of Pennsylvania, spoke about anti-lynching legislation. Other notable orators included another white man, Vito Marcantonio, President of the International Labor Defense, who spoke about civil liberties and the Negro people, and Tuskegee Institute president F. D. Patterson, who offered remarks about problems of the rural Negro in America.

Unfortunately for the National Negro Congress, an innocuous topic, a symposium on war and fascism appeared on the program, demonstrating that left-wing activists could undermine the organization. Probably few black attendees seriously reflected about war and fascism in 1937. Nevertheless, the topic revealed a significant Communist Party influence in the NNC, a reality that eventually dominated the organization and caused black leaders to leave the National Congress in droves. When NNC president and staunch unionist A. Philip Randolph realized the National Negro Congress had become a CPUSA tool, he refused to stand for reelection and withdrew from the organization. With Randolph's departure, the NNC slid into oblivion, and by 1940, the National Negro Congress had become moribund.[75]

The collapse of the National Negro Congress and the betrayal of African Americans by the Communist Party left an indelible, negative impact on the black masses. Certainly, African Americans who attended NNC meetings intended to assist disadvantaged African Americans. White communists who risked life and limb for African Americans during the 1930s and advocated for the creation of a forty-ninth state, however, placed communist ideology before black amelioration.[76] The CPUSA's concerns for the African American masses quickly dissipated. Blacks, in turn, seldom again flirted with communism. Thus, the National Negro Congress represented the last concerted effort of African American organizations and leaders to work collectively on behalf of the low-income black masses.

With war clouds hanging over Europe and the justifiable wariness of the CPUSA, the black bourgeoisie refocused and devoted their attention primarily on specific middle-class interests. A small contingent of black leaders like celebrity Paul Robeson, union activist A. Philip Randolph, and T. Arnold Hill of the National Urban League still dedicated themselves to helping the black masses. Most middle-class African Americans and black leaders, however, would focus more on achieving civil rights for African Americans in the forthcoming war than ameliorating the condition of the masses. Valiant efforts to help and serve destitute blacks ended with the demise of the National Negro Congress.

CHAPTER 6

The World War II Decade

World War II existed as a potential watershed period in the lives of impoverished African Americans. For those who entered the armed services, the military removed thousands of black Southerners from the limiting confines of the rural South. Black servicemen and women would acquire "a knowledge of wants" and become covetous of previously denied material goods attributed to their long-standing poverty. More significantly, between 1941 and 1945, approximately 330,000 African Americans, and eventually 1,447,229 blacks during the World War II decade, would vacate the South to find work in defense industries located in the Northeast, Midwest, and Far West.[1] Few migrants would realize, however, that they traded the hell of the rural South for the mean streets of urban America.

Changes wrought by the Second World War initially proved threatening for African Americans who labored under the infamous sharecropping system. During the years prior to the commencement of hostilities in Europe, scores of sharecroppers had been pushed off the land. By 1940, 192,000 fewer black tenants existed in the United States than in 1930.[2] With the United States hovering on the edge of war, the federal government recognized that technology would be essential to assure victory. With the increased importance of technology required for the war effort, associated domestic needs for technology also occurred at home. As Southern landowners sought the means to maximize future profits, more and more cotton growers introduced mechanized cotton pickers and tractors for harvesting. Mechanization, therefore, pushed even more black tenants and sharecroppers from the land.[3] Sharecropping headed toward an eventual demise. For better or worse, destitute, exploited blacks mired to the land as exploited laborers had cause to flee the agrarian South.

When the United States finally entered the war, the military and American industry would eventually have an augmented need for black service personnel and workers. During the 1940s more than one million African Americans vacated the Deep South. And for the first time in the nation's history, more unskilled and marginally skilled blacks would reside outside the rural South.[4] With this Great Migration, the specter of black poverty shifted from the rural South to cities in the Northeast, Midwest, and Pacific Coast. From this era forward, impoverished African Americans would reside primarily in urban metropolises outside Dixie.

Ironically, the diminution of the tenant and sharecropping system could hardly occur at a more propitious time for African Americans. War in Europe, combined with threats to United States interests emanating from the Empire of Japan, suggested that the national need to prepare for hostilities would augur well for job-seeking blacks. Initially, opportunity for work did not seem readily apparent to the black masses. While Southern states nearly contained one-third of the United States population in 1940, less than a fifth of all war supply and facility contracts existed in the South.[5] Since most heavy industries were located in the North, Southern blacks faced two distinct dilemmas. Those who had jobs as farm laborers and were familiar with customary racism could remain in the South. Though experiencing demeaning racism, this faction could enjoy relative comfort and support from family and friends. On the other hand, Southern-bred African Americans who decided to relocate would face the challenges of surviving in an unfamiliar milieu. Given the challenging choices available, many blacks willingly took risks and prepared to migrate.

Despite the demise of sharecropping and prospects for a better working environment, problems still existed for job-seeking blacks. Northern and Southern whites alike displayed hostility toward placing African Americans in war production industries.[6] In 1940, 657,000 blacks acquired jobs in manufacturing—but were limited to working in unskilled, menial jobs. This became specifically true for lily-white machinist and boilermaker unions that confined blacks to the dirtiest, most contemptible aspects of work. In addition, while the federal government poured millions of dollars into vocational training for war preparation, the allotment for African Americans proved abysmally small. As late as December 1940, educational, business, labor, and political leaders opposed providing African Americans with vocational training. Thus, blacks comprised only 1.6 percent of trainees in pre-employment and supplementary vocational courses.[7] For many impoverished African Americans the lingering joblessness evident during the Great Depression continued.

After learning that training programs established for prospective defense work employees excluded blacks, race leaders became disgruntled.[8] As the nation prepared for war, blacks had been virtually eliminated from most armament industries. With jobs available and necessary to sustain the war effort, blacks had cause to decry racist treatment when only whites seeking jobs obtained work. Unlike the Great Depression when universal unemployment meant everyone suffered, existing discriminatory policies applied specifically to black workers seeking employment.

White industrialists and labor leaders placed far greater importance on confining blacks to lower status than preparing the nation for war. In October 1940, for example, only 5.4 percent of all employment placements involving twenty defense industries—comprising automobiles, airplanes, ships, iron and steel, and chemicals—contained nonwhite help. By April 1941, the percentage of nonwhite employees declined to a meager 2.5 percent.[9] Equally disconcerting, African Americans learned that industrial workers could contribute to the newly devised Social Security program and collect unemployment checks while agricultural workers and domestics—overwhelmingly black in composition—were unprotected by unemployment insurance and thereby ineligible for Social Security benefits.

Recognizing a strategy must be devised to combat racist policies, blatant discrimination forced black leaders to act on behalf of their entire race. As early as the winter of 1940–1941, African American leaders decided to act. Goaded by fulminations of the late Robert Vann of the *Pittsburgh Courier,* A. Philip Randolph of the Brotherhood of Sleeping Car Porters and NAACP executive secretary Walter White launched an onslaught against racist hiring practices. Mindful that acquiescence to national unity failed to quell white hostility toward blacks during the First World War, African American leaders became more militant and demanded immediate equal rights concessions.

Given the downward trend regarding black employment, A. Philip Randolph threatened to march on Washington and draw attention to racism that limited opportunities for African Americans. Fearing the march would come to fruition and embarrass the government, President Roosevelt agreed to Randolph's demands that blacks be hired to work in industries that received government contracts. On June 25, 1941, President Roosevelt issued Executive Order 8802, which called for a ban on discrimination in defense industries. In order to enforce the directive, on July 19, 1941, Roosevelt appointed the nation's first Fair Employment Practices Committee (FEPC), enabling the long-sought-after federal support for employing blacks in defense industries to become a reality.

Making a proclamation and having the directive enforced with measurable results proved elusive, if not impossible. Indeed, black prospects for work plummeted almost immediately after the United States entered the war. As late as June 1942, the publication *The Labor Market,* reported that in April 1940, blacks comprised 9.8 percent of the population, 10.7 percent of the national labor force, and 12.5 percent of the unemployed. By 1942, however, African American unemployment increased, reaching approximately 20 percent because war industries almost exclusively recruited white workers into the labor force.[10] Equally disconcerting, black unemployment in the North exceeded numbers in the South.

Unlike the NAACP that advocated for the legal rights of African Americans, the National Urban League had the responsibility for placing blacks in jobs.[11] As the war continued, fortunately wartime necessity enhanced black prospects for finding work. The NUL used the war as means to garner support on behalf of unemployed blacks. In a memo referencing Negro contributions to winning the war, the Urban League called on President Roosevelt to discuss the negative implications of racism that undermined the nation's military effort. Black leaders also produced a slate of objectives designed for the president's approval. Roosevelt, however, refused to act on the overtures, fearing a Southern backlash from white conservatives would occur in Congress. And because heads of the armed services believed that black inclusively would undermine white servicemen's resolve to fight, Roosevelt sensed race riots would take precedent over fighting the Axis powers.[12] An impasse existed between the government and black leaders endeavoring to find gainful employment for their race.

With discrimination practiced and condoned in the federal government, all other prospective hiring agencies—state, municipal, or private—engaged in similar restrictive practices. All blacks—professionals, street-corner folk, habitués in beauty parlors and barber shops—seemed equally disgruntled by the treatment accorded African Americans.[13] The least sophisticated African Americans must have pondered how white people could verbalize the love for democracy and the need for freedom abroad while simultaneously practicing discrimination against loyal, black United States citizens at home. Even discontented African American rubes like those of Holtuka in rural Oklahoma envisioned the conflict as a white man's war in which blacks should not participate. These cynical blacks concluded that whites sought African American participation only if they would "cook for the white man and clean up after him while he did the fighting." Disdain for the American version of Nazism appeared in the black press, providing candid remarks about white racism that angered African Americans throughout the nation.[14]

Although the federal government eventually realized that every able-bodied worker would be needed to produce necessary war materials, racist restrictions that excluded blacks from the workforce remained strong throughout the United States. Bell Aircraft, headquartered in Buffalo, New York, agreed to hire two thousand blacks in its Atlanta plant, but local authorities refused to train African Americans. Brooklyn manufacturers received $300 million in war contracts by end of 1941 but excluded blacks from working in factories. Unions in Kansas City only hired union labor and unions refused to admit skilled blacks into the fold. Racism transcended nationalism; without employing the entire workforce, the nation's capacity to wage war proved limited.

Eventually, with the aid of activist civil rights groups, the FEPC forced some employers to hire black workers. Rather than face the embarrassment of public scrutiny that would be created by FEPC investigations, war industry corporations eventually hired scores of African Americans. Equally significant, the Policy Commission enabled blacks to retain newly acquired jobs. In 1943 and 1944 the agency squelched at least twenty-five hate strikes organized by whites who resented the hiring of black employees.[15]

Securing gainful employment appeared as the most pressing issue for jobless African Americans. The key to success depended upon the ability of blacks to enter unions. Initially, the possibility for attaining work seemed better for unskilled rather than skilled black workers. The American Federation of Labor excluded blacks, but the fledgling Congress of Industrial Organizations appeared to take a more progressive approach toward incorporating blacks into their ranks. For those unskilled African Americans fortunate to join the CIO, prospects for becoming a solid member of the working class and possibly acquiring middle-class status, appeared to improve. Nevertheless, local CIO leadership focused on protecting the white rank and file; African American workers became admitted into the union but still experienced discriminatory restrictions. Seniority and favorable job assignments for established white employees prevented the advancement of African American workers.[16] Ambitious blacks who coveted a higher station in life remained at a disadvantage.

Despite the inconstancy regarding African American membership in unions, heightened war demands dictated that more blacks must be included in the workforce. Eventually, scores of underprivileged African Americans from the South would vacate their native region and take advantage of job opportunities never previously realized. A sense of optimism prevailed as the Southern exodus suggested life would improve immeasurably for the African American masses.[17] Newcomers arrived from varied backgrounds and ventured into cities throughout the nation. Between 1940 and 1950, the black populations of the Northeast, Midwest, and Far West cities increased exponentially. New York City acquired 211,153 new black inhabitants followed by Chicago (166,322), Detroit (130,272), and Los Angeles (112,648). The black urban population supplanted African Americans living in rural environs.[18]

The success of migrant adjustment to industrial cities depended primarily on their Southern origins. Newcomers who moved to Chicago came directly from decidedly impoverished rural backgrounds and would find adjustment to the new urban environment difficult.[19] Thus, the "Bronzeville" world of lower-class blacks in Chicago, with uncouth, disrespectful youths and dissolute adults, differed little from migrants attracted to the Windy City during previous migrants.[20] Meanwhile, most of the migrants who ventured to Los Angeles came from Southern cities and towns, rendering the transition from the

South somewhat less arduous. Given the race, class, and regional differences between the migrants and established residents, the newcomers would still find adjustment difficult.[21]

Although African Americans vacated the South seeking freedom and fortune elsewhere, black ghettos, with all the massive problems attenuated with migration, impacted cities throughout the entire nation. In addition to Southern blacks moving into Chicago, Philadelphia, New York, and Detroit, the influx of migrants became most apparent on the West Coast. Los Angeles, San Diego, Oakland, and Long Beach, California, witnessed enormous increases in the black population.[22] The numbers of migrants and the intensity of their impact upon established residents and the urban infrastructure proved unprecedented. Cities already overcrowded with white workers who became the first to find employment in war production industries now became visited by what the white and African American establishment perceived as a black scourge. With housing, recreational facilities, consumer goods, and transportation services already overtaxed during the war, an already fulminating public would react harshly toward the new black arrivals.[23]

The established black bourgeoisie from the east to the far west became particularly aggrieved by the newcomers. In some locales like Los Angeles, the number of migrants exceeded the native black population. Negative opinions varied. Some feared newcomers would inject a countrified behavior and thereby embarrass established black residents seeking integration with the white elite.[24] Others reviled the overcrowding that existed in their black neighborhoods, blaming newcomers for undermining the acceptable pre-migration status quo. And still others feared the aggressive nature of repressed Southern blacks who perceived an unintended slight as a racist affront that demanded redress. One observer declared, "The new-comers have a freedom they haven't experienced before, and sometimes they become wild."[25] Obviously residual effects of the World War II migration further widened the gap between middle-income African Americans and the masses.

The shortage of suitable housing units in black communities nationally proved particularly acute as black ghettos commenced a steady decline into slums. Slum clearance programs and the erection of new housing structures failed to resolve the crisis. With slum dwellings razed and residents displaced, scores of people remained without proper shelter. Even when the federal government endeavored to mitigate the housing shortage by constructing the Sojourner Truth Homes in Detroit to house low-income blacks, whites sought to claim the newly erected apartment units for their race. Riots erupted in the Motor City, resulting in three deaths, more than five hundred injuries, and millions of dollars in damages.[26]

The housing crisis became particularly grating because the increased density of African Americans in cities resulted in entrenched segregation and greater restriction to black mobility. With complicity from local housing authorities, realtors and landlords avoided federal regulations by dividing units and defining the changes as mere remodeling. Indeed, the lines of segregation had been so deeply drawn that landlords and realtors lost money by limiting black opportunities to secure housing. Still, those who owned property in African American neighborhoods forced black residents to continue paying higher rentals for inferior, run-down accommodations.[27]

As black neighborhoods became more inhospitable, housing specialist Robert Weaver lamented about the increasingly difficult conditions that evolved. In Chicago, Weaver observed, World War II caused "slum conditions [to be] introduced, blight . . . accelerated [causing] deteriorated communities and family life [to] ensue."[28] Similar problems befell black migrants who moved to Los Angeles. After Japanese citizens had been uprooted from Little Tokyo and moved to reclamation camps, black migrants occupied the vacated homes. Unscrupulous landlords crammed migrants into tiny living spaces and forced newcomers to pay exorbitant rents. A contemporary journalist observed,

> In place after place children lived in windowless rooms, amid peeling plaster, rats, and flies that gathered thick around food that stood on open shelves or kitchen [or] bedroom tables. There was no bathtub . . . As many as forty people shared one toilet. Families were separated only by sheets strung up between beds. Many of the beds were "hot" with people taking turns sleeping in them.[29]

An area originally designed for thirty thousand residents in 1940 housed seventy thousand in 1945.[30]

The Federal Public Housing Authority (FPHA) exacerbated the housing dilemma by engaging in racist practices. With insufficient space and funding for new housing, the FPHA failed to enforce guidelines designed to make affordable housing available for newly arrived migrants. In addition to Chicago and Los Angeles, segregation became even more entrenched in cities like Cleveland, Detroit, Philadelphia, and San Francisco.[31] In those cities where FPHA directors were more progressive and enlightened in regard to public housing, the changes proved too uneventful to make a significant difference.[32] With national public housing authorities hostile or indifferent toward making apartments available for established low-income blacks, local housing officials cared even less about providing suitable shelter for impoverished African American migrants.

Without proper guidance offered by federal housing authorities, municipal leaders and bureaucrats found creative ways to discriminate against African Americans. Restrictive housing covenants easily became implemented. Real estate boards and realtors instituted practices, agreements, and codes of ethics that limited the prospects for low-income blacks to acquire suitable housing. Moreover, since the Federal Housing Authority accepted restrictive housing covenants, few private builders and financers had the incentive to erected low-income housing for blacks. Even when money became available to private contractors willing to erect low-income housing for African Americans, the builders decided not to erect accommodations for blacks. These contractors simply sought to avoid placing their businesses in jeopardy by angry white residents willing to use violence and political clout to maintain a "lily white" community. Local governments also feared that low-income housing would lure more impoverished black migrants into their city. Consequently, ambitious politicians recognized that voicing opposition to housing low-income blacks elicited public support and enhanced political careers.[33]

Racism in regard to housing created a self-fulfilling prophesy that justified white aversion toward African Americans. The more whites confined blacks to restrictive ghettos causing neighborhoods to deteriorate, the more whites felt justified in limiting African Americans to segregated black enclaves. White aversion toward African Americans became compounded by evidence of squalor, vice, and crime in black neighborhoods. To improve the negative perception whites held toward African Americans, the National Urban League called for better recreation and housing conditions in cities containing black migrants. Unfortunately, communities experiencing an influx of African Americans failed to address NUL concerns. Job seeking migrants basically became pariahs. The Urban League even had to attack vilification of migrants by the white press including *The New York Times*. The *Times*, like other mainstream newspapers, justified its negative reports on African Americans by proclaiming black crime is what people wanted to read.[34]

An additional problem, the anti-intellectualism of the impoverished black masses, surfaced as another continuing factor that lessened prospects for low-income black amelioration. Unlike predecessors who participated in the previous Great Migration and vacated the South in search of jobs and educational opportunities, new migrants focused on work at the expense of educational attainment. During World War I scores of newcomers entering Chicago enrolled their children in day schools and attended night schools themselves.[35] A far different attitude toward education existed among World War II migrants. Deeply impacted by the Great Depression, focused on the desire to make money, and burdened with the educational inadequacies attributed to poverty and residence in the rural South, recent migrants had little reason to champion the cause of education. After being destitute during the "Depression Decade," acquiring money took precedence over obtaining a high school diploma.

Equally debilitating, other factors inhibited the learning process for the children of the low-income migrants. Indignity and embarrassment became commonplace for virtually every migrant child who enrolled in a regular public school outside the South. In integrated schools, the inadequate preparation of migrant children resulted in lower achievement scores, placement in remedial classes, and, often, reduction to a lower-grade level. Migrant students consequently became identified by white teachers and student peers as being subnormal and ignorant.[36] Migrant children also suffered from the ignominy of Southern birth in segregated black schools. Black students who vacated the impoverished, backward schools of the South found themselves attending classes with similar transplanted children. By attending schools with students of the same socioeconomic class and value system, anti-intellectualism and the desultory academic performances remained in place. Uninformed, rustic, impoverished parents produced unenlightened children. These factors, combined with racism, and classist sentiments imbued among established teachers and students, provided the foundation for sustained, wretched, academic performances among low-income black youths. Blacks with bucolic origins appeared inadequately educated for urban living.[37] Despite new surroundings, discouraged, dispirited low-income children, remained indifferent toward education.

Additional problems occurred when overwhelming numbers of working-class whites and blacks simultaneously flowed into cities. Domestic warfare resulted. Shortages in housing, limited access to recreational facilities, and overcrowding in schools heightened racial tensions.[38] The first significant racial disturbance occurred in Detroit, Michigan. On June 20, 1943, a large black crowd comprising one hundred thousand people trekked to Belle Island, an amusement park located on the Detroit River. Feeding upon the resentment toward whites generally and the police in particular, angry black teens spoiled for a fight. Black belligerence erupted when young African Americans allegedly robbed a white couple of two dollars and assaulted whites playing on an athletic field. Perhaps one of the more egregious acts of unmitigated black resentment toward whites occurred when an eighteen-year-old black boy from Alabama called a white woman riding on a bus a “motherfucking son of a bitch.”[39] After that brazen pronouncement and other acts showing disrespect toward white people, fights erupted. Both races went berserk. Whites fought to maintain the status quo. Blacks, many from the South, conversely, felt liberated. Now able to off-load confining shackles attributed to their Southern heritage, black youths defended their dignity by engaging in violence and wreaking revenge on white people.[40] The riot resulted in 34 deaths, more than 700 injuries, and an estimated 2 million dollars lost in destroyed property.

On August 1, 1943, New York City served as the scene of another infamous riot as low-income blacks identified as being undignified fought to acquire respect. Unlike the 1943 riots in Los Angeles, Detroit, Mobile, and Beaumont, where racial tension resulted in violence and mayhem, the confrontation in Harlem pitted lower-class blacks against the police.[41] Frustrations attributed to poverty, combined with rage fostered by a history of racial affronts created a tinderbox in Harlem. An uprising attributed primarily to the frustrations inherent among the impoverished, Harlem erupted when African Americans heard an erroneous rumor that a white police officer killed a black soldier.[42] Although the resulting mayhem resulted in less injuries and loss of life than in Detroit, three to four hundred blacks were injured and at least five people died. Approximately five hundred people—three hundred African Americans and one hundred women—were arrested.[43] The riot revealed a continuing contempt for the police, and interestingly, a significant number of black women engaged in the unfortunate melee. The Harlem riot proved unique because blacks directed their anger toward white-owned property rather than to individuals.[44]

In the wake of the New York City disturbance, between 1943 and 1944 riots broke out in such disparate cities as St. Louis, Baltimore, Mobile, San Francisco, Indianapolis, Philadelphia, Houston, Port Arthur, and Beaumont, Texas.[45] Angry blacks fought whites over segregated housing, job assignments in defense industries, and discrimination that denied African Americans the use of parks and toilets. Blacks recognized that unrepentant, racist whites placed discrimination toward blacks as a greater priority than defeating Germany, Japan, and Italy. Despite the drama associated with racial discrimination that impacted all African Americans, the people most inclined to display anger in the streets presumably had the least to lose. Logically, this group comprised impoverished race members who resided in ghettos.

Illicit activities that occurred in transitional neighborhoods also bolstered racial tensions and negative stereotypes toward blacks. The so-called Bronzeville in Los Angeles, for example, became a center of vice, prostitution, gambling, and drinking. Thrill-seeking war workers—black and white—flocked to the neighborhood for debauchery and entertainment. An impressionistic white woman declared, "I hear colored people control all the [vice] . . . ."[46] Avaricious established residents, rather than newcomers, owned the burgeoning liquor stores, provided drugs, and maintained the shoeshine parlors that functioned as brothels. Migrants, however, received the blame for promulgating white beliefs of black immorality and inferiority. Local whites indeed held blacks responsible for the perceived increase in crime. White people residing in the West and Southwest regions of the United States, interestingly, deemed Mexican laborers during the war a necessary evil. Blacks, however, were perceived as being both unnecessary and evil.[47]

Patriotism, combined with the desire to escape from undesirable low-income black communities, encouraged African Americans with martial ardor to enlist in the military. Educational deficiencies, however, prevented scores of African Americans from joining the armed services. By the end of 1943, nearly half (46 percent) of eligible African Americans—as opposed to 30 percent of whites—experienced rejection from military service recruiters. The Army General Classification Test (AGCT) that evaluated a recruit's ability to learn proved disadvantageous for thousands of African Americans. Low-income Southern blacks who comprised a majority of the rejects had fallen victim to a Southern heritage rife with inadequate schools, limited educational opportunities, and woeful inexperience with customary middle-class practices and norms.[48] Blacks who met the minimal educational requirements and became inducted into the armed services still faced difficulties. A disproportionately high percentage of African American inductees scored low in AGCT tests. Blacks with low test scores were placed in the lowest grade category and reduced to menial work assignments earmarked for "low intelligence Negroes."[49]

In a positive sense, the armed services served as a prospective employer for jobless young black men. Nutritious food, ample clothing, and higher pay than in most occupations available for impoverished blacks certainly made the military attractive. And for those eager to acquire a better education, service in the army and navy made prospects for an enhanced life seem feasible.[50] With hope beckoning for armed service inductees and with the knowledge that black men placed their lives on the line for their country, the war caused African Americans to be more self-respecting and less inclined to accept white racist practices with impunity.

Eventually the war enabled impoverished blacks to make some gainful measures against racial discrimination within unions. The National Urban League organized an extremely successful Victory through Unity conference that addressed racial inequities and received extremely high attendance and national publicity.[51] The conference resulted in the establishment of more than three hundred human relations commissions in states, cities, and towns to deal with inequities attributed to racism. Because of gains made with unions, the Urban League had reason to feel prideful. By 1945 more than one million African Americans acquired union cards—the AFL boasted 650,000 black unionists and the CIO, 500,000.

African Americans in Washington, DC, specifically benefited from expanded job opportunities in the federal government. The number of employed African Americans increased from approximately eighty thousand in 1938 to three hundred thousand by 1944.[52] Although racial discrimination and deficient educational qualifications limited the majority to toiling in unskilled positions, scores of struggling African Americans acquired work and enjoyed greater prospects for achieving dignity, respect, and middle-class standing.

Despite the successes aspiring African Americans achieved because of the war, circumstances dictated that a black majority still faced continuous problems securing employment as World War II drew to a close. Richard Russell, a racist senator from Georgia, introduced an amendment in June 1944 declaring that no funds could be allotted to any agency established by an executive order and in existence for more than one year.[53] Russell clearly attacked FEPC and was not alone in his opposition. Even President Harry Truman, Roosevelt's successor, opposed the federal mandate. Truman and the Democratic Party engaged in ritualized lip-service gestures of support before the public. In actuality, the Truman administration did nothing concrete to sustain FEPC legislation that benefitted disadvantaged African Americans. Thus, when employers offered preferential hiring to white workers and ignored FEPC regulations, African American appeals to municipal, state, and federal governments proved ineffective.[54]

Unfortunately for certain impoverished African Americans, race advances in unions and housing became divisive, separating the more resourceful from those inclined to accept the economic and social status quo. Ambitious blacks made preparations to elevate in status by working hard, saving money, stressing the value of education, exercising patience, and embracing other norms indicative of middle-class standing. With jobs allowing for greater access to money and better housing opportunities on the periphery of the ghetto, industrious African Americans made strides to enter the black bourgeoisie. Others who failed to use mitigating racism as a window of opportunity, however, experienced an incipient and widening gap between the black bourgeoisie and themselves. A majority of African Americans would remain alienated, dispossessed, and poor.

A temporary decline of the NAACP during the 1930s and early 1940s and the concomitant rise of the Communist Party in postwar America created another dilemma for working-class blacks. Although a guarded relationship existed between the two organizations, when circumstances warranted, the NAACP and the American Communist Party worked collectively on behalf of the black masses. By the late 1940s, however, ideological differences created divisions that rendered a vigorous, sustained effort to help disadvantaged African Americans impossible. Since the Scottsboro Boys incident and its role in the National Negro Congress during the 1930s, the more radical and aggressive Communist Party gained popularity among the masses at the expense of the NAACP. By 1945, however, the NAACP regained popularity and received tremendous support from African Americans generally, and the black working-class in particular.[55] Meanwhile, as the Cold War evolved at the close of World War II, any association with the Communist Party raised concerns among patriotic citizens and politicians. The CPUSA pushed relentlessly and uncompromisingly for black justice at the close of World War II. The Cold War and the stench associated with communism, however, eroded public sympathy for the Communist Party generally, and the black masses in particular. Mutual endeavors between the NAACP and CPUSA to aid the working class fostered a guilt-by-association stigma. As the CPUSA became a pariah, the NAACP would distance itself from efforts that focused on the black working class to avoid the pejorative anti-American sobriquet.[56] Any ameliorative efforts the communists made on behalf of impoverished blacks would receive condemnation rather than praise. Race-conscious blacks doubted the sincerity of Communist Party advocates, and white Americans soon disdained communism as a political and economic ideology.[57]

As the CPUSA lost credibility within white America, the black masses correspondingly suffered. By 1948 the newly formed Civil Rights Congress (CRC), a Communist Party affiliate, became established in New York City. Low-income blacks appreciated the new agency that actively endorsed equality for black laborers and opposed police brutality. The CRC staged pickets, organized strikes, and garnered a bevy of lawyers to operate as a legal defense team.[58] Unfortunately for the masses, the CRC appeared more concerned about confusing and embarrassing Americans and the American government than promoting the cause of black people.[59] Even when communists cooperated with the NAACP, given the atmosphere of extreme anticommunism, the party proved more a liability to the masses than an asset.[60] With the NAACP distancing itself from the CRC, and the Communist Party in national disfavor because of the Cold War, disadvantaged African Americans lost needed support.

During the 1940s increased automation evolved as another phenomenon that adversely affected the African American masses. Blacks who vacated farms and migrated to cities became part of the new but unfortunate working class—an assembly of factory and service workers on the verge of obsolescence.[61] Labor-saving machinery on the farm and in the factory contributed to underemployment and eventually unemployment. Unskilled blacks became unwanted laborers in the great centers of urban America. Recent migrants during the postwar era found themselves on the horns of a dilemma—deciding whether to return to the inhospitable South or remain in less offensive Northern locales to "eek out" a meager existence in urban ghettos.

At the end of WW II black unemployment soared because of automation and the "last hired first fired" policy.[62] Blacks who found jobs with the greatest promise and highest wages, as in aircraft production and shipbuilding, would be among the first to be laid off during the postwar years.[63] Equally important, the postwar recession caused blacks with marginal skills to suffer from downsizing. Black workers occupied the lowest-paid sectors of the postwar economy and had insufficient funds to withstand layoffs. Black women specifically became vulnerable to downsizing because of race and gender.

Perhaps the most significant and consequential impact of World War II existed in the hydra-headed dilemma working-class black women encountered. Initially, the war provided significant opportunities for black female workers as jobs created during World War II enabled African American women to enhance their earning capacity. By 1945, 46 percent of all black women were full-time employees as opposed to 31 percent among whites. Black women obtained financial independence, acquired unemployment insurance, became incorporated into the Social Security program, and received more benefits previously deemed impossible as traditional service workers. The euphoria would be short-lived. Given the need to hire returning veterans, all female employees, including black women, became expendable. After enjoying the fruits of gainful employment, black women, specifically those functioning as primary breadwinners lost jobs in the post war economy suffered grievously.[64]

Although single black women who retained jobs could survive, females with children faced adversity within their families that extended into the community. Children of a single working mother who retained a job during the war or returned to service work suffered from neglect. Indeed the entire neighborhood experienced discontent caused by rambunctious youths. Without adult supervision in the home, black children demonstrated a greater tendency to engage in delinquent behavior and establish a trend that continued throughout the twentieth century.[65]

Philadelphia's Thirtieth Ward provided evidence of increasing disruptions in the neighborhood caused by young toughs. As early as June 1946, YWCA leadership observed and complained about an increasing crime wave promulgated by idle youths. The impact of unruly juveniles on middle-class children who customarily attended YWCA events became obvious to the executive director, who said, "Many girls [will] not venture out, many parents refuse to let them go and even committee women timidly pass dark corners and loiterers . . . [N]o age feels safe."[66] Without the problem abating, an extremely frustrated executive director recorded her observations by declaring, "Gangs—not one but three—have made life generally miserable for us. We have turned to community agencies—Crime Prevention, Anderson Special Detective Squad, Police District #1—without success."[67] Prominent leaders within the Thirtieth Ward endeavored to resolve problems involving black youths by organizing a community meeting to address concerns in the neighborhood, an effort with inconclusive results.

Heightened evidence of juvenile delinquency also represented a concomitant increase of class disparages within black neighborhoods. Similar to the black YWCA in Philadelphia that disdained the problematic lower class, venerable civil rights organizations like the National Urban League and

NAACP became increasingly middle class in focus and approach. Leading men in each organization—Lester B. Granger and Walter White, who headed the NUL and NAACP respectively—declared an affinity for the masses but, instead, represented the black bourgeoisie. As representatives of middle-class blacks rather than the masses, impoverished blacks were devoid of any prominent black or white who spoke for or represented the interests or concerns of lower class African Americans.[68]

After the war American politicians also demonstrated less concern about placating low-income blacks than placating the concerns of the black bourgeoisie. In preparation for the 1948 presidential election, the Republicans spoke out against lynching, the poll tax, and segregated units in the armed services. The GOP presented the voting public with a constructive, conservative platform. At their National Convention the Democratic Party presented a liberal platform committed to eradicating all racial, religious, and economic discrimination. Platitudes declaring the right of minorities to live, work, vote, and have equal protection under laws guaranteed in the Constitution appealed to progressive-minded African Americans. Nevertheless, something more substantive would be required to address the needs of the African American masses.

Unfortunately for impoverished African Americans, only third parties out of favor with the voting majority addressed the needs of disadvantaged blacks. Indeed, third parties alone kept the role of low-income blacks in mind when devising party platforms. The Communist and Progressive Parties presented platforms designed to ameliorate the condition of the underprivileged black masses. The CPUSA spoke of a democratic agricultural program that offered land and other forms of assistance to thousands of farm laborers. Meanwhile, the Progressive Party advocated for special programs designed to raise the standards of health, housing, and educational facilities for African Americans. The voting public, however, ignored the platforms of the Communist and Progressive Parties. And to make matters decidedly worse for Democrats with negritude sensibilities, disgruntled Southerners broke from the Democratic ranks and founded the States' Rights Democratic Party (Dixiecrats) in an effort to maintain segregation and return blacks to the long-standing servile status of previous generations.

In retrospect, the 1948 election represented a watershed period in regard to the condition of the Negro. The election left an indelible impact on the nation's insensitivity toward disadvantaged African Americans. The Dixiecrat defection that garnered thirty-eight electoral votes for presidential candidate Strom Thurman failed to blunt President Truman's reelection. Nevertheless, progressive Democrats in the Eighty-First Congress feared the possibility of a Southern filibuster and did little to improve conditions for downtrodden

African Americans. The black masses faced a daunting future.[69] While President Truman's reelection proved comforting to the loyal black middle-class electorate, a final blow for the black masses' amelioration occurred with the failed candidacy of Henry Wallace. Running as the Progressive Party candidate for president, Wallace supported labor as well as African American rights. Wallace's overwhelming defeat (winning only 2 percent of votes cast) represented a devastating blow for labor and marked the demise of a cooperative labor-based civil rights movement.[70] Equally important, middle-class blacks eschewed the Progressive Party's radicalism and remained unequivocally supportive of the Democratic Party and its gradualist approach toward civil and class amelioration for downtrodden African Americans.

Even as signs of racial progress appeared for middle-class African Americans, countervailing forces dashed hopes for the black masses. While more and more states banned racial segregation and discrimination during the late 1940s—though minimal enforcement occurred—little, if any, attention was given to the employment concerns of black workers. The demand for unskilled and semiskilled labor declined more rapidly than blacks could acquire an education to upgrade into broader areas of work. Many occupational advances black workers achieved after 1940 were eliminated by automation.[71] Indifference toward the African American working class became evident just as FEPC policy enforcement efforts lapsed. Blacks eager for work only heard lip service—the federal enforcement policy had no teeth.[72] Although the National Urban League encouraged employers to make symbolic, high-level black hires designed to create a favorable impression in society, affiliated unions voted down a resolution calling for the end of Jim Crow. Union leaders failed to curtail heightened racism. By the 1950s FEPC became defunct, virtually eliminating all concerns for the black working class for more than a decade.[73]

The decade of the 1940s marked an era when the black ghetto began the steady deterioration into a slum. Because African Americans already resided in blighted ghettos prior to the war migration, newcomers caused the neighborhoods to further deteriorate. As the decay of black communities accelerated, dens of inequity, characterized by vice and underworld activities—purposely concentrated in the black community by law enforcement and the white establishment—heaped greater scorn upon African Americans. Problems for the black masses became compounded as private real estate boards, lending agencies, and home builders associations abhorred federal funds being designated to erect low-income housing. At best, these groups reasoned that undo government influence undermined private enterprise. In actuality, however, a different reality emerged. City planners ignored the increasingly slum-like conditions evolving in Negro ghettos.[74]

Unfortunately at this time, organizations and individuals on the left, like the CPUSA and the National Negro Labor Council, that traditionally championed the rights of downtrodden African Americans in housing and employment had lost influence. The Cold War caused left-wing progressives to become wary about their actions. Therefore, leftists could only offer tenuous support for impoverished blacks as communists and socialists in the United States became marginalized. Anticommunist sentiment consequently hastened the withdrawal of social activists from the side of downtrodden blacks.

Six years of global conflict enabled scores of underprivileged blacks to leave the restrictive South. Every migrant coveted success. But by the end of the decade, the thrifty, more sophisticated African Americans benefited from the opportunities made possible by World War II. Civil rights organizations used the scourge of Nazism to break down racist barriers. But activists focused primarily on areas that could enhance the quality of life for the Negro elite rather than the black masses. Leaders in the National Urban League circulated resumes of respectable, well-educated African Americans to encourage employers to hire blacks in breakthrough white-collar jobs.[75] The NAACP became actively involved in civil rights cases to acquire dignity for all African Americans. Nevertheless, the National Association's efforts had greater impact for the "better" class of Negroes. The NAACP proved instrumental in opening graduate and professional schools in Oklahoma, Delaware, Arkansas, and Kentucky, and terminating restrictive real estate housing covenants that confined blacks to ghettos.[76] These efforts to gain access to white-collar jobs, entrance into graduate and professional schools, and the opportunity to move into decent homes located in white neighborhoods established a foundation that created an ever-widening gap between the African American masses and the black bourgeoisie.

Chapter 7

From Ghetto to Slum: Urban Black America at a Crossroad

Although 1940s marked a period of promise for African Americans as scores of migrants left the South for a more promising future outside "Dixie," the fortunes of low-income blacks declined precipitously after World War II. Despite economic opportunities derived from the war effort and the increase in disposal income to satiate the taste of boundless consumers, low-income blacks would be unable to sustain benefits that accrued from the vibrant postwar economy. While the black bourgeoisie took advantage of diminished racism and enjoyed greater social, economic, and political rights, opportunities for the black masses languished.[1] The residual effects of Southern sharecropping characterized by ignorance and limited marketable skills, combined with increased migration to overcrowded ghettos, severely curtailed future prospects for low-income blacks. The plight of underprivileged African Americans continued throughout the postwar decade.

Discrimination attributed to federal housing policies enacted during the New Deal proved instrumental in confining the African American masses to ghettos. While the Home Owners Loan Corporation of 1933 provided funding for American citizens, blacks were denied access to federally backed loans and mortgages. And when the 1937 Wagner-Steagall Housing Act established the United States Housing Authority to finance slum clearance, blacks again suffered. Monies earmarked for slum clearance in African American neighborhoods were allocated by local (white) housing authorities. These housing directors either refused funds to eradicate African American slums or restricted black housing projects to unsavory segregated enclaves located near industrial sites, railroad tracks, or marginal lands near waterfronts.[2] Thus, African Americans who migrated out of the South to urban milieus in other regions of the country would expand black neighborhoods from ghettos to slums.

Between 1950 and 1960, approximately 1.5 million African Americans moved from the South to Northern, Midwestern, and Northeastern cities in the United States.[3] While the 1940s migration was related directly to the war, African Americans who migrated between 1950 and 1960 had different reasons for leaving the South. During the 1950s agricultural and fiber production increased by more than 25 percent; but automation, new chemicals, and cotton pickers reduced the numbers of gainfully employed workers by 27 percent. The agrarian revolution reduced employment by 50 percent, displacing thousands of black farmworkers.[4] By 1959 jobs held by approximately 500,000 sharecroppers had been eliminated. As individuals victimized by the horrendous peonage system vacated the countryside and faced unknowns in the city, they faced daunting challenges that made Southern brutality appear less extreme. Migration, nevertheless, continued.

As Southern migrants exited the South, several factors had a deleterious influence on venturesome travelers. First, technological and market changes allowed those who recently acquired work to be dismissed. Technology that eliminated menial jobs in the rural South had a corresponding impact on manual laborers in the urban America. For example, Philadelphia lost ninety thousand jobs between 1952 and 1962, with many blacks experiencing unemployment as factories closed or relocated to suburbia. Second, workers with marginal skills and a limited education became the last hired, first fired, and most inclined to remain unemployed.[5] Anticipating the difficulties that would lie ahead as early as 1951, native Tennessean Carl T. Rowan, an eyewitness to the migration, expressed grave concerns about the future of his race. Sitting in the car of a passenger train headed North, Rowan said, "I knew that I was leaving the South, land of my birth and childhood, never to return. And as I looked at the hundreds of Negroes milling about the train stations of cities along the [Mason-Dixon] boundary, I knew that I was not alone. Thousands of other Negroes were, and are, leaving the South." And then recognizing the pitfalls that lay ahead he noted, "This had not blinded me to the evils of the North, and I knew that because of these evils many of these pilgrims would not be so lucky as I had been. Some would get caught in the undertow of big-city brutality—brutality that I had seen in many forms and had learned to despise."[6]

Rowan's words of doom proved prophetic for many migrants. Concomitant with the good fortunes enjoyed by skilled white laborers and business enterprises in postwar America was the growing and omnipresent black slum. Black slums increased in size and taxed every aspect of social service. Housing, recreational facilities, and schools were severely impacted by the continuous influx of newcomers. Established citizens, in turn, deemed migrants the cause for social problems that plagued the neighborhood. Migrant behavior provided long-term residents with evidence that raised concerns. The migrants' inability to adjust to the urban industrial milieu, demonstrated by erratic work habits, ignorance of deferred gratification, indifference toward hygienic norms, and other nefarious practices derived from the inhumanity of sharecropping made the transition from the rural South to the urban North difficult.[7]

Migrants and other low-income African Americans would reside in ever-increasing segregated, impoverished neighborhoods. Being confined to old, deteriorating neighborhoods and unable to acquire mortgages from the Federal Housing Authority, the Veterans Administration, or private banks like white peers, low-income African Americans could only purchase homes in black neighborhoods. Never able to enjoy the appreciation in home values enjoyed by whites, as African American communities deteriorated, black home values in inner cities declined.[8]

Impoverished blacks faced a continuous problem in postwar America—finding work—that nagged previous generations of African Americans. In Philadelphia, Pennsylvania, the Armstrong Association, the city's branch of the National Urban League, witnessed age-old tribulations inherent within the burgeoning black populace. The association reported that most indigent African Americans lacked sufficient skills and training to meet the job requirements in an urban, industrial society. These blacks often failed to demonstrate sufficient initiative to obtain educational opportunities that would enhance prospects for finding work.[9] Equally astonishing, scores of low-income people had difficulty communicating their problems or knowing how to acquire essential information from social service agencies.[10]

In Philadelphia and other cities, the increasingly inherent problem within black communities of the 1950s may be traced directly to the declining interest of the Congress of Industrial Organizations in the economic fortunes of unskilled African Americans. Blacks who envisioned hope for a better future by joining the CIO faced a rude awakening. Businesses amenable to unionization during the prosperous war era increased productivity through automation and thereby eliminated jobs. Therefore, CIO locals became less concerned with expanding the union base with African American workers.[11] Instead, the CIO became increasingly conservative and focused primarily on protecting the established membership. A time for consolidation within the ranks and working with industrialists took precedent over incorporating unskilled blacks into the union movement.

In 1955 a harbinger of doom for the unskilled masses occurred when the CIO merged with the American Federation of Labor. As the preeminent labor union that represented skilled workers, the AFL traditionally restricted black entrance into the labor movement. CIO leaders, however, recognized the union's future existed with the AFL rather than with the Negro. With increasing automation prompting the need for more highly skilled workers, the CIO understandably embraced protection under the AFL umbrella. The CIO had therefore cause to abandon direct action to benefit unskilled African Americans.[12] As palliatives to African Americans, the AFL-CIO offered black leaders like A. Philip Randolph and Willard S. Townsend prestigious posts as vice presidents in the newly merged organization. Their promotions, however, had little direct effect on enhancing work prospects for unskilled African Americans. Marginally educated, poorly trained blacks remained on the periphery of the labor movement.

Traditional African American leaders also appeared disinclined to perceive union membership as essential for the black working class. With favorable experiences that accrued from Roosevelt's New Deal, black spokespersons placed greater emphasis on having the government make provisions for African Americans rather than rely on union beneficence.[13] The black bourgeoisie also sought to distance their race from the CIO, which had the taint of communism during the McCarthy era. The AFL-CIO merger, combined with job-limiting automation and black leadership's aversion to unions, collectively proved inimical to the black working class.

In addition to long-standing difficulties in finding work, the flight of the black bourgeoisie from African American neighborhoods also adversely impacted low-income African Americans. As the black bourgeoisie found opportunities to leave burgeoning ghettos, the quality of life in African American neighborhoods declined.[14] Evidence of the black bourgeoisie's exodus occurred noticeably in the predominately black Thirtieth Ward in South Philadelphia. Viewing the migration firsthand, directors of the Southwest-Belmont YWCA observed scores of young women leaving the ward to find professional opportunities elsewhere. Miss Margaret D. Barbee, resident director of the Elizabeth Frye House, declared, "We hate to see them go, but each one leaving has been for a step forward. The latest one to leave went to New York to enter nurse training."[15]

Further evidence of middle-class black flight from the Thirtieth Ward was provided by Executive Secretary Milton Washington of the Christian Street YMCA of South Philadelphia. Recognizing the increasing mobility of more affluent YMCA members, Washington observed, "For many years [Negro] members lived in close proximity to the building. Recently, however, movement of Negroes to West, North, [and] Northwest Philadelphia and to Delaware, Bucks, Montgomery, and Chester Counties, has spread the base of the branch's membership to all corners of the Delaware Valley."[16] Consequently, typical YMCA board meetings during the decade occurred with at least one-third of its members missing. By 1957 only three of fifty-two influential men associated with the Y lived in South Philadelphia.[17] In 1958, Mrs. Robert J. Patience of the

YWCA registered a similar concern regarding her organization. She candidly stated, "Many of our members who gave years of service to Southwest have moved away and some have joined branches nearer to their homes."[18] Obviously, integration and declining racial barriers contributed to the black professional exodus.

Statistics proved the observations of YWCA and YMCA directors correct. In 1940, for example, 494 blacks with college degrees resided in the Thirtieth Ward. By 1950, 49 college-trained residents vacated the neighborhood. However, by the end of the decade 236 additional college professionals left the Ward, resulting in a 72 percent reduction of highly trained African American professionals.[19] Y leaders obviously faced significant challenges because of demographic shifts in the black neighborhood as the numbers of lower-class blacks who frequented the YMCA increased while middle-class members moved away.[20] Milton Washington initially endeavored to reflect positively about the exodus of black professionals but realized that the YMCA could no longer adequately meet the needs of the local populace. He then raised a disturbing question by asking, "How much longer will members continue to travel across so many miles to participate in the Association's program?"[21]

Astute Y directors recognized that the comforting aspects and racial homogeneity of the ghetto waned without the positive influences of the black bourgeoisie. During the late 1940s a sufficient number of prominent blacks who resided in the ward expressed outrage when a taproom was scheduled to open across from the YWCA. The Y Executive Committee protested the unwelcome neighbor because of the liquor joint's ability to attract "an undesirable element deemed unsuitable for close proximity to a youth serving agency."[22] Y directors succeeded in having the bar project terminated. But a few years later when a neighborhood committee met at the Southwest-Belmont YWCA with the primary purpose of keeping the community clean, orderly, and well maintained, few outspoken leaders resided in the neighborhood to address the problem adequately. Now opportunity beckoned to self-serving opportunists intent on bringing questionable business enterprises into the black community. A reduction in the aura and significance of the black YMCA and YWCA occurred simultaneously with the decline of the black neighborhood. A distinct but unfortunate trend developed from the middle-class exodus; voices that customarily addressed concerns about the quality of life in the neighborhood fell silent.

Low-income African Americans who filled the vacated properties of the black professional class lacked the expertise, pride, and means for maintaining the neighborhood. With little money for home maintenance, impecunious black homeowners failed to make necessary repairs and with the natural complicity of slum lords hastened the decay of long-standing black communities.

Throughout urban America, the vibrancy of the ghetto vanished and gave way to the sordidness of the slum.[23]

Like middle-class African Americans, white people in close proximity to black communities fled to suburbia. The police and media reinforced white fears by posting information on crimes committed by black men and publicizing the irresponsibility of black women who produced scores of illegitimate children.[24] A white girl in Philadelphia voiced her fears about changes in the neighborhood and observed, "Children stealing anything they can lay their hands on. Fighting and arguing all through the night. People sitting on their front porches watching everyone else go to work."[25] Thievery, interpersonal dissension, and idleness, in her opinion, appeared as unfamiliar characteristics in a milieu where blacks and whites traditionally resided peacefully in close proximity. White flight became symbolized by For Sale or vacancy signs posted on apartments, single family homes, and retail businesses. Whites incapable of flight became increasingly insecure and reacted to their plight by identifying the black newcomers—rightly or wrongly—as a populace that lacked the sensibilities of previous African American residents.

Evidence of declining fortunes representative of low-income blacks nationally could also be observed through ten randomly selected families residing in federally subsidized Richard Allen Homes in North Philadelphia between 1941 and 1960. Each family that dwelled in the projects had been carefully screened, requiring someone to be employed in the defense industry and dedicated to hard work. The John Smith (names of all the families residing in the projects have been changed to protect individual identities) family moved into the projects in October 1941. The family consisted of a thirty-year-old male head of household, a nineteen-year-old wife, and two children—a boy of four and a girl aged one. Smith worked as a laborer in the Philadelphia Navy Yard, later became a baker's helper, and then acquired work as a porter for the Lit Brothers Department Store. Although Mr. Smith worked hard to get ahead, paying strict attention to family finances and paying rent on time, he and his wife suffered grievously from the troubles caused by their children. By 1958 the children (now aged nineteen and sixteen) had fallen prey to the negative influences of a changing neighborhood. The son had been sent to a house of correction and the daughter became a teenaged mother. By the end of the decade the family would purchase a home, but the future hardly looked promising for the children.

Additional difficulties attributed to unforeseen circumstances awaited black families residing in the projects. For example life seemed fortuitous for the Jones family in 1941 when a thirty-six-year-old grandmother and seventeen-year-old mother with a year-old baby moved into the development. As late as July 1944 a case worker for the Family Society of Philadelphia could report, "We are particularly interested in this family as they have been trying very hard to improve their condition." During the war the older woman's separation from her husband, her subsequent heart condition, and her daughter's illegitimate child had failed to deter the family's desire to succeed. Rather, the family's most distressing moments occurred later when the daughter left home intending to be self-sufficient. Finding low-paying jobs as a storekeeper, laundry worker, and later as a school crossing guard exacted an enormous price from the young woman, resulting in a nervous collapse. The grandmother, incapacitated after a heart attack in 1945, died at age fifty-four in 1959. Soon afterward, the daughter abandoned their apartment, owing $90.30 in back rent. This perceived irresponsibility had been classified as a federal offense. By the end of the decade the Jones family met with increasing problems and never experienced the bountiful life.

With all the prospects for a better future created by World War II, troubling experiences became commonplace among other residents in the North Philadelphia projects. Malcolm Williams, a young man employed as a rigger's helper at the Navy Yard, earned $2,588.69 annually, a substantial salary in 1944. Despite his training and skills, four years later he suffered a slight reduction in salary ($2,555.47) as a Yellow Cab Company driver in Philadelphia. Although his base salary, combined with customer gratuities, enabled Williams to take home more money than during the war era, the added aggravations associated with being one of the first black cab drivers in the City of Brotherly Love hardly afforded him pleasure. Williams left his wife and two sons, preferring to spend his time running with women. A dutiful father nonetheless, Williams continued to support his family and eventually took over sole responsibility for his elder son. Meanwhile, his estranged wife performed day work, earning $1,935 in 1954. The wife retained custody of the younger son and the family never reconciled.

Occasionally violence marred relationships within a family. In 1950, George Johnson, a twenty-nine-year-old veteran of World War II who attained the respectable rank of staff sergeant, moved into the projects with his twenty-four-year-old wife, a three-year-old daughter and a one-year-old son. Despite evidence of leadership he displayed in the war, Johnson shifted from one job to another, first as a laborer for the Chemical Fire Proofing Company, and then as an unskilled employee of Gimble Brothers Department Store, and finally as a rug cleaner. By March 1953 Johnson's job prospects seemed to improve; he was hired by the Bald Manufacturing Company to work as an assemblyman. Unfortunately, the Johnson family fortunes soon declined. After two additional children were added to the family and a seventy-seven-year-old aunt moved into the apartment, George Johnson became unemployed. When Johnson finally found another job, his employer deemed his workmanship poor and terminated Johnson's employment. But after finding another job making a relatively comfortable income of $4,795.40 annually as a filter plant operator in 1959, his disgruntled wife shot at Johnson, wounded one of their sons, and injured two visiting friends. The media allegedly reported, "Mrs. Mae Johnson was jailed for assault with intent to kill. [Her husband] was jailed too for disorderly conduct."

Only Thomas Elliott headed a family that met with some success. In December 1940 the thirty-six-year-old Elliott moved into the projects with his wife Dora (thirty-two), their fourteen-year-old step-daughter Jill, sons Leon and Harold (seven and four respectively), and four-month-old daughter Kate. The familiar pattern of constant job movement occurred as Elliott worked as a garage attendant, as an unskilled worker employed in the Foster Brothers Clothing Store, and, by 1942, found work as a machinist's helper and ship welder in the Philadelphia Navy Yard. By 1945 Elliot annually earned $2,624.44 working for the navy. By 1946, however, he lost his job, found work as a truck driver, but only earned $1,400 in annual pay. In October, Elliott left his family, forcing his wife and children to accept welfare from the Department of Public Assistance (DPA). When employed, Elliott tried to supplement his family's income by sending them $15.00 each month. By 1951 the elder son Leon (now seventeen) acquired odd jobs at the Royal Crown Lamp Company as a delivery boy and a janitor. In 1953 Leon Elliott had earned $1,808, and eventually purchased a home and moved his mother, wife, and son into accommodations away from the projects. Meanwhile, Harold Elliott earned a scholarship to La Salle College and, by the end of the decade, entered Brown University as a graduate student.

The story-book experience of the Elliott family proved far more the exception than the rule. Of the ten families surveyed, eight had three to seven children; five contained heads of households who were constantly changing jobs; five felt the sting of frequent and/or extended unemployment; four were missing a husband or wife from whom the head of household was separated; three were forced onto the DPA rolls; and two reported cases of mental illness. Only one of the three veterans took advantage of the GI Bill, attending a school for painting and paper hanging. The veteran never practiced the newly acquired trade.

Although only one of the thirty-six children observed in the study had a criminal record, the future looked exceedingly dim for the residents of the Richard Allen Homes. Leaving aside the four families who eventually left the projects to purchase homes and the one child who eventually obtained a college education, the majority of those sampled experienced no more than a marginal existence. These low-income people knew frustration, sorrow, and failure after enjoying the highs of the war years. Despite initial prospects for success—husband/wife separations, mental illness, unemployment, and erratic work records—disorientation plagued the majority of those who lived in the North Philadelphia housing development during the 1940s and 1950s.

While the experiences of families residing in the Richard Allen Homes proved unfortunate, prospects for shelter appeared extremely dire for those denied access to public housing. Federal guidelines restricted public housing to two-parent households. Therefore, single mothers found housing difficult to obtain. Although a small number of separated mothers could legally qualify for public housing, unmarried mothers were entirely excluded.[26]

Residents in the Richard Allen Homes also suffered from overcrowding and niggardly expenditures for maintenance. Thin walls contributed to a lack of privacy and disagreeable relationships between neighbors. Littered areas, acts of vandalism, unsupervised children, and omnipresent evidence of crime created an unseemly appearance that correspondingly caused residents to feel slighted, inferior, frightened, and, subsequently, angry.[27]

The experiences of residents in the Richard Allen Homes might have been slightly better than low-income blacks who resided in Washington, DC, during the 1950s. As the most northern Southern city, Washington contained scores of impoverished blacks deeply imbued with the unkempt, rustic lifestyle emblematic of the impoverished rural South. Newspaper reporter and eyewitness Carl Rowan observed, "Even though [Washington] represents the greatest concentration of college trained Negroes in the world, the community's basic problems are filth, poverty, squalid slums, and disease—problems more reasonably part of a less able, less literate community."[28] But Rowan omitted that local housing authorities failed to obtain sufficient funds for maintenance, or to keep public housing clean and respectable in appearance.[29]

Residents within the segregated black Washington community known as Burke's Court fared no better, and perhaps worse, than counterparts in Philadelphia's Richard Allen Homes. Burke's Court—a slum located in northwest Washington—appeared so filthy that a visitor, after leaving the premises of some of the wretched homes, would be advised "to bathe in DDT."[30] Squalor existed everywhere. Although Jim Crow provided blacks with business opportunities and the security of intra-racial relationships, a combination of factors related to poverty rendered living conditions less than satisfactory. Accustomed to living in squalor, residents failed to recognize that the use of soap, water, paint, and elbow-grease allowed for an agreeable neighborhood. Unfortunately, blacks residing in the unsavory conditions of Burke's Court lacked the dignity, energy, and initiative to maintain a clean, salubrious residential community.

The perceived indifference Burke Court residents displayed toward the despicable condition of their homes and neighborhood appeared inexcusable except for extreme, restrictive policies and indifferent posture displayed by federal authorities. Although the federal government insisted that tenants keep the premises tidy, federal managers failed to provide suitable funding for cleaning materials and utensils too expensive for low-income residents living a marginal existence to afford.

Consciously or unconsciously, the federal government contributed to urban blight during the postwar decade. In 1934 the Federal Housing Administration enforced a policy of homogeneous neighborhoods in a manual that stated, "If a neighborhood is to retain stability, it is necessary that properties shall continue to be occupied by the same society and race group."[31] This restrictive practice continued unabated and became enhanced by the 1948 code of ethics of the Washington Real Estate Board that declared, "No property in a white section should ever be sold, rented, advertised, or offered to colored people. In case of doubts, advice from the public affairs committee should be attained."[32] Congressional lawmakers and others in positions of authority had few qualms about maintaining segregation, to the disadvantages of impoverished blacks, in metropolitan America.

Although the United States Supreme Court eventually declared restricting covenants unconstitutional, lax enforcement in the District of Columbia prohibited black residential expansion and adversely affected living standards in African American communities. Overcrowded neighborhoods gave rise to unremitting problems as evidence of increased social malaise in black neighborhoods materialized. Though comprising only 30 percent of the population, blacks resided in 70 percent of the slum dwellings. And because of the low pay working-class blacks received that rendered them too impecunious to enhance living conditions, tuberculosis rates increased.[33] When diseases exploded in slums, the decidedly inferior segregated black hospital meant adequate treatment would be difficult, if not impossible, to attain. Segregation and marginality in the nation's capital affected African American residents in additional ways. Blacks comprised at least two of every three felons arrested in the projects. Additionally, one of every three juveniles arrested and serving time were black as well.[34]

Educational limitations attributed to segregation in Washington, DC, also contributed to the dysfunctional lifestyles and social malaise inherent in low-income black communities. Like the aforementioned families in Philadelphia, few among the black masses in the District of Columbia perceived education as a ticket for success. Given the anti-intellectualism that pervaded low-income African Americans, civil rights activist Floyd McKissick had reason for demanding school integration in the District's schools when he declared, "If you put Negro with Negro you get stupidity."[35] Presumably, McKissick spoke for a black bourgeoisie disgusted by the anti-intellectualism and hostility to advancement through education that characterized the thinking and behavior of low-income African Americans.

Because the Washington DC Board of Education reported directly to the United States Congress, national lawmakers condoned inequality in the

District's public schools. Congress enabled severely overcrowded schools to limit instruction given to African American students, forcing some to attend school on a part-time basis. The situation became particularly odious because segregated white schools contained a paucity of students with vacant seats unavailable for black youths.[36] Given the extreme differences in physical appearances and expenditures between black and white schools in the national capital, African American leaders felt impelled to denounce segregation.

Pressures exerted by angry black leaders upon the District's Board of Education forced educational administrators to consider integrating schools. African American parents had justifiable cause for concern. Although teachers' salaries, standards for promotion, length of the school term, and textbook selection were similar in black and white schools, officials responsible for overseeing the District's schools spent $240.27 per capita for white pupils as opposed to $186.17 for black students.[37] Given this discrepancy, students in black high schools, understandably, scored lower (45th percentile) in national tests than students instructed in white schools (95th percentile). Given the inequity of funding for black students and the inferior instruction offered in overcrowded African American schools, black anger could be understood.

Black parents from the Anacostia neighborhood became incensed when the Board of Education refused to integrate the newly constructed John Philip Sousa Junior High School. Aggrieved parents formed the Consolidated Parents Group and filed suit against the board. On December 10–11, 1952, the United States Supreme Court heard arguments for what became known as the *Bolling v. Sharpe* case. Although the most cogent argument on behalf of Bolling existed in the reality that black schools were inferior to facilities occupied by white students, integration became the primary thrust of plaintiff attorney James Nabrit Jr. On May 17, 1954, Bolling became enjoined with the landmark *Brown v. Board of Education* case that declared segregation unconstitutional.[38] Decades of civil rights work undertaken by the NAACP to achieve integration came to fruition with the *Brown* decision.

Upgrading inferior schools rather than integration, however, should have been the primary issue argued on behalf of low-income blacks. Yet prior to the celebrated *Brown* case, seeds had already been planted that suggested low-income blacks would not necessarily integrate well into middle-class white schools. Even before the first black child entered a white school, African American students functioned at a disadvantage. Ignorance attributed to Southern sharecropping stunted the intellectual development of black youths by forcing young black children to spend more time working in fields than in the classroom. This practice resulted in subpar intelligence quotients for black children. With IQ being determined by environment, heredity, and poverty, rural Southern blacks functioned academically at a disadvantage. Students became unable to acquire the learning necessary for success in an industrialized society. Children would experience the same academic limitations imposed on their parents in the segregated, rural South. As in the past, the new generation of African American students in Washington, DC, remained educationally deficient.[39] Additional difficulties pertaining to black students attending public schools in the District of Columbia surfaced when the Department of Education explored the feasibility of integrating public schools. Black students exhibited IQ scores decidedly lower than white peers. In black elementary schools, for example, African Americans achieved a mean IQ score of 87, 18 points lower than students enrolled in white schools.[40]

Had members of the black bourgeoisie been more cognizant of Charles S. Johnson's study of African Americans from the rural South, they might have delayed the push for school integration. Since Johnson reported that approximately two-thirds of all black youths interviewed intended to leave the South, black children attending public schools in Washington, DC, could easily be counted as the progeny of those academically challenged and ill-informed boys and girls of the 1930s. If the children of the 1930s held true to their word and exited the South as adults, the presence of their children had devastating consequences for the municipal educational system in Washington, DC.

While the Warren Court's rulings in integration specifically enhanced educational opportunities for middle-class blacks, little, if any, thought seemed directed toward how school integration would impact African American youngsters from low-income families. Before the epic cases found resolution with the Supreme Court, underprivileged black children displayed little knowledge about the significance of education and cared even less about promoting the efficacy of integration. The harsh aspects that poverty had on the District's depressing black neighborhoods demonstrated that severe damage had already been done that severely impeded learning for African American students.

Civil rights activists also failed to anticipate that the initial group of blacks who integrated predominately white schools would cause problems. Low-income blacks seemed comfortable with segregation and hostile to mingling with white children. With an obvious sense of inferiority attributed to poor academic training and poverty, black students created mayhem. Many students used profanity excessively and overtly displayed disdain toward white students, faculty, and staff. In response, white students, teachers, and administrators expressed concerns about the conduct of African American children, noting that black students engaged in thievery and seemed more inclined to engage in sexual intimidation. The principal of McFarland Jr. High School testified that "boys would bump against girls" and "put their hands upon them." And white girls in Anacostia High School expressed resentment about "being touched by colored boys in a suggestive manner when passing . . . in the halls."[41] Aside from the mischievous behavior of black children, low-income African Americans acted comparably to some within the third world that abhor westernization.

Further evidence justifying white objections to school integration appeared when health tests revealed that black children appeared to be excessively promiscuous. African American students demonstrated abnormally high incidences of venereal disease (98 percent of gonorrhea cases in the District involved African Americans). White people had an additional cause for angst when discovering that black students produced 26 percent of the illegitimate children in the District as opposed to only 4 percent for whites, and that African American girls comprised 90 percent of the pregnancies in public schools.[42] Unfortunately, black girls in the District of Columbia might have represented a microcosm of African American females in the United States; more than 10 percent of black females nationally at that time failed to graduate because of pregnancy.[43] Understandably, white parents felt justified in offering strong opposition to integrated public schools.

White people perceived problems inherent with school integration exclusively from the perspective of race rather than class. Because numerous low-income blacks entered white schools, African American students were measured by the worst element of the race. With the white schools accustomed to enrolling high-achieving students, few arrangements existed to assist the disadvantaged and academically challenged African American pupils. Because middle-class white parents recognized their academically oriented children were insufficiently challenged by slow-learning blacks, a logical choice came to fruition—white flight. Parents with resources fled public schools in the District of Columbia, enabling Washington, DC, to become the first predominately black urban public school district in the United States.

Evidence of black children's disregard for education and integrated schools appeared in cities outside the national capital. A confluence of heightened slum conditions and problems educating black youths also occurred in Chicago, Illinois. As the city that boasted the greatest increase in the black population since 1900, the South Side of Chicago in 1950 had become a Negro slum. Segregated residential areas resulted in an impoverished neighborhood that contained inferior schools. Depressed slums produced a high proportion of juvenile delinquency and problematic schoolchildren. When black children were removed from underachieving schools and placed in integrated settings, the social adjustment became difficult; academic prowess not only lagged, but also defied measurement.[44] Again, the negative deportment displayed by black students from slums provided credibility for white resistance to school integration.

Black Philadelphia's tenderloin area also exhibited the similar educational malaise as African Americans in Washington, DC, and Chicago. Benjamin Franklin High School in North Philadelphia represented all the negative characteristics of a dysfunctional school. Containing rundown, unseemly, antiquated homes, Ben Franklin existed in a neighborhood that possessed all the characteristics of a slum. Half the households lacked the presence of an adult male, and 40 percent of the families were migrants. Virtually all the students resided in households where parents rarely held a high school diploma. In 1951, for example, 80 percent of parents had not finished high school and approximately 33 percent never finished elementary schools.[45] Understandably, their children did not fare well academically. Ben Franklin students recorded a median IQ of 87, and 40 percent registered IQ scores below 86.[46]

Institutional problems also plagued inner-city schools. Although the national media focused primarily on school segregation in the South, blacks attending public schools in Northern cities fared as bad, if not worse, than Southern counterparts. Deeply ingrained inequities and school board resistance to change impeded the academic progress of low-income African Americans.[47] Thus, pupils attending segregated neighborhood schools instructed by dispirited teachers encumbered by a lack of institutional support caused many students to drop out of school.[48] Moreover, students who graduated usually received a substandard education that kept them mired in the lower class. Those problems became compounded by fiscal conservatism inherent in school districts where many white voters refused to support tax increases to provide money that could enhance the quality of inner-city public schools. Indeed, in the City of Brotherly Love, many elementary school students scored lower in IQ tests after four years of education than as preschoolers.[49]

The woeful deportment and dismal academic performance of African American children in the District of Columbia, Chicago, and Philadelphia mirrored the pathetic academic performance of black students in New York City's Harlem. Educational problems evident in Harlem involved poverty rather than integration. A blue-ribbon committee headed by Dr. Kenneth Clark, consisting of university professors, religious leaders, social workers, artists, professional educators, and civil rights activists, endeavored to explain the dismal academic performance of black youths in a study authorized by the Harlem Youth Opportunities Unlimited organization (HARYOU). Researchers found that the children harbored deep feelings of inferiority and accepted personal failure as commonplace. Consequently, students rarely performed well in Harlem's elementary and junior high schools.[50]

Virtually everyone in Harlem agreed that public schools in the community were horrendous, and that students entered senior high school several years below grade level.[51] Two drastically different explanatory interpretations emerged. On one hand, some attributed pathologies inherent in low-income communities as the cause for failed schools. Others, however, placed the burden for student failure primarily on the educators within the school system.

Those who espoused social pathology as the cause for low-academic performance believed handicaps related to poverty severely limited progress. Most of the young children revealed a dearth of educational experience prior to entering school. The retarded learning process continued as students exhibited a tendency to be withdrawn and uncommunicative. Researchers found that disadvantaged students refrained from answering teachers' questions, revealed a hostile reaction to authority by exhibiting bad conduct, and displayed little motivation to perform well in school.[52] Moreover, impoverished, unprepared black students engaged in a distorted effort to maintain independence, pride, and power by rebelling against societal norms.

Researchers further explained that without positive adult role models, the children behaved in ways that made learning virtually impossible. Schools became outlets for hostility derived from negative relations with adults. Disorderly conduct, intimidation, and violence became customary as recalcitrant students responded to actual or perceived rejection from parents. Inattentiveness attributed to insufficient experiences with play or work tasks, combined with the absence of books in the homes to stir imagination, also limited academic development. Negative influences transmitted by parents and blemished neighborhoods fostered a sense of hopelessness to succeed and indifference to violence and criminality.[53] HARYOU researchers provided a prescient observation when declaring,

> There is a condition of anti-intellectualism which is widespread . . . throughout the country. The prevailing interest is in learning how to make money—not learning as such. This attitude is passed from parent to child so that the child looks at the school experience and says, "What's all this worth to me?"[54]

Negative factors associated with poverty—impecunious households, hostile street cultures, and decrepit housing conditions—contributed to disproportionably low intelligent quotients and poor academic performance. Out of perceived necessity that provided familiarity and comfort at the expense of success, low-income black children appeared to cling relentlessly to negative cultural and class norms.

Public school teachers and administrators also bore some responsibility for the abysmal performance of African American children. Investigators found that, directly or indirectly, teachers conveyed negative imagery about the learning capacity of black children. This, coupled with the newest and least qualified teachers being assigned to inner-city schools, certainly contributed to academic failure.[55] Those who contended that inner-city schools operated at a minimum of efficiency could not ignore poverty as a factor for low-academic performance. The universality of poverty in slums throughout the nation trumped the most dedicated teachers' and sincere administrators' devotion toward motivating slum children and encouraging them to seek academic enrichment.

Regardless of the veracity of the opposing positions on educational theory, the 1950s represented a decade when disadvantaged African American youths appeared to plant the seeds for self-destruction. The black bourgeoisie valued learning, but low-income black children and adolescents eschewed potential opportunities gleaned from acquiring a sound education. The emerging youth culture that surfaced was sullen, disrespectful of adults, excessively hedonistic, and delinquent. A common sub-cultural trend appeared among low-income black youths that focused instead on illicit, asocial practices that stifled access to what should have been a coveted middle-class lifestyle.[56] The primacy of unruly black youth as a dominating force in slum communities would prove devastating as future generations of inner-city children eschewed polite, futuristic, middle-class norms.

During the 1950s the slum became firmly established as the locale where middle-class blacks became replaced by scores of low-income African Americans. For the black bourgeoisie, the postwar decade marked a time when life commenced to become bountiful. African American professionals who possessed marketable skills benefited from opportunities that occurred during and after World War II. The exigencies of war began to blunt racist traditions. Ambitious, competent middle-class blacks began to acquire responsible positions in federal, state, and municipal governments. Black professionals also gained access to private-sector jobs where they demonstrated prowess and efficiency. But for the masses of African Americans, the euphoria of the 1940s, highlighted by the massive move to urban milieus where jobs abounded, had dissipated. Squalor in the black urban North equaled or surpassed the horrendous living conditions experienced by impoverished African Americans in the rural South.[57] The need for unskilled employees declined, sending the African American masses into despair. Seeds had been sowed to enable disadvantaged blacks to embrace a sense of nihilism in the marginalized, sprawling urban slum.

By the end of the decade scores of African Americans remained trapped in slums because of continuous, sinister, bank policies. Banks throughout the nation refused to offer working-class blacks lines of credit. Real estate agents who sold Negroes homes in white neighborhoods were subjected to harsh recriminations by the National Association of Realtors. Therefore, opportunities afforded working-class white families to enhance personal wealth by purchasing homes where real estate values appreciated were denied African Americans.[58]

Ironically, the transformation of African American neighborhoods from ghettos to slums appeared gradual and instantaneous simultaneously. For decades, African Americans from all socioeconomic classes were confined to a life in rundown black neighborhoods. The sights, sounds, and smells inherent in ghettos conveyed an unmistakable reality evidenced by long-standing poverty. The higher classes of African Americans learned how to function as a distinct class within a community defined exclusively by race. But compared to the long existence of black ghettos, the reduction of a ghetto to a slum seemed instantaneous. The large influx of Southern migrants, overcrowded residences, congested streets, turmoil in public schools, and eventual job losses attributed to automation wreaked havoc on African American neighborhoods. The transformation of a black community from a holistic intra-racial enclave to an impoverished, low-income residential neighborhood occurred within a generation, and became most apparent during the 1950s.

Problems inherent in segregated black communities represented challenges far more profound than alienated youths. Social scientists of the 1940s seemed prescient when they proclaimed that segregated blacks were inflicted with a disease caused by prejudice. Scholars found that African Americans victimized by prejudice revealed irrevocably damaged self-esteem and displayed "psychosexual dynamics that deformed Negro culture."[59] Oppression created feelings of inadequacy and inferiority among black adults. Adults, in turn, passed on these characteristics to children, contributing to eventual male emasculation and a female matriarchy with tragic results. These psychological maladies became manifested in self-hatred, dysfunctional families, unemployment, crime, and continuous poverty. When black children internalized aforementioned slum pathologies, youths demonstrated frustration by exhibiting delinquent, hostile behavior. Thus, blacks residing in disadvantaged neighborhoods exhibited what would come to be known as slum behavior.[60]

Despite the trek north in search of economic opportunity, blacks fell far short in attaining the enhanced lifestyle expected in the Promised Land. And while the civil rights movement proceeded, advocating for the integration of public schools and establishments, and pressing for the right of black Southerners to vote, problems encountered by the black masses outside the South were ignored. On many fronts, blacks at the bottom rung of African American society would be forgotten during the trials and tribulations of the ensuing decade. Soon the slums of black America would bear witness to the anger and frustration of impoverished blacks impacted by the changes inherent in postwar America.

CHAPTER 8

The Quixotic Revolution of the 1960s

The 1960s marked a time when a civil rights movement offered great promise for middle-class African Americans of the South but failed to enhance the quality of life for the disadvantaged black masses above the "Mason-Dixon Line." Using Freedom Rides, marches, rallies, and lunch-counter sit-ins, intrepid blacks risked life and limb in the unreconstructed South to acquire social respect and political rights. President Kennedy imposed the power of the federal government to protect African American activists. Kennedy's successor, Lyndon Baines Johnson, instituted the Great Society initiative, a program designed to provide low-income African Americans with opportunities never previously realized. Yet despite noble intentions of Presidents Kennedy and Johnson to redress African American grievances, a significant segment of the low-income black population—particularly those who resided outside Dixie—still felt alienated, forlorn, and forgotten.

The decade commenced—for the first time in United States history—with the largest percentage (40 percent) of African Americans residing outside the South and in urban centers.[1] Despite the population shift, media coverage focused on direct action that occurred in the South, evident in the Greensboro sit-ins, the Freedom Riders, and Eugene "Bull" Connor's treatment of protesters in Birmingham, Alabama. Savvy black leaders like Dr. Martin Luther King, Jr., head of the Southern Christian Leadership Council, knew how to focus the national media on situations that courted sympathy for the civil rights cause. Hardened, insensitive white Southerners seemed eager to play villainous roles. They brutalized civil rights activists, defied federal mandates calling for racial equality, and earned the righteous indignation of Americans who believed Southern racists prevented democratic principles espoused in the United States Constitution from being realized.

Civil rights activities in the South captured the nation's attention and forced President Kennedy's hand, causing him to react positively on behalf of civil rights activists. Kennedy denounced racial discrimination, placed blacks in key administrative posts, and met with prominent African Americans like Vice President A. Philip Randolph of the AFL-CIO, Roy Wilkins of the NAACP, and King to address and assuage their concerns. The aforementioned leaders planned a march on Washington that occurred on August 28, 1963. Although the primary focus of the rally pertained to jobs and freedom, employment concerns became less relevant to participants and observers than freedom manifested in the middle-class interpretation of civil rights.

As media attention focused exclusively on the South during the initial throes of the civil rights movement, other regions where impoverished blacks resided went unnoticed. Those who migrated from the rural South to more opportune urban environments in the Northeast, Midwest, and Far West never received the skills to function successfully in an economy driven by automation. Schools outside the South also failed to provide the proper training to help migrants or long-term residents make adjustments necessary for finding work in a rapidly changing, post-industrial society. An era that boasted greater opportunities for the black bourgeoisie also witnessed a downward spiral for low-income African Americans that pushed those farthest down deeper into poverty. Low-income blacks unfortunately represented an island of poverty in a sea of affluence.[2]

Indifference toward the black masses could also be attributed to circumstances that had far less to do with race than chance. At a time when blacks exited Dixie, Northern manufacturers like General Motors and the Radio Corporation of America moved South to benefit from access to a cheap, nonunion workforce. Moreover, employers needed a more highly skilled, educated working class to meet labor demands in a post-industrial society. The cybernetic revolution of the 1960s, for example, resulted in structural unemployment for the American workforce, resulting in a permanent loss of jobs rather than casual layoffs. Therefore, African Americans who resided in segregated neighborhoods, attended inferior schools, and received a marginal education had little value for employers.[3] Despite comprising a fraction of the national population in 1962, nearly half (46 percent) of the five million unemployed workers in the United States were black. Because African Americans lacked seniority and held the lowest-skill-level jobs, blacks faced difficulty being rehired. In addition, blacks forty years of age or older became particularly vulnerable to layoffs, being more inclined to be let go permanently during the remainder of their working years.[4] Publicity garnered from the civil rights movement suggested that all blacks would be beneficiaries of civil rights reforms. This never happened. Since an estimated one of every nine black males experienced joblessness, the persistent wretched condition of the masses continued.[5]

At the commencement of the decade, underprivileged African American had few black advocates who championed their cause. African Americans who voiced concerns about the plight of the black underclass often existed as spokesmen identified as being on the periphery of American society. The messages of Minister Elijah Mohammed and Malcolm X appeared more as a diatribe against white people than as advocates for marginalized African American men who needed a sense of pride, satisfaction, and meaningful jobs.[6] Others who spoke on behalf of poor blacks by criticizing wealthy Americans received the customary anti-American indictment—accused of being a card-carrying communist.

Fortunately for impoverished Americans generally, and poor blacks in particular, the election of John F. Kennedy to the White House initially provided African Americans with hope. The Democratic Party, proud of the social welfare programs that harkened back to the New Deal, endorsed the Kennedy administration's intent to offer federal development funds to depressed Northern industrial towns and cities. Moreover, Kennedy's domestic policy staff, in addition to addressing poverty, reflected on the best means for resolving issues regarding the employment of America's youth. Although not a frontal assault on black poverty, a foundation had been established to address the needs of disadvantaged Americans.

With the assent of Lyndon B. Johnson to the presidency after Kennedy's assassination, prospects for the black masses appeared even brighter. A Texan who personally understood the ravages of poverty, Johnson recognized that most African Americans would remain poor unless black unemployment could be adequately addressed. But as a Southerner, Johnson also perceived the multiple aspects of racism being a contributory factor for black poverty. Johnson's impressions were reinforced by the news media, as television showed racist Southerners beating civil rights demonstrators. Thus, the Johnson administration decided to focus on voting rights, black access to public facilities, and the termination of racial discrimination in the South. These key proponents hopefully would ameliorate the black condition in the well-intentioned Great Society programs and move the nation toward a more egalitarian society.[7]

The woeful condition of underprivileged blacks presented a significant challenge for the new president. Between 1940 and 1960 more than three million marginally skilled blacks searching for work moved North and relocated to tenderloin areas of major cities. Therefore, by the mid-1960s more than 70 percent of blacks employed nationally worked in blue-collar and service occupations. Unfortunately, two of every three Northern blacks resided in slums and toiled in jobs being phased out of the economy.[8] Working-class people engaged in minimum-value labor would not only face unemployment and underemployment, but also, to the chagrin of all in a comparable situation, experience "unemployability." African American workers ironically gained access to jobs previously restricted by racism at the same time the jobs became obsolete.[9]

Sensing the severe employment challenges African Americans faced, President Johnson attempted to address the problem of black poverty directly. Mindful of his hard scrapple origins, the president perceived poverty as the nation's enemy and proposed to do something about rectifying this national quandary.[10] In his first State of the Union address to Congress delivered on January 8, 1964, Johnson declared a War on Poverty. Blacks had reason to be encouraged. With 55 percent of blacks (versus 18 percent of whites) living below the poverty line, and 83 percent of African Americans perceiving the federal government as being sensitive to black plight, the time seemed propitious for a federal mandate that would aid impoverished blacks.[11] Administrative officials sincerely believed that proper training would enable the hard-core unemployed obtain gainful employment. Through the Great Society manifesto, Johnson persuaded the federal government to become directly involved in job-training programs to enable marginally skilled blacks to find work. Few officials, however, ruminated about the availability of jobs for prospective black employees.

Great Society expenditures proved insufficient to provide a satisfactory balm to eliminate the wounds created by poverty and racism. During the early 1960s blacks were disproportionably represented as the most impoverished and unemployed Americans; 10.8 percent of African Americans as opposed to 5 percent whites lacked jobs.[12] Federal job-training programs, however, failed to reach the large category of hard-core, unemployed black laborers who sought work. After the Great Society training program was announced, more than three hundred thousand applied for the ten thousand available slots. Unfortunately, those accepted into the program still encountered difficulties. With a paucity of funding committed, few African Americans stood to gain from the training programs. And for those who successfully completed the programs after three years of training, problems remained. Many African American participants were still impoverished and maintained a sense of worthlessness attributed to the demeaning and persistent scourge of racial discrimination.[13]

Several additional factors undermined the Great Society's prospects for success. First, altruistic government officials intent upon ameliorating persistent problems pertaining to African American unemployment came to realize that more blacks sought jobs than prospective employers had to offer. Evidently few federal administrators anticipated the number of jobs that would be lost to automation. Despite the best intentions for keeping unskilled people on the payroll, the introduction of automation into the work place to save time and money logically proved far more important to manufacturers than following

Great Society recommendations. Businesses focused on making money rather than placing marginally skilled African Americans in jobs. Second, when jobs became available, the social and psychological aspects of slum life rendered retraining difficult, if not impossible. The habitually unemployed found gainful employment uncustomary and arduous. Third, housing restrictions that confined blacks to inner-city slums created costs and distance limitations. Impoverished blacks had difficulty securing money and traveling to suburban areas where factory jobs relocated. And finally, city mayors and ward heelers invariably existed as uncooperative partners with the federal government. Local politicos resented federal funding that undermined their ability to wield power through the traditional spoils system. These collective factors resulted in structural unemployment for the black American workforce. Rather than experiencing casual layoffs like many white employees, blacks lost jobs permanently.[14]

The Great Society failed to increase significantly the number of gainfully employed blacks and extricate the African American masses from poverty. Yet perhaps the most egregious failure of the Great Society's War on Poverty appeared with the Elementary and Secondary Education Act (ESEA). On April 9, 1965, Congress passed ESEA, a program designed to aid deprived children. This legislation was intended to provide equal access to education and minimize the achievement gap between blacks and whites. Unfortunately, ESEA became a billion-dollar boondoggle that benefited suburban whites rather than the black urban poor.[15] Johnson's good intentions proved noble but ineffective.

Tragically for low-income blacks, the United States at this time moved closer toward a two-tiered economy. Essentially, middle-class black and white Americans experienced economic stability and enjoyed a comfortable standard of living. The black masses, conversely, remained part of a marginal economy, employed in low-level jobs that paid minimum wages in service occupations. For blacks with limited job options, the proverbial wolf resided outside the door. Thus, lower-class blacks declined from being economically exploited to economically irrelevant.[16]

As early as 1964 the marginalized condition of the black unskilled worker appeared finalized. Two social scientists, S. M. Willhelm and E. H. Powell, observed,

> The tremendous historical change for the Negro is taking place in these terms: he is not needed. He is not so much oppressed as unwanted; not so much unwanted as unnecessary; not so much abused as ignored. The dominant whites no longer need to exploit him. If he disappeared tomorrow he would hardly be missed. As automation proceeds it is easier and easier to disregard him . . . .The historical transition for the Negro . . . is a movement out of the southern cotton fields, into

> the northern factories and then to the automated urbanity of "nobodiness."[17]

A disproportionate number of African Americans never escaped poverty and functioned in an existence devoid of hope.

Other continuous problems surfaced related to poverty and racism that rendered objectives enunciated in Johnson's Great Society unrealistic. Social and psychological factors endemic in slums prevented the government from enabling disadvantaged blacks to make a positive transition from job training to full employment.[18] Generations of families plagued by long-term poverty and unemployment lacked sufficient training and experience to hold jobs. In addition, the paucity of education precluded young adults and previously employed men and women with limited job skills from remaining competitive in the workplace. Hence, the inability to acquire familiarity with high-tech machinery and instruments again confined the black poor to low-level jobs. Despite President Johnson's good intentions, prospects for an expanded workforce of marginally educated, unskilled African Americans seemed doomed.

As the decade of the 1960s progressed, the unemployment gap between whites and blacks expanded. During the final throes of the Great Depression in 1940, the discrepancy between white and black unemployment proved miniscule—a mere 1.5 percent (13 percent white versus 14.5 percent nonwhite). By 1964, however, the unemployment differential increased exponentially, registering 5.9 percent for whites as opposed to 12.4 percent for blacks.[19] Logically, expanded gaps between white and black employment contributed to wider differentials between the races in income. In the early 1960s, approximately two of every three African American families had annual incomes below the $3,000 poverty level. And by 1963 nearly half (43 percent) of all nonwhite families (most of whom were black) in the United States lived in poverty as opposed to 16 percent of white Americans. Moreover, pay differentials between whites and blacks performing identical lines of work ranged between $1,000 and $2,000.[20] Given these financial discrepancies in wages, redressing irregularities in regard to race would prove easier and less expensive than rectifying omnipresent poverty evident in low-income black neighborhoods.

Another issue negatively impacting impoverished African Americans existed in the national focus on maintaining hegemony as an international superpower. Because of the Cold War, political leaders insisted on maintaining a strong military and spent large sums of money to court favors with allies and unaligned nations. These decisions received priority over enhancing the quality of life for impoverished African Americans. While the federal government spent millions domestically through Great Society efforts to create opportunities for impecunious blacks at home, the executive and legislative branches of government spent billions to safeguard national interests abroad.[21]

The private sector also engaged in activities inimical to low-income African Americans. A survey conducted on twenty cities with large black populations found that in eleven metropolitan areas, African Americans functioned at a disadvantage. Unable to afford an automobile to acquire services outside the slum, poor blacks became victimized by retailers who sold inferior goods at inflated prices. For example, an item selling for $100 wholesale and $165 retail could cost $250 in a low-income neighborhood specialty store. Moreover, because many among the poor could only purchase items on credit, impoverished African Americans became subjected to enormously high interest rates. Slum residents paid for items at least 50 percent above retail costs.[22] The cost of the most inexpensive automobile would enable slum residents to engage in comparative shopping and save thousands of dollars. However, the inability to obtain an automobile limited black purchasing opportunities and kept impoverished African Americans mired in the slum to remain perennially poor.

Retail establishments that provided bargains to white suburbanites failed to offer similar inducements for slum residents. People confined in poor neighborhoods lacked sufficient information to understand that usurious credit rates constrained them to an impoverished existence. Thus, low-income blacks thought primarily about satisfying immediate needs rather than having concerns about future indebtedness. Evidently, fatalism that accrued from the infamous sharecropping system remained ingrained among black urbanites that migrated from the rural South. Even those aware of the economic discrimination and usurious practices visited upon impoverished blacks acquiesced to their condition and tended to remain pliant and mute.

The 1960s also represented a period when a substantial number of businesses vacated inner cities and relocated to the suburbs. As businesses transported factories to suburbia, jobs not only became available to the predominately white suburban residents at the expense of black workers, but other equally important dynamics occurred to the disadvantage of inner-city black residents. First, taxes generated by businesses no longer became available for those responsible for maintaining the economic and educational affairs of the cities. With a declining tax base, necessary social services that customarily aided the poor diminished. Second, the bevy of wholesome consumer products evidenced by well-maintained supermarkets declined. The quality of food products not only diminished, but equally important, slum residents paid higher food costs because of pilfering expected from an economically destitute and desperate clientele.[23] Third, bank loans customarily proffered for property maintenance became unavailable. Consequently, black neighborhoods resembled third-world slums. And finally, with jobs being displaced and unemployment increasingly common, Darwin's survival-of-the-fittest doctrine prevailed. Unsavory conditions evident in inner cities contributed to higher incidents of property crime, causing insurance rates to soar exponentially. The criminal behavior of desperate, selfish, uncaring people—though poor and few in number—negatively impacted the law-abiding majority.[24]

Black slum residents also experienced problems when unable to make steady payments to merchants by having their wages garnished. In twenty states, creditors could legally have debtors' wages directed to creditors without an advance hearing being provided to the black employee. In New York City, for example, retailers specializing in credit sales of furniture and appliances to low-income consumers used the courts to garner wages from one of every eleven black debtors. Meanwhile, large department stores frequented by higher-income patrons used the courts to redress debts in only one of more than fourteen thousand customers.[25] Obviously, class inequality existed to the detriment of disadvantaged African Americans in a unique and unfair manner.

In response to the deteriorating economic situation and ill treatment of downtrodden blacks evident during the 1960s, scores of black men became sullen, frustrated, and prone to vent pent-up anger resulting in violence. Danger lurked in urban America when the black masses acquired televisions and visual evidence of the comfortable lifestyle of middle-class white Americans. Television also heightened ire among African Americans who observed the inhumane treatment directed toward Southern blacks demanding civil rights. Black males residing in the North displayed their rage in the streets while their Southern counterparts practiced passive nonresistance. But another significant difference between passive Southerners and African Americans residing in the Northeast, Midwest, and Pacific Coast existed in the class differences of protesters. Southern black activists drew participants from the better-educated, upwardly mobile section of the black community. In contrast, urban riots outside the South contained activists from the lower socioeconomic strata.[26] Unlike the disciplined, organized, middle-class activists of the South who acted with passive aggression to attain human rights, counterparts elsewhere thought less about civil rights and acted out of blind rage to exact vengeance euphemistically against "the man."

For various reasons, black anger commenced with a series of riots in 1964. Although the initial riot that year occurred in Jacksonville, Florida, the wave of anger soon spread to other regions of the country. In early July, fighting erupted in Harlem and Brooklyn in New York City, followed by racial disturbances in Rochester, New York. Eruptions also appeared in Jersey City, Patterson, and Keansburg, New Jersey; Dixmoor (a Chicago suburb), Illinois; and Philadelphia, Pennsylvania.[27] Here, anger, as in subsequent riots, conflicts occurred between impoverished blacks and the police. In part, problems between low-income blacks and law enforcement were situational. Historically, the white power structure prohibited vice from existing in white residential areas and confined numbers running and other illicit activities to black ghettos. Consequently, a minority of African Americans engaged in questionable activities to make a living and survive. The police, correspondingly, under the guise of protecting society's welfare, had the singular responsibility of keeping law and order and imposing their moral will—often by force—on black communities. Blacks, in turn, viewed police impositions on their communities as unwarranted racism. Therefore, police brutality directed toward black civil rights activists in the South contributed to enhanced frustration and anger among young African Americans who took to the streets in violent protests.[28]

The most devastating and significant riot of the decade occurred in the Watts section of Los Angeles, California. Watts evolved as a black ghetto during the early 1940s when hundreds of Southern blacks migrated to the City of the Angels in search of jobs in fledgling war industry plants. By 1947 blacks comprised five-sixths of the Watts population. Many newcomers occupied three inexpensive two-story residential projects—Nickerson Gardens, Jordan Downs, and Imperial Courts—that housed the burgeoning African American population. At that time residents had no control over services, markets, or had little prospects for finding better-paying jobs.[29] People, however, appeared sufficiently satisfied to have found work and enjoy a more comfortable life outside the extremely demeaning South.

Watts appeared as a precursor to potential problems encountered in other cities. After World War II, jobs available for marginally skilled blacks on the West Coast declined. Already disadvantaged by holding lower-income service jobs, blacks had little margin for error. Low-income blacks in Portland, Sacramento, San Diego, Seattle, and in inland cities like Spokane and Denver experienced unemployment similar to cities of the Northeast, Midwest, and South.[30] Unemployed blacks, consequently, appeared increasingly disillusioned and angry. Because recently urbanized unskilled and untrained blacks could not find work, a restive pall would be cast over inner-city black residents.[31]

When World War II industries closed, Watts specifically began a downward economic spiral that continued throughout the 1950s. Segregated and crowded with impoverished blacks, Watts revealed unseemly qualities that portended future difficulties. Typical slum businesses—storefront establishments characterized by low-quality clothing and food—became commonplace. In addition, police harassment, combined with inadequate public services, created a tinderbox destined to produce a violent eruption.[32]

On August 11, 1965, the Watts riots encapsulated the frustration and anger of impoverished and forgotten African Americans. Despite enormous strides African Americans made in acquiring civil rights, the black masses found themselves unable to enjoy the social and economic amenities comparable to middle-class whites or the black bourgeoisie. Rather than demonstrate jealousy toward the accomplishments of their middle-class brethren, however, low-income blacks directed their ire toward white people and blamed whites for their sordid condition. Hostility toward white people received constant reinforcement when those who dominated the black community—the police, absentee landlords, retailers, and influential moneyed interests—were authoritarian whites who resided outside the African American neighborhood. Substandard wages and marginal jobs devoid of excitement, when juxtaposed with the honorable, steady, and rewarding employment white people enjoyed further stimulated black rage.

Feeling alienated, entrapped by omnipresent poverty, and devoid of training that could improve opportunities for acquiring work, young men of working age had little cause for optimism. These negative factors, coupled with institutional racism, caused blacks to explode at any perceived slight.[33] The sense of profound anger voiced by a young black Watts resident spoke universally on behalf of peers nationwide when he said, "Shit, ain't nothing happenin' out here, just the same old bullshit—no jobs, no money, no good food—and the jive-time brothers, and the man, just running games about what they're trying to do. Shit, we ought to burn this mother, and rip off some things."[34]

Although white people could be perceived as the object of black wrath, the response to the inequities evidenced in slum life became inner rather than outer directed. Frustrated young black men started fiery conflagrations within their own community, demonstrating limited knowledge of where anger might have been directed. With generational poverty long in evidence, factors characterized as institutional racism became difficult to comprehend. Without knowledge of feeder systems that connected prospective employees with the primary labor market, the black urban masses never identified institutions like unions, civil service agencies, and banks that continuously inhibited prospects for upward mobility. Moreover, buildings that housed institutions responsible for connoting power, demonstrating influence, and providing residents with the means for upward mobility were conspicuously absent in the inner-city slum. Devoid of logical thinking, blacks attacked buildings in close proximity to their own homes and apartments without taking into consideration the reality of communal self-destruction.

Riot participants defied the norms expected from a permanent black underclass. Most rioters ranged between fifteen and twenty-fours of age and were not the most impoverished residents. Those arrested were better educated than most inner-city residents but recognized the hopelessness of low-end jobs and unemployment.[35] Removed from the South and too young to comprehend the ugly and direct aspects of racism, young black adults engaged in rioting acted without thought or direction. These young people also lacked an understanding of self-sufficiency. Requirements to receive the benefits of food stamps and welfare payments became constant and tedious for those only accustomed to welfare. At the same time these people became dependent on the caprice of welfare supervisors intent on maintaining the status quo rather than providing clients with incentive and ambition to improve their lot in society. Additionally, rustic parents recently from the South failed to provide the sufficient sophistication and positive instruction to offspring, enabling their progeny to cope with the new urban milieu without direction. Also impacted by the pitfalls of a changing economy, black parents proved unable to play the role as sagacious providers who offered proper guidance for children and young adults.[36]

Watts and subsequent riots failed to produce constructive results for low-income African American residents. Black communities characterized by poverty and unemployment continued the decline from ghettos to unsavory slums. Those who failed to acquire the education and necessary job skills that resulted in decent wages remained as slum dwellers devoid of work and prospects for success. Idle blacks lacked time-management skills, possessed little understanding of punctuality, and represented the chronically unemployed. Since employment status determined the pride and wealth of an individual or family, the jobless, impoverished, hard-corps inner-city black population became increasingly dispirited. Inner-city blacks seemed resigned to a deplorable state of nothingness. These African Americans had become accustomed to the cycle of failure, continuous unemployment that rendered black slum residents inconsequential.[37]

Frustrated by the harsh black response to the initiatives taken by his administration, President Johnson commissioned Assistant Secretary of Labor Daniel Patrick Moynihan to investigate causes for the malaise inherent in low-income black families. In 1965, the controversial Moynihan Report was published, identifying the black matriarchy as the primary cause for black duress and failure.[38] Moynihan contended the omnipresence of a black matriarchy had a pejorative impact on low-income African Americans. He argued that dependence upon black women resulted in stifled ambition and resultant complaisance among black males. Without a plethora of visible black men working as skilled artisans or in respectable jobs, thoughts about the industrious, law-abiding, male family provider serving as a positive role model became illusionary rather than real. Thus, low-income, emasculated black men who fathered children and avoided responsibility for their care was related directly or indirectly to female dominance in black families.

Moynihan's conclusions absolved President Johnson from failing to ameliorate the pathos evident among low-income African Americans. But more significantly, the report ignored the constant plight encountered by black women. Employment problems within the race became magnified because of the multiple challenges African women experienced. And like impoverished black men, racial discrimination in employment and housing severely impacted black women. But women, unlike most men, were placed in a disadvantageous position because of gender. A disproportionate number of women also faced domestic violence inflicted by dispirited black men. And when these women had the added responsibility for raising children in an abusive household, problems became magnified. Flight hardly became a panacea. By leaving furniture, clothing, and all material possessions in the vacated residence, women incurred additional debt by endeavoring to furnish a new apartment and purchase necessary clothing.

The Moynihan Report also failed to note that black females realized that many public institutions responded to women in need with hostility. Some government officials refused to appropriate adequate funding for programs serving black women. Thus, overburdened black social service associations like the YWCA proved unable to provide sufficient support for desperate black females. These pressures caused black women to experience unique health issues at an early age, particularly because unemployment rendered access to adequate health care problematic. Actions limiting funding for welfare and public housing kept black women and children mired in poverty.[39] Therefore, blaming black women for the disadvantageous status of African Americans and black families, in retrospect, appeared as a ludicrous, propagandized notion eagerly embraced by conservative forces in the country.[40]

Given the volatility of the civil rights movement in which white people were exclusively deemed responsible for racial inequities, the Moynihan Report conveniently blamed the victims, particularly black women, for the race's lack of progress. The report also ignored sharecropping, hostile unions, and the political and social inhibitors attributed to racism that rendered many African Americans destitute.

More than a critique on the black family would be required to extricate African American slum residents from perdition. The most obvious solution appeared in placing scores of unemployed people in menial jobs. While the suggestion appeared meritorious, no easy panacea existed. The low-income black response to performing menial tasks appeared more self-defeating than constructive. Some blacks who perceived low-paying menial jobs as a stigma voluntarily elected not to work to demonstrate a sense of personal independence, empowerment, and pride.[41]

Black men confined to menial jobs blamed their woeful condition on enduring racism. These concerns had validity. Surveys conducted by the Department of Labor revealed that inequities existed between low-income black and white employees. An excessively high proportion of blacks—including part-time workers looking for full-time work, full-time workers earning less than $3,000 annually, and people who dropped out of the workforce—were designated as being underemployed. In order to elevate African Americans to an economic status comparable to working-class whites, the Department of Labor concluded that 923,000 jobs would have to be created. Consequently, the problem appeared less about poverty than inequality, as 40.6 percent of blacks—as opposed to 11.9 percent of whites—had incomes below the poverty level.[42]

The black male's inability to acquire gainful employment wreaked hardships on the African American family. For husbands who found work, many suffered the humiliation of earning less money than their wives. Wives who worked and earned more than their spouses invariably lost respect for their husbands. And like mothers who became primary breadwinners, children also perceived fathers as being less-than-capable providers. These pressures caused men to stop looking for work; many relinquished the responsibilities of husband and father. Incapable of providing adequate support for their families and eager to garner some modicum of respect, some men gravitated to the streets and found comfort with other women. Others drifted away completely from the family. Hence, the greater the incidences of black unemployment, the higher correlations appeared where husbands abandoned wives and children.[43]

Discrimination in hiring, low wages, and unemployment negatively impacted African American families and correspondingly contributed to the limited education of black youths.[44] But attribution for the low academic performance of black children and young adults could also be attributed to parental child-rearing practices. Single mothers as well as families with two or more adults recognized the difficulty in protecting children from the harsh realities of slum life. Consequently, low-income blacks innocently used child-rearing practices that placed African American children at a decided disadvantage in school. After bestowing love to a child after birth, low-income mothers withdrew affection. By age three children had little interaction with their parents. In fact, mothers invariably pushed children away emotionally as a means for preparing them to become independent, self-sufficient, and capable of achieving personal preservation in the disagreeable slums. In response, children learned to protect themselves acting as adults. But children also mistrusted adults, refusing to respect elders and learning not to depend on older members of the family for emotional support. Consequently, impoverished children became less emotionally attached to adults and would recoil from adult supervision.[45]

Elementary school children grew up fast, becoming self-reliant and independent. They became unruly, sullen, enormously self-centered, disrespectful, and disinclined to accept the disciplined regimen of the classroom.[46] Frustrated by ill treatment at the hands of adults and filled with rage emanating from the confining slums, children subsequently became scarred. Neither the withdrawal of emotional support from adults nor physical punishment deterred black children from unseemly street parlance and peer influence. Indeed, within low-income African American families, older siblings held greater significance than parents, the opposite of the parental role played in middle-class households.[47]

Although the racial divide between blacks and whites became mitigated by the gradual movement toward civil rights and school integration in the South, the difficulty in educating low-income black children outside Dixie remained. Being ill prepared to meet more rigorous educational standards in white schools, impoverished black families out of the South had cause to be fearful of integration. Families bonded together for mutual support, keeping children in line to respect Southern mores and avoiding trouble with white people. But rather than focus on the most efficacious manner for instilling children with a renewed interest in education, black mothers focused on proper decorum and punished children for displaying aggressive behavior and showing disrespect for elders.[48] The positive features derived from strong family ties and respect for adults became irrelevant for children who left the South.

Residential segregation outside the South kept children at an educational disadvantage as well. In low-income urban black communities parents taught children to be forceful and aggressive. Northern adolescents and adults separated rather than bonded with relatives. Moreover, disrespect for adult authority figures like schoolteachers and law-enforcement officers were condoned. When mutual assistance occurred, help was based on economic necessity rather than shared Southern values.[49] Eventually children and young adults from Dixie aped the behavioral patterns of Northern counterparts rather than the behavior and mannerisms of the South.

Another unfortunate reality that plagued the black family pertained to children continuing to lack adequate supervision. In inner-city households, fatherless families had a greater tendency to be larger than families containing responsible male adults. This meant that when circumstances forced women to head households, the natural role as a nurturing mother would be neglected. When latchkey children came of age, they gravitated to life in the streets and thus became more inclined to engage in violence and crime. For impressionistic youths, dope dealers, numbers runners, and others who preyed upon impoverished slum residents appeared as successful, respected entrepreneurs. Given the exodus of positive African American role models who left the ghetto, self-indulgent hustlers supplanted well-mannered adults and instilled scores of black youth with wayward flaws.[50]

With necessity requiring mothers to work, public schools bore the responsibility of preparing low-income black students for the eventualities of adulthood in a competitive postindustrial society. Deeply embedded racism, however, stymied black students and interfered with the process. African American students residing in slums throughout th experienced difficulties regardless of whether the schools were integrated or predominately black. Administrators and teachers reinforced the low self-esteem that characterized disadvantaged students, a situation that made failure a self-fulfilling reality. Low IQ test scores placed a disproportionably large number of black students in lower academic tracts. Teachers, most of whom were white, believed that low intelligence hampered learning and consciously or unconsciously conveyed pejorative beliefs to students. Students, in turn, sensed that teachers did not like them and, in response, engaged in rebellious behavior.[51]

Blacks dwelling in slums experienced a marginal economic existence and lacked sufficient funding to withstand physical and psychological disorders. At least 30 percent of all families earning less than $2,000 annually during the late 1960s suffered from chronic health conditions as opposed to only 8 percent with a family income comprising $7,000 or more.[52] Naturally, large impoverished black families requiring food, clothing, and other necessities had less money available for medical emergencies.

Because poverty affected African Americans 3.5 times greater than the white populace, higher incidences of illness occurred.[53] Deficient diets, less-than-satisfactory clothing and shelter, and ignorance of proper health maintenance had a catastrophic effect on impoverished African American urbanites. Also, slums contained homeless people who lived on the streets, providing additional congestion and clutter that rendered customary trash removal, street cleaning, and sanitation difficult. With a higher population density, the lack of well-managed buildings, less-than-satisfactory garbage collection services, and the high volume of refuse left on the streets led to the natural infestation of vermin. Because garbage and refuse provided feeding grounds for rats, disease-ridden vermin plagued low-income residents. In 1965 alone, more than fourteen thousand people reported being bitten by rodents. Black slum residents, therefore, suffered from greater indexes of disease, a lower availability of medical services, and, consequently, experienced higher morbidity rates than middle-class Americans. The visual effect of unsavory slums devoid of proper sanitation reinforced a feeling of insecurity and hopelessness.[54]

By the end of the 1960s the transition of black ghettos into slums had been finalized as evidenced by higher rates of crime.[55] Inner-city crime caused African Americans to be viewed as habitual criminals who victimized anyone within proximity of an impoverished black neighborhood. While statistics revealed a direct correlation between lower-income areas and higher incidents of crime, impecunious black residential areas registered higher crime rates than comparable white neighborhoods.[56] In Northern, Midwestern, and Far

Western cities, black reformers and activists extolling African American pride, dignity, self-respect, and the demand for Constitutional rights had little, if any, impact upon the minds of alienated blacks. Young African Americans between fourteen and twenty-four appeared most inclined to participate in crime. In 1966, those under twenty-five committed 37 percent of the murders, 60 percent of all rapes, 71 percent of robberies, 75 percent of larcenies, 81 percent of burglaries, and 80 percent of all auto thefts.[57] Because the majority of those who suffered at the hands of the predatory criminal element resided in slums, the elderly, infirm, and innocent suffered alike without quarter being rendered by perpetrators.

Unfortunately for the disadvantaged black masses, strident, conservative white Americans believed a relationship existed between civil rights protests, black anger, violence, and crime. Few seemed to notice that the focus on black amelioration in the South excluded the impoverished African American masses residing in cities. Meanwhile, outside the South blacks suffered more from indifference than oppression. Even progressive white observers perceived urban violence to be a response to unrequited achievements of the civil rights movement rather than as an impoverished black populace recognizing civil rights was irrelevant to its existence.

Although the primary cause for urban conflagrations could be attributed to rising unemployment and poverty among young black men, the media overlooked the root causes for President Johnson's War on Poverty. Instead, the media, conservative politicians, and the comfortable middle class viewed angry African Americans as an ungrateful race that demanded entitlements at the expense of industrious, law-abiding, moral, and fair-minded people. An outraged American public would call for law and order rather than for sympathy and understanding for rioters.[58]

Toward the decade's end, government and corporate interests coalesced in mutual agreement to support military efforts and ignore disadvantaged African Americans. The public appeared far more interested in safeguarding national interests by winning the Vietnam War than finding money to ameliorate the condition of low-income African Americans. For example when two B-52 bombers valued at $18 million crashed on a return from saturating bombing in Vietnam, the loss totaled more than all the expenditures on poor blacks and whites in Cleveland reclamation projects.[59] Expenditures on the war effort continued.

While the nation focused almost entirely on the middle-class concerns and the war in Vietnam, long-standing negative characteristics evident in the slums of urban America continued festering and spiraling out of control. For real or imagined slights, angry, low-income blacks rioted in cities throughout America. Young people brought up on the mean streets exhibited a sense of independence, coveted respect, and demanded power. This spiri independence, however, functioned as a mask to hide deep-seated insecuriti derived from poverty, ignorance and hopelessness.[60]

By the end of the decade, the deleterious impact of low-income Southern blacks migrating to metropolitan areas throughout the nation had become complete. Sadly, the progeny of these migrants failed to perform effectively in schools or work cooperatively with others in a constructive and positive manner. Outside of gangs, long-lasting, mutually satisfying bonding friendships rarely materialized.[61]

The Black Power movement presented an interesting contrast to the Moynihan Report and the sensibilities of middle-class Americans. The clenched fist, Afro hairstyle, and occasional military garb, as reflected by male members of the Black Panther Party in Oakland, California, fostered a sense of pride in African ancestry and an appreciation of African American culture. The movement also demonstrated the ability of African Americans from the voiceless masses to organize for justice. With women purposefully showing deference to males, Black Power presented an effort, though illusionary and fanciful, to provide black men with a sense of significance, importance, and dominance.

Ironically, the anti-intellectualism that became evident during the 1960s could be attributed partially to the Black Power movement. An unforeseen by-product of the male-generated focus on Black Power became manifested in the refusal of low-income African Americans to "code switch." Racial pride became exhibited by maintaining all the earthier aspects of black culture. Hence, the more speech patterns reflected a black dialect, mannerisms, and sordid expressions on sexuality evocative of slum life, the greater acceptance and respect received from black peers.[62] For the African American masses, unfortunately, the negative connotations of black speech patterns and style became fixated in white minds that young black men appeared edgy and uncouth. Although the 1960s would prove essential for the augmentation of the African American middle class, the decade represented the seeds of destruction for the black masses.

Perhaps the greatest irony of the civil rights movement of the 1960s could be observed in the contradiction to its genesis, a focus on elevating the race through education. Although blacks with middle-class values benefited from school integration, the black masses eschewed education and opted instead upon self-destructive anti-intellectualism. Teenage black males particularly demonstrated indifference, at best and at worst, an outright hostility toward formal instruction. Eager to acquire immediate wealth and convinced that education provided no tools necessary for surviving the slum's mean streets, young black men deemed academic achievement unmanly, inconsequential,

With national economics governed by needs inherent in a ociety that demanded a highly intelligent and informed ning for black educational Luddites would prove disastrous. ..owing about the high value freed slaves placed on book learning, ..w-income blacks eschewed education, seemed resigned to an ignominious future, and appeared hell-bent to travel on a road to perdition.

The characteristics of black unemployment proved telling. At least fifteen million workers in the United States, approximately half being black, were unemployed by the end of the decade. Moreover, black youths between eighteen and twenty-five, dogged by marginal skills, were three times more likely to be unemployed than white peers. In some cities 70 percent of working-age black youths appeared on unemployment registers.[63] This new black populace, functioning outside the union movement and basic United States economy, served as a precursor to the marginalized black underclass throughout the remainder of the decade and into the twenty-first century.

CHAPTER 9

The Regression Decade of the 1970s

For low-income African Americans, the 1970s represented a decade when conditions degenerated from bad to worse. In central cities where a significant number of blacks resided, households with incomes that dropped below the poverty line increased from 9.8 to 14 percent between 1970 and 1980.[1] The inability to obtain gainful employment severely impacted lower-class blacks. Between 1947 and 1977, twelve of the largest Northwestern and Midwestern cities lost 2.1 million retail, wholesale, and manufacturing jobs, as opposed to acquiring only 316,000 jobs within that thirty-year span.[2] Unemployment among African Americans proved twice that of corresponding white counterparts.[3] Despite the aforementioned realities, conservative forces terminated programs geared to find jobs for chronically unemployed African Americans.[4] Some prominent black leaders basking in the success of the civil rights movement failed to realize or recognize a permanent black underclass existed.[5] These factors created a blueprint for black slums from which escape became virtually impossible.

The 1970s also represented an aversion to the turmoil of the previous decade. Rather than embracing racial reconciliation, the nation focused on displeasure with the Vietnam War, the impeachment of President Richard M. Nixon, the incoherent blandness of President Gerald Ford, and the naïve incompetence of President Jimmy Carter. But equally significant, white Americans displayed an enormous backlash toward blacks and black achievement. Influential white leaders refrained from advocating funding to maintain high-quality urban public schools and refocused attention on street crime. Conservative white spokespersons decried the effectiveness of Great Society programs and contended that disproportionate amounts of middle-class tax money went to an undeserving African American populace.

During this same decade, those who sought black amelioration would be ignored because the nation's embarrassment in regard to the racist

South dissipated. The presidential election of 1976 placed Jimmy Carter, a native Georgian, in the White House. The flow of rust-belt industries to the South swelled the population and made the region more agreeable to native Southerners and émigrés alike. The media also contributed to mitigating the Southern image. Television programs like the *Beverly Hillbillies* and the Waltons projected a positive image of Southern families and family values. Popular TV evangelists rooted in the South addressed moral and social values and the significance of family that could be embraced by Americans nationwide. Other Southern cultural norms impacted a broad spectrum of Americans as well. The simple, moral lyrics of increasingly popular country-and-western music, combined with the homey marketing of Kentucky Fried Chicken, helped those who resided outside the Sunbelt to forget and overlook the region's recent racist and heinous past.[6]

The acceptance of Southern themes and norms in popular culture also provided the illusion that the racist veil had been lifted off black Southerners. Indeed, life for Southern African Americans appeared significantly better than daily experiences of their Northern counterparts. Racial conflict shifted from Dixie to the Far West, Midwest, and Northeast cities like Los Angeles, Detroit, Chicago, and Boston.[7] Although pockets of resistance to the new racial order in the South existed, the incorporation of black athletes on Southern college football and basketball teams, and the gradual but steady influx of African American children into previously all-white schools, provided progressive Southerners with the means to forget a sordid, racist past.

In contrast to reconstructed white Southern norms, black culture hardly conveyed moral values. While country-and-western music warned about the consequences of cheating, adultery, divorce, and the failure of love and family—containing a strong religious admonition to engage in corrective behavior—black soul music spoke of passion, sex, drugs, and alienation. In addition, the genesis of rap music and its contentious lyrics portrayed the black masses in a negative light. By projecting black men as aggressive male chauvinists, white people could justifiably perceive the African American masses as a hostile, belligerent, fearful populace that required restrictions and control. A white backlash toward African Americans commenced.[8]

At the same time, cultural norms of low-income African Americans revealed a socioeconomic class insufficiently prepared to benefit from advantages derived from the civil rights movement. In the 1890s Du Bois prophetically proclaimed that "if discriminatory racial barriers were suddenly removed, some blacks would attain higher socioeconomic status, others might make modest gains, but the mass would remain stagnant."[9] Du Bois' observation appeared in a previous century and proved prescient years later. Slum-related problems—joblessness, concentrated poverty, family dysfunction, and welfare dependency—worsened between 1973 and 1980.[10] A sordid historical past exemplified by race and class inequities could hardly be erased within a century, let alone a generation.

During the economic recession of 1970–1971, the labor market declined, causing older manufacturing plants located in central cities to close. In response, Congress passed the Manpower Development and Training Act (MDTA), and in 1973 introduced an experimental program known as the Comprehensive Employment and Training Act (CETA) to provide local governments with employment training funds. Unfortunately for African Americans, more qualified and employable white males with high school diplomas received most of the jobs rather than undereducated blacks.[11]

By 1973 conditions became even more severe for impoverished Americans. With the sharp rise of oil prices, incidences of poverty among the nation's poor increased. Neither President Ford nor Congress elected to defend the American consumer by challenging big oil. This meant that people on the periphery of the United States economy—specifically low-income African Americans—would be severely impacted by rising fuel costs. The poor faced destitution as several additional factors reduced impoverished blacks into deeper penury.[12] Jobs programs declined, enhancing the social, political, and physical isolation of indigent blacks. In addition, the lack of marketable skills attributed to an increasingly dysfunctional educational system undermined disadvantaged blacks' prospects for obtaining work and being accepted into mainstream society. And finally, continued white disdain and antipathy for impoverished African Americans caused the lowly masses to remain destitute.[13]

Meanwhile, liberal New York senator Daniel Patrick Moynihan initiated and justified the nation's indifference toward underprivileged blacks. Moynihan coined the term "benign neglect" regarding the treatment of impoverished blacks, an opinion that provided credibility to conservative forces intent on reducing federal services to low-income African Americans.[14] Correspondingly, middle-class blacks had cause for contentment: President Johnson's efforts created thousands of government jobs, public payroll positions filled by the black bourgeoisie rather than the masses.[15] Influential African Americans who struggled for decades to achieve equal opportunity even momentarily debated whether or not the venerable National Association for the Advancement of Colored People should continue its existence.[16] Also, as civil rights efforts morphed into electoral politics where scores of blacks became elected to state and municipal offices, impoverished blacks became inconsequential. Like white politicos, black politicians ignored class differences between wealthy and impecunious African Americans and focused instead on forging a close relationship with corporate leaders. By offering developers and corporations tax breaks to do business and remain in the cities, necessary resources seldom became distributed to poor and working-class neighborhoods.[17] With these pervasive realities a foreboding trend appeared: poor, destitute blacks would be forced to fend for themselves.

A decline in the condition of the African American masses commenced simultaneously with civil rights successes. After sociologists coined the term "underclass" during the 1960s, this designation attained national significance by the decade's end. A permanent African American underclass became evident as the rate of unemployment among black male teens of working age increased from 22.5 percent in 1966 to 39 percent by 1974. Meanwhile, the arrest rate for black males between thirteen and thirty-nine increased 49 percent from 1966 to 1974.[18] Other disturbing statistics surfaced. The percentage of illegitimate black children increased from 16.9 in 1966 to 27.1 by 1976. And simultaneously, the percentage of black female headed households rose from 34.8 in 1965 to 60.6 in 1973.[19]

Low-income African Americans would also be most adversely affected by the white backlash that commenced in the presidential election of 1968. Running on a third-party ticket, Alabama governor George Wallace nearly received 25 percent of the vote, with a considerable number of voters from rust-belt states supporting his candidacy.[20] Although Wallace lost, he made an impressive showing, a reality hardly lost on the victorious candidate—Richard Milhous Nixon. Nixon utilized a Southern strategy that appealed to white Southerners and a white working-class electorate angry at "indolent" African Americans responsible for causing riots.[21] Consequently, the Nixon administration retreated from civil rights to court the favor of white voters. Although the president had expanded affirmative action for minorities, he slowed desegregation in Southern schools, curtailed busing, endeavored to undermine the Warren Court by placing conservatives on the bench, and redirected funding for special projects to weaken the liberal establishment.[22] Members of the black bourgeoisie immediately recognized that Nixon's policies would have an adverse effect on their race and class. Yet the blacks impacted most significantly and profoundly by Nixon's policies comprised the helpless, downtrodden members of the black lower class.

After Nixon applied his Southern strategy and certain facts became public about the horrendous condition of the African American masses, black leadership decided to help underprivileged members of the race. President Nixon became a convenient target for an aggrieved African American leadership. In 1971 the NAACP reported that African American unemployment proved comparable with joblessness of the Great Depression. Two years later the organization learned that approximately 30 percent of the black population and more than five hundred thousand African Americans lived below the poverty line. Firmly believing that license had been granted whites to practice discrimination, NAACP leaders endeavored to expand job opportunities for low-income blacks. The association engaged in numerous suits to obtain employment for jobless African Americans. Despite noble efforts of NAACP leadership, the masses experienced more unemployment after civil rights efforts of the 1960s than during the immediate years before the civil rights movement gained traction.[23]

While many black leaders identified Nixon as the culprit responsible for the socioeconomic problems the black masses encountered, the president could actually be praised for promoting policies coveted by the black bourgeoisie. Desegregation continued and legal segregation declined. Hotels, restaurants, and other establishments open to the public served all races—including African Americans. Simultaneously, the economic gap between blacks and whites narrowed as the income of middle-class African Americans increased exponentially. Moreover, the federal government specifically moved in a positive direction to terminate legal segregation. By 1972 every department in the federal government had established an equal-opportunity office. Funds for the Equal Employment Opportunity Commission ballooned from $3 million in 1966 to $111 million by 1979.

Nixon presided during part of a decade when African Americans possessing middle-class values experienced enormous growth and achievement. These ambitious African Americans voted, acquired an education, and earned sufficient funds to enjoy a comfortable lifestyle. Affluent blacks became the primary beneficiaries of largess emanating from public and private sectors of the national economy. Between the Great Depression and the 1970s, African American households with an income in excess of $50,000 increased by more than 400 percent.[24]

Nixon failed to receive credit for the gains achieved by African Americans in part, because the black underclass could not take advantage of the nation's economic growth and merge into the larger society.[25] Even avowed efforts of business leaders to find work for the hard-core unemployed African Americans failed to materialize because of inadequate support from federal and state governments. Blacks who remained poor largely suffered from intergenerational poverty, experienced a continuous disconnect from the larger society, and occasionally fell victim to political forces far beyond their control.[26] The economy went from manufacturing, wholesale, and retail industries to technical services that comprised advertising, management consulting, computer data advances, and various aspects of research and development.[27] With corporations no longer requiring an extensive unskilled labor force, the number of low-entry jobs diminished.

Despite establishing a positive record beneficial to the black bourgeoisie, Nixon would be excoriated for his public opposition to busing. Nixon's pronouncements on education gave credence to the anti-busing sentiment that caused Caucasians to vacate the cities in droves. While desegregation progressed in areas where whites and blacks had casual contact—restaurants, hotels, and airports—schools and neighborhoods largely remained segregated. Public opinion among white people became outrageously clear. They would, as the blues refrain declared, "rather drink muddy water and sleep out in a hollow log" before they permitted their children to be bused to inferior and predominately black neighborhoods and schools. The exodus of white people with means became assured with the *Milliken v. Bradley* case of 1974, when the Supreme Court declared that busing could no longer occur between black Detroit and adjacent white suburbs. This legal decision caused affluent whites to seek residence in the pure, pristine suburbs and ignore concerns of people relegated to life in inner-city slums. Impoverished blacks, in turn, voluntarily or involuntarily remained in the familiar confines of their neighborhood.[28] Since neither whites nor poor blacks coveted integration by the decade's end, entrenched segregation continued. And as the gaps in wealth between blacks and whites increased during the 1970s, the quality of schools attended by African Americans correspondingly declined. Factors that had a continuing adverse effect on indigent African Americans caused impoverished blacks to remain mired in slums.[29]

Other circumstances dictated that white people would think less about integration and the welfare of African Americans than self-preservation. By mid-decade economic stagnation occurred, limiting the nation's economic progress and seriously impacting the black underclass. Recognizing the declining fortunes of all destitute citizens, Senator Hubert Humphrey of Minnesota and black California congressman Augustus Hawkins decided to apply their legislative skills. They introduced the Humphrey-Hawkins Full Employment Act to Congress with the purpose of employing all citizens who sought work. The liberal senator Humphrey, and Hawkins, a founding member of the Congressional Black Caucus, purposely intended to aid low-income African Americans. But public sentiment cared less about the conditions of indigent blacks. Instead, mainstream Americans focused on ameliorating conditions for individual citizens rather than endorsing altruistic efforts for low-income African Americans.[30]

Cities in the North and Midwest encountered additional recession-related problems that seriously impacted low-income African Americans. Disadvantaged blacks continued experiencing layoffs, underemployment, and joblessness.[31] Low-income African Americans also became victims to the debilitating results of the evolving global market economy where physical labor became cheap and abundant. Without work, these blacks experienced unemployment.[32] But marginal blacks residing in slums faced other concerns that transcended the job market. Toxins, hazardous waste, airborne carcinogens, noise, and high-population densities also contributed to debilitating conditions that impinged on the black urban poor.[33] Although additional funding would be required to treat people suffering from harmful changes in the environment, few funds became available to treat the new urban environmental pathologies.

Unfortunately for the black masses, white Americans responded to the previous decade by embracing conservatism stances. Conservatives endorsed low taxes, demanded funds for national defense, voiced anti-elitism opinions, and promoted the need for a culture that placed primacy on morality and family values rather than social services. New Right conservatives also opposed Planned Parenthood, the Sierra Club, and the NAACP.[34] But most significantly for inner-city blacks, white conservatives equated liberalism with socialism. They particularly resented hard-earned middle-class taxpayers' money being used to provide sustenance for the underpaid, indigent, and nonworking poor. Conservative politicos blamed generous welfare practices of the Great Society for creating a disincentive for work.[35] More open-minded Americans, however, also held a conservative view toward people on welfare. In a Harris poll taken in 1972, nearly 90 percent of the respondents favored making people on welfare go to work. Seven years later, an NBC poll revealed that 93 percent of the respondents felt that able-bodied welfare recipients should be required to work at public jobs. Those who believed the nation spent too much money on welfare programs increased from 61 percent in 1969 to 81 percent in 1980.[36] The rising tide of conservatism would hardly bode well for dependent African Americans.

When the economy shifted away from manufacturing to service-oriented jobs during the 1970s, banks helped maintain segregation. Banks in the private sector manipulated Home Owners Loan Corporation guidelines in order to redline or refuse loans to working-class African Americans. While scores of white people used federal funds and moved from cities to suburbia, many African Americans were denied access to HOLC funding. Without loans to purchase or enhance properties, home values in inner cities collapsed. White speculators recognized the devaluation of home prices, abandoned center-city housing, or, to avoid tax payments on speculated properties, allowed the houses to remain vacant. Subsequently, as loan officers refused to extend credit to prospective African American homeowners, inner-city landscapes deteriorated further into sordid slums.[37]

As heightened residential segregation enabled black mayors to be elected in many cities, the concomitant white tax revolt had a deleterious impact on low-income African Americans. Anti-tax legislation initially appeared in California with the 1978 passage of Proposition (Prop) 13. The lower tax mantra of Prop 13 reverberated throughout the nation. At a time when cities needed funding to educate students to fill postindustrial jobs, funding disappeared. With diminished resources, the ability to improve schools already deemed inadequate proved impossible. Despite the large increase of black mayors, this neophyte political corps could not garner sufficient funding to prevent the decline of municipal infrastructures. Buildings and roads deteriorated, and equally important, the quality of public schools declined.[38]

When the Nixon agenda stressed individualism and looked to private enterprise rather than the federal government to mitigate domestic challenges, the suffering of impoverished blacks continued unabated. Neither President Nixon nor the voting public entertained extending opportunities to poor Americans. Since a consensus suggesting African Americans comprised a disproportionately high number of welfare recipients, few local, state, or federal politicians offered constructive ideas to ameliorate problems associated with being black and poor.[39] Because funding from private foundations and corporations could hardly match financial assistance comparable to the federal government, poor blacks remained marginalized. Blacks residing in the inner cities of America particularly bore the brunt of public indifference and administration callousness that directed the masses toward a continuous, downward spiral. Destitute blacks became convenient scapegoats, as Nixon and Southern strategy proponents recognized the efficacy of associating poverty with race and gaining favor with impressionistic segments of the white electorate.

The individualism that President Nixon proposed had nothing to do with the significance of an individual's address. As white people vacated cities, a less-affluent black populace devoid of job training and experiences rented housing accommodations in the declining urban neighborhoods. With an education gap already in evidence, employers appeared disinclined to hire young African Americans who resided on streets with inner-city addresses. This would explain, in part, why only four of every ten black teens found jobs and more than 60 percent of all unemployed African Americans between sixteen and nineteen resided in slums. Even residence in a slum castigated young black men, marring their future and forcing them to think about individual survival within the confining slum rather than seeking legitimate work outside the neighborhood.[40]

Without governmental assistance, black slum residents collectively possessed insufficient tools and training to escape poverty.[41] Evidence of the decline of an inner-city black community devoid of federal, state, or municipal support again became apparent in the Thirtieth Ward of Philadelphia. While New Deal administrators exhibited compassion for downtrodden urban blacks, a generation later the sensitivity of government officials abated. Given the decline of two-parent households, higher incidences of venereal disease, heightened violence, and other harmful factors apparent in slum life, concern for the poor hardly proved a government priority. For example in 1933, the most severe year of the Great Depression, approximately 2,500 people in the ward were arrested for criminal offenses, but only 75 had been charged with serious transgressions (36 larcenies, 30 aggravated assaults, and two each for auto theft, burglary, robbery, and rape, and a single homicide). By 1977, however, the propensity for violence became underscored when 599 people had been arrested on serious charges (152 larcenies, 94 aggravated assaults, 47 auto thefts, 127 burglaries, 140 robberies, 25 rapes, and 14 homicides).[42] Blacks residing in the ward during the 1970s fared worse than predecessors who lived there during the Great Depression.

If federal and state governments were indifferent to impoverished African Americans, segments of the white populace and municipal leaders proved hostile. Unsympathetic white Philadelphians, for example, initiated a practice known as neighborhood control, a concept declaring that neither the municipal or federal governments had the right to encourage racial integration. Furthermore, a conspiracy existed between white residents of the Whitman Park section of South Philadelphia and the city administration of Mayor Frank Rizzo. Collectively the conspiratorial parties prevented blacks from returning to a redeveloped area that previously housed African Americans.[43] These secretive developments undertaken by municipal leaders like Rizzo placed blacks in a defenseless position.

The indifference municipal leaders in Philadelphia demonstrated toward inner-city black residents could also be observed in New York City's South Bronx. Life in the Bronx proved particularly unsavory and harsh during the 1970s. By mid-decade the borough lost approximately six hundred thousand manufacturing jobs, and the average per capita income dropped to $2,430.[44] With apartment-building owners selling their property to slumlords, a pernicious cycle developed that fostered and enhanced bitterness between residents. Slumlords realized personal profits would increase and money could be saved through certain nefarious practices. Therefore, avaricious apartment owners withdrew funding for heat and water, withheld property taxes from the city, and, on occasion, employed arsonists to destroy buildings in order to benefit from fire insurance policies.[45] Those who observed the pattern of arson in New York City concluded, "There is simply no incentive for banks, insurance companies, or anyone else with money to invest in building or rebuilding dwellings at reasonable rents."[46]

Many individual decisions low-income blacks made appeared as natural responses to poverty and a lack of direction. Perhaps one of the more egregious directionless acts occurred when teens and young adults produced children out of wedlock. Given the enormous need to acquire unconditional love, scores of black girls welcomed pregnancy and looked forward to having a child.[47] During the 1970s illegitimate births involving teenage girls within the black community increased by 50 percent.[48] This phenomenon placed enormous stress on the African American community and undermined the viability of the black family. Although low-income African Americans faced less condemnation for having bastard children than people with middle-class values, young mothers residing in inner-city slums still faced enormous survival challenges.[49]

Young mothers without a proper means of support remained in poverty. Even those who worked experienced unrelenting difficulties. Teenage mothers who failed to graduate from high school in all likelihood never obtained a high school diploma. Since marginally educated young mothers could only acquire low-paying jobs, the parent and child remained in a penurious state. In 1977, for example, the median family income for central-city families was less than $14,000. But for female-headed households, the family income averaged only $5,125.[50] The overburdened young mother and occasional father characteristically seemed overwhelmed by daily obstacles. The smell of refuse in the streets, shabby appearance of homes, omnipresent vermin, overcrowded conditions, and deficiencies in food and medical care contributed to antisocial behavior. Those seeking escape through alcohol and drugs hardly seemed prepared to assist children or provide their progeny with a positive self-image and constructive norms of behavior.[51]

By the mid-1970s weaknesses within black families residing in slums became unabashedly evident. A disproportionate number of African Americans failed to find work.[52] Fathers specifically displayed characteristics that negatively impacted everyone in the household. Generally, the presence of a father residing in a slum household appeared, at best, symbolic. Jobless husbands garnered no respect. Even when husbands and/or fathers found work, tensions hardly abated. Husbands who eventually became employed and endeavored to reassert authority over wives faced resistance. These mothers refused to revert back to secondary roles and respect men with inconsistent work records.[53]

Given the perceived irresponsibility of husbands, fathers, and male friends, black mothers experienced psychological disorders. Women with children had reason to be insecure. By the time a child reached four or five some mothers lost a deep psychological connection with their offspring. Unable to protect the child from the harsh realities of slum existence as the child matured and became an adolescent, all too frequently role reversal occurred. Half the women on Aid to Families with Dependent Children (AFDC) had problems that prevented them from handling simple responsibilities, 30 percent exhibited limited cognitive abilities, 13 percent experienced daily bouts of depression, 10 percent displayed medical disabilities, and 9 percent became addicted to cocaine. Therefore, vulnerable mothers became dependent on their progeny, lacked personal esteem, and lost respect when the children became young adults.[54]

While most children suffered when raised in a fatherless single-parent household, boys particularly appeared damaged. In households without fathers, boys lacked proper male role models who could instill them with positive, manly attributes. Instead, boys represented the negative manifestation of a father who deserted the family and failed to provide material or emotional support. Invariably, mothers projected anger toward the adult male on to the child. In response, boys became defensive, stubborn, and self-assertive. Denied access to developing self-esteem at home, boys joined peers in the streets and gained acceptance by signifying and playing the Dozens, a word game disrespectful of mothers.[55]

For the mother, a daughter received more care than a son. And like the mother, the girl learned to be self-sufficient. Consequently, daughters attained more self-confidence than sons. Girls acquired discipline and a sense of achievement by performing household chores and gained satisfaction by performing acceptable, matronly duties.[56] Unfortunately, impoverished mothers seldom advised daughters about sex, invariably enabling them to fall prey to sexual advances of immature boys and self-indulgent men disinclined to practice safe sex. But wayward girls, like irresponsible fathers and mothers, also manifested negative qualities, being sassy, stubborn, self-indulgent, and promiscuous.[57]

Sadly, both adolescent boys and girls of childbearing age succumbed to the sexual rituals of the impoverished. Boys focused on impressing their peer group by "running a game" to obtain sexual favors. Girls generally understood the game being played, but many risked pregnancy to acquire affection and prospects for the traditional family comprising a husband, wife, and child. In the final analysis, the entire community suffered. Young men who fathered children possessed few economic means for acting as a responsible parent, and the young mother became saddled with the burden of being a single parent facing a limited future.[58]

With fathers abdicating responsibility for raising children and mothers reeling from the constant pressure of being the primary breadwinner, children had to fend for themselves. Collectively young people seized power from irresponsible adults. Thus, life in inner-city black slums throughout the nation became dominated by young people rather than their elders. Customarily rebellious and understandably immature, black youths from the slums exhibited uncultivated, feckless behavior, projecting an attitude middle-class Americans failed to comprehend. Extremely adroit in establishing paradigms that measured success under the guise of being cool, black youths displayed purposeful irresponsibility and conspicuous hedonism, norms that essentially prohibited slum residents from extricating themselves from perpetual poverty.[59]

Perhaps the most egregious effects of a male being cool may be observed by men who had children by different women and had their wages garnered for child support. Experiencing hard-earned funds going elsewhere, these men quit their jobs and returned to the street. Even when some friends exerted influence to encourage a man to take responsibility for his offspring, the biological father prioritized his need for individual freedom and maintaining ties with peers.

Other evidence of neglect appeared in the on-going doleful academic performance of black children. During the 1960s Harvard president James B. Conat announced that inner-city schools failed to reach student clients, a trend that continued into the 1970s. Schools acted more as holding stations designed to keep students off the streets rather than as institutions that provided direction, guidance, basic knowledge, and inspiration. Schools proved unable to provide children with sufficient motivation to achieve self-sufficiency and strive for upward mobility. Conat recognized that most inner-city schools failed at their mission. In the urban slums, academic success depended almost entirely on the socioeconomic condition of the family rather than the instruction rendered in public schools. Influential students with hostile intentions toward authority invariably had greater influence than teachers.[60]

Lacking in motivation, exhibiting deviant behavior, and revealing disrespect for authority, students enrolled in inner-city schools engaged in a myriad of negative activities. Many boys fought, drank, and stole to demonstrate courage and a sense of manhood. Girls, meanwhile, decided to become women by engaging in premarital sex and possibly producing a child. Students eager to perform well in school, unfortunately, faced badgering and intimidation, leaving them ill informed, unprepared to meet workforce demands, and devoid of the discipline necessary for a successful college career.[61]

Believing school unnecessary, some inner-city youths emulated irresponsible adults to seek escape by using drugs. While drugs provided a momentary high, habitual offenders invariably lost interest in school, work, or any kind of constructive activity. Students who succumbed to drugs appeared destined for a life of crime. Others denied attention in dysfunctional households responded to being ignored by engaging in disruptive behavior at school and accepted failure as a badge of honor. And still others attended classes sporadically until reaching sufficient age to withdraw. Students with the aforementioned characteristics and behavioral patterns faced unemployment, prison, and a nonproductive existence.

With inner-city public schools failing to prepare students for the competitive job market, young people learned survival lessons in the streets. Education acquired in the streets, however, could not be transferred directly to legitimate employment. Highly skilled streetwise youths consequently failed to perform adequately when securing a job. To avoid being terminated many youths quit work and returned to the familiar confines of the street. Obviously the discipline offered on job-training programs failed to instill black youths with the required work ethic. Being punctual, dependable, patient, and industrious on mundane, entry-level jobs held little allure for young people accustomed to the excitement of street life.[62] Without proper training in basic math, science, and English, and operating as functional illiterates, African Americans of working age who resided in slums had difficulty finding and securing jobs.[63]

Even young people fortunate to find employment appeared lost and forlorn. Low-income blacks lacked proper social graces, causing scores of black workers to be simply let go. Since African American deficiencies were not countered by favorable qualities like leadership, ingenuity, tenacity, and highly developed verbal skills, slum residents appeared to potential employers as useless drones devoid of redeeming qualities that enhanced production in the workplace.[64]

Given the enormous burdens inner-city blacks faced, a unique survival technique became resurrected during the 1970s, the art of remaining calm under the guise of being cool. For African Americans, remaining cool under pressure enabled ancestors to survive the Middle Passage, endure the dehumanization of slavery, and transcend generations of racial discrimination. Black males residing in slums, the "cool pose" practitioners of the 1970s, mimicked the historical behavior of predecessors and made necessary alterations to survive challenges within the impoverished urban milieu.[65]

Blacks used being cool as a defense mechanism to exhibit pride, demonstrate strength, and show control without revealing emotion. By presenting a stoic, indifferent demeanor, "cool" activists conveyed mastery of a problematic environment. Boys in particular embraced "cool pose" because of the profound need to appear stoic and self-assured. Burdened with the internalization of personal failure, cool posturing masked insecurities, kept potential opponents off balance, and garnered support from current or prospective allies.

Being cool appeared as the most apropos escape mechanism in the rough-honed slum society; but "cool pose" also produced negative results. The "cool" person engaged in self-deception and demonstrated an inflated sense of self-worth. Those who exuded confidence without portfolio exaggerated prowess. When challenged, ridiculed, or forced out of the "cool pose" persona, an individual could become surly, paranoid, aggressive, and likely to engage in black-on-black violence. "Cool" inner-city residents rejected progressive whites and blacks who could have a constructive impact on the community. "Cool pose" practitioners were also reticent and perceived candor as a weakness. Blacks who embraced the negative ramifications of "cool pose" and fiercely endorsed the "cool" persona invariably made decisions that placed them beyond redemption.

"Cool" became institutionalized by hustlers who thrived in low-income black neighborhoods. The hustlers adopted a swagger, wore the proper hip-hop attire, exuded style, and flashed money.[66] Hustlers became role models in inner-city black America because of conspicuous displays of wealth. Ostentation exhibited by expensive cars, flashy clothes, and gold jewelry without holding a steady, traditional job seemed alluring to impoverished, impressionistic youths.

Hustlers, therefore, held far more prestige than adults performing mundane work in dead-end jobs that garnered meager pay.[67]

Hustlers operated in the criminal underground, engaging in drug dealing, pimping, and gambling. Desperate, ambitious young men with the profound need to make money cast caution to the wind, sold drugs, and accepted risks that could culminate in incarceration or death. Pimps, on the other hand, took fewer risks than drug dealers and enjoyed the glamour and prospects for acquiring wealth. Successful pimps, though street-smart, appeared hardened and completely self-indulgent. Petty hustlers who earned a living running numbers and operating as pool sharks enjoyed a relatively safe existence. But with less resources than dealers and pimps, petty hustlers appeared weak and, without a strong vice lord, could still be subjected to danger and disaster.

The more a boy or young adult embraced the "cool" persona of a hustler, the greater the propensity to experience ultimate personal failure. Unfortunately, the lucrative payoff, prospects for glamour, and the risk of being arrested for illegal activities seemed preferable to the relatively non-lucrative, degrading, disappointing, and boring work associated with traditional employment. Scores of young African Americans chose to practice being "cool" and accepted a marginalized lifestyle that could have negative consequences.[68]

Those who embraced the "cool pose" persona gave credence to middle-class America's negative impression of low-income blacks. Young residents of inner-city slums placed themselves in an untenable situation. While blacks believed the lackadaisical nature of "cool pose" provided coping mechanisms for the vicissitudes of slum life, middle-class people viewed slum residents as being irresponsible, uninspired, insipid, violent, and unconcerned. Too cool to work and too cool to study, inner-city blacks possessed few socially redeeming qualities that induced employers to recognize the ebony masses as a dependable workforce. Thus, African Americans who adopted the "cool" stance to mask insecurity and a sense of defeatism created a negative, self-fulfilling prophesy for themselves.[69]

As products of dissolute families who resided in untenable apartments and experienced failure in school, alienated blacks joined gangs to capture a sense of identity and self-worth. Gangs offered succor to those who sincerely believed the system conspired against African Americans. For angry young blacks a systemic conspiracy against their race and class existed. High rates of unemployment, few municipal recreational facilities, unfair judicial sentencing practices, and public schools that presented curricula with little, if any, appeal for boys and girls battling for daily survival, provided convincing evidence of societal indifference to the plight of underprivileged African Americans.

Gangs addressed the marginalization of black youths by restoring pride, providing the means for empowerment, and guaranteeing mutual support. Although gangs augmented the self-esteem of alienated youths, gang activity failed to direct members toward positive activities. Participation in criminal activity became commonplace. Serving time in prison garnered respect rather than scorn. Gang members, therefore, seldom perceived their behavior as being deviant. Instead, members took pride in being pariahs within the larger society, embraced the role of outsiders, reveled in illegal activities, and viewed the police solely as a hard-core phalanx hired to keep young blacks subservient. Invariably, gang members accepted incarceration as a badge of honor.[70]

Gentrification also contributed to black marginalization. Corporate developers purchased strategically located real estate in which low-income African Americans resided. They had blacks removed from rented properties, razed slum dwellings, and erected expensive luxury neighborhoods. Impoverished, inner-city blacks were caught in catch-22 situations determined by the location, estimated property valuation, and vision of moneyed interests. If the black neighborhood lacked proper proximity to downtown businesses and cultural centers, the community would be ignored. This would be evidenced by boarded homes, deteriorating structures, vacant lots, and other unseemly characteristics. Yet if municipal leaders and speculators envisioned the locale favorably with the potential to lure Americans with means into refurbished downtown properties, low-income blacks became victims of gentrification and removed.

Black marginalization, anger, and frustration caused by difficulties in accessing decent housing and finding jobs exacerbated young people and caused them to raise voices in protest.[71] This protest morphed into a cultural norm that spawned an art form destined to be known as hip-hop or rap. The origins of rap evolved innocently in New York City during the early 1970s. Masters of ceremonies and disc jockeys at block parties held in the South Bronx rapped between songs, mesmerizing the audience by telling jokes, speaking in anecdotes, encouraging people to dance, and used a poetic, rhythmic cadence to keep those present entertained. Though initially a counter response to disco, the emerging musical genre became the voice of angry blacks left to fend for themselves in an increasingly impoverished neighborhood.[72]

Rap music emerged as the most pronounced and significant means of protest, an art form that originated with low-income black youths. As the last element to emerge from hip-hop culture, the music's unmistakable significance influenced the attitudes, style, and meaning of life for young black people. With origins in New York City, rap evolved from the pathos of urban life. Soon, alienated young black people throughout the East Coast, West Coast, the Midwest, and eventually the South became captivated by the raw, unconventional, piercing lyrics. Rap centers appeared in Los Angeles (Compton), Oakland, Detroit, Chicago, Houston, Atlanta, Miami, Newark, Trenton, Boston (Roxbury), and Philadelphia.[73] An indifferent federal government, a comfortable and complaisant black bourgeoisie, a dysfunctional

NAACP, decaying neighborhoods, and unrelenting poverty compelled young people to find solace in hip-hop music.[74]

The neighborhood posse and crews who created hip-hop culture also found personal identity through graffiti, dance, and music. Maintaining the raunchy, confrontational edge, hip-hop became extremely competitive. The music, rap lyrics, and graffiti conveyed the hard-core experiences of the inner-city and created tension among competing groups. Fist fights occurred among break dancers, rappers, and DJs. Yet despite evidence of discord, all parties seemed devoted to promoting a unique style to garner acclaim and boost individual or group status.[75]

A new cultural norm known as graffiti that commenced in Philadelphia also served to provide nameless, inconsequential youth with an identity. The symbols, names, and images painted on subway trains, walls, and other public facades eventually extended to New York City and other metropolitan areas. Writers known as taggers conveyed various styles of graffiti that marked a hip-hopper's identity. Moreover, the commonality between gangsters and taggers proved unmistakable. Both sought recognition from peers, used aliases, participated in illegal activities, and perceived themselves as noble outlaws. Inner-city youth from cities throughout the United States embraced tagging and antagonized city officials responsible for maintaining urban aesthetics. While taggers gained notoriety, city officials deplored the defacement of property and viewed graffiti as a scourge representing signs of urban decay.[76]

Of all the activities that attracted urban youth, break dancing seemed least likely to offend the sensibilities of the general public. Although dance crews occasionally clashed, the practice itself embraced athletic, entertaining moves appreciated by viewers and participants alike. Eventually, break-dancing schools would be created to introduce and instruct enthusiasts throughout the United States, Europe, and Japan.[77]

Incipient black cultural norms that evolved during the 1970s failed to terminate the downward spiral of impoverished African Americans. While a unique protest movement that eventually produced millions of dollars for artists and promoters, the hip-hop culture did nothing to inspire black youths to seek normal channels for success. Few artists advocated staying in school, respecting proper authority, using language devoid of profanity, or appealing for peace and tranquility. Instead, as the civil rights era ended, hip-hop artists naturally focused on making money rather than providing a positive direction that could serve as a positive beacon for impressionistic youths.

During the 1970s the civil rights movement ended. Antipoverty programs like Model Cities, the Comprehensive Employment and Training Act (CETA), and the Office of Economic Opportunity (OEO) that spent billions to rehabilitate slums would be severely cut back or dismantled. Equally important, a consensus appeared among the white public suggesting that enough had been done to address black grievances.[78] Political capital for the War on Poverty had been expended. Conservative forces would gain ascendancy and commence dismantling training programs sorely needed to enhance employment prospects for marginally skilled African Americans. Ultimately, by the end of the 1970s, a disproportionate number of blacks entered prison, and the final transformation of African American communities from ghettos to slums had become finalized.[79]

CHAPTER 10

Abandonment: The 1980s

The decade of the 1980s marked a confluence of four factors that had a deleterious effect on low-income African Americans. First, policies adopted by national leadership evidenced in the Reagan administration and conservative influences conveyed an aversion to African Americans.[1] Second, the continuing decline in industrial jobs traditionally available to blacks with limited training and education reduced prospects for employment and further diminished the ability of black men to function as adult providers.[2] Third, African American leaders and civil rights organizations relinquished their role as "race advocates" and ignored the black masses. And finally, heightened impoverishment contributed to an increase of harmful, self-inflicted decisions made by disadvantaged blacks that severely undermined African American communities.[3] Although the Reagan administration espoused harsh bombastic Negrophobe rhetoric to curry support from the reactionary white base, it endorsed certain measures to aid indigent African Americans.[4] In the final analysis, the negative rhetoric, coupled with the conservative ideology that sustained primacy of white elites, prevented the administration from providing necessary assistance to disadvantaged African Americans.

African Americans comprising the underclass of the 1980s differed significantly from poor blacks of previous generations. These people largely resided in central-city neighborhoods or communities with increasing rates of chronic poverty exemplified by social isolation, hopelessness, the crack epidemic, and dysfunctional behavior.[5] Blacks comprising this degraded population included the passive long-term welfare recipients; hostile street criminals consisting of school dropouts, drug addicts, and dealers; nonviolent hustlers; and the "traumatized," consisting of drunks, drifters, homeless shopping-bag ladies, and released mental patients who roamed city streets.[6]

Alarmed by the prospects of a Reagan victory in 1980, the NAACP requested the candidate's presence at their national meeting. Reagan declined to address the NAACP but decided instead to honor the request of the more conservative National Urban League. Many blacks in attendance at the NUL convention seem enthralled by Reagan's speech. First, Reagan declared he would strengthen the national economy so that the cities could be revitalized with the insertion of self-help initiatives.[7] Furthermore, Reagan declared that he intended to make African Americans more economically independent by encouraging blacks to enter the private sector. While some in attendance declared that Reagan dispelled the notion he held a "Neanderthal approach to black issues," others appeared far less impressed.[8]

The NAACP had cause for trepidation. After Reagan handily defeated Jimmy Carter in the 1980 presidential election, victorious Republicans prepared to implement conservative policies. Right-wing ideologues who represented the embodiment of Reagan Republicanism's New Federalism called for localized responses to social problems.[9] A return to laissez-faire without federal protection presented a comfortable reality to self-centered industrialists, social conservatives, and subliminal racists. Reagan would be unsympathetic to alienated and dispossessed citizens. As Reagan policies afforded wealthy Americans free reign to acquire and retain riches, the administration displayed comparable indifference to all poor and disadvantaged people.[10] States' rights and the concept of "home rule" shifted power from cities to suburbs. These policies caused an increase in urban poverty, resulting in a poorly educated, inattentive hostile workforce and a counterproductive, dependent African American citizenry.[11] When civil rights activist Marion Wright Edelman challenged President Reagan about cuts that undermined programs protecting the poor, the president wryly declared, "In the war on poverty, poverty won."[12] But rather than using a quip to make his point, Reagan would have been more appropriately accurate if offering the rejoinder, "Quotas rarely benefit the poorest, the most unskilled, the most economically" in need of help.[13]

Harboring opinions that blamed the victim, Reagan Republicans endorsed the long-held tradition that low-income blacks were responsible for their own shortcomings. Social mobility programs designed to improve labor prospects for chronically unemployed blacks were targeted for elimination. Reagan intended to eradicate CETA and, with it, the Public Service Employment Program (PSE). Only the newly created Job Training Partnership Act (JTPA) remained to employ jobless people. Funding, however, was directed to the affluent white suburbs and rural towns rather than big cities where impoverished minorities abounded. Reagan conservatives then added insult to injury by earmarking funds for law enforcement and enacting funds for new jails rather than improving inner-city schools and increasing the number of job-training centers.[14]

Playing to individualistic and moralistic sentiments of their conservative base, the administration deemphasized the social concerns about citizenship involving the right to employment, economic security, education, and health care. And though Reagan opposed the 1964–1965 Civil Rights Acts, Reaganites now believed that voting rights and integration of swimming pools, restaurants, and hotels would be sufficient to appease African Americans.[15] In addition, the administration contained people who professed to believe equal economic opportunity existed between African Americans and whites. Blacks devoid of resources, Republican conservatives reasoned, demonstrated slothful work habits or engaged in poor moral practices. Ascribing to the adage that individual initiative determined success or failure, Reagan and the Republicans ignored factual realities like inferior public schools, low wages, the absence of jobs, and an unhealthy physical environment that explained the continued existence of a black underclass.[16] Indeed, a meanness that belied Reagan's jovial public persona would have harsh consequences for poverty-stricken African Americans.

The newly elected Reagan Administration found a convenient rational to avoid the ignominy of being deemed racist or blatantly indifferent to African Americans. Reaganites used the conservative theoretical construct that the growth of liberal social policies of the 1960s—the Great Society and civil rights legislation passed during the Johnson Administration—heightened, rather than decreased, slum conditions. Reagan's theorists contended that social programs made the underclass less self-reliant and consequently contributed to greater unemployment.[17] Unfortunately for the black masses, liberals offered no satisfactory rejoinder to the conservative doctrine. As the largest disproportionately underserved and disadvantaged group in the United States, the black masses suffered grievously from the administration's hostile rhetoric directed toward low-income Americans.

Reagan policies that allowed for an inequitable distribution of wealth directly impacted impecunious African Americans.[18] As the wealthiest United States citizens became wealthier, a concomitant rise of persistent poverty and an augmentation of the underclass occurred.[19] Incidences of homelessness, characterized by long-standing poverty, disconnection from family, psychological impairment, and drug and alcohol addiction increased throughout the decade and comprised a disproportionate number of young African Americans.[20]

Policy makers in the Reagan administration also devastated black Americans by reducing social expenditures by 20 percent.[21] The reductions occurred without enormous public clamor because the larger American society believed that indolent, undeserving blacks received an excess in social benefits and drained welfare coffers. In reality, however, more than half the federal dollars were spent on programs that had nothing to do with poverty. Social Security, Medicare, veterans' benefits, workmen's compensation, and federal retirement programs received the bulk of the national government's largess.

Politically, Reagan strategists saw advantages in playing to their base by focusing on cuts to black welfare mothers rather than selecting other fiscal reductions the American public might abhor. African American women disproportionably bore the brunt of social welfare cuts because a steady decline in money to Aid to Families with Dependent Children severely impacted prospects for survival. The administration initiated a cost-cutting trend inimical to poor people that continued throughout the decade. But contrary to public opinion, the number of births among unwed mothers declined. Still the myth put forward that black girls and women deliberately produced babies to acquire additional AFDC funds persisted.[22]

Recognizing that the conservative victory at the polls had limitations, Reaganites realized the election could not be mistaken as a mandate for a return to racist Southern norms. Reagan Republicans deftly prepared to stave off criticism from African Americans by finding opportunistic blacks willing to endorse their conservative agenda. Black conservatives seized the opportunity to ingratiate themselves with the Reagan administration. Therefore, on December 13 and 14, 1980, a month prior to Reagan's presidential inauguration, a black think tank, with Reagan confidant Edwin Meese scheduled to provide the keynote address, met at the Fairmont Hotel in San Francisco to show compliance with and support for the new administration. While impossible to assess accurately the motives of individual blacks who attended the gathering—profound political beliefs, opportunism, or self-hatred—a basic truth existed. Reaganites enlisted the support of blacks who would militate against those who would accuse the forthcoming administration of racism.

The Fairmont Conference initiated a fall from grace in regard to black leadership. While some of those in attendance like Chuck Stone and Tony Brown represented the black media and the intellectual professor Charles V. Hamilton of Columbia attended, most attendees were black conservatives. Economist Thomas Sowell, Clarence Thomas (aide to Senator John Danforth of Missouri), Clarence M. Pendleton of the San Diego Urban League, and others of like mind gathered to forge a new direction in leadership that differed significantly from civil rights activists of the 1960s and 1970s. After knowledge of the meeting became public, progressive African Americans failed adequately to challenge the ideas presented at the Fairmount Hotel gathering. Consequently, blacks who endorsed a "conservatism" that promoted individualism and ignored expected fairness from a sympathetic federal government operated with impunity.[23]

Though little could be done to stem the tide of Reagan conservatism during the 1980s, pliant blacks eased the administration's conscience, enabling Reaganites to restrain and minimize opportunities for indigent African Americans.

Black appointments in the Reagan administration also proved disquieting to those concerned about the welfare of poverty-striken African Americans. Clarence M. Pendleton Jr., president of the San Diego chapter of the National Urban League, became an immediate target for being a questionable appointee. Pendleton's conservative ideology made him attractive to members of Reagan's staff. Pendleton opposed building a $308-million-dollar hospital in the black community, suggesting that the cemetery lot would be more useful for possible industrial or residential development.[24] Vernon Zukumo, a disgruntled San Diego resident, complained, "Whenever there was a chance for him to do something on civil rights, he has opposed the black community and the black community's sentiments."[25] Despite Zukumo's misgivings, Pendleton received an appointment as chair of the United States Civil Rights Commission. During Pendleton's tenure as the Civil Rights Commission chair, congressional funding was significantly reduced. Staff members, moreover, were either dismissed or resigned in opposition to Pendleton's disquieting policies.

Housing and Urban Development (HUD) appointee Samuel R. Pierce Jr. had also been perceived as a black tool that did the bidding of conservative Reaganites. Congressman Henry Gonzalez, chair of the Banking Subcommittee on Housing, called Pierce a "Stepin Fetchit," a most derogatory name that personified a shiftless, lazy Negro.[26] In addition, the *Impact Journal*, an independent, bimonthly publication out of Washington, DC, stated that over 50 percent of HUD employees rated Pierce as incompetent, and nearly three of four found the secretary a poor leader. Specifically, the employees reported Pierce to be indifferent or hostile to HUD recipients (73.1 percent), subservient to the White House (80.8 percent), and rarely existed as a cabinet voice for civil rights (90.4 percent).[27]

Equal Employment Opportunity Commission (EEOC) chair Clarence Thomas evolved as the most renowned of the black Reagan appointees. After graduating from the College of the Holy Cross and Yale Law School, Thomas gained the support of Senator John Danforth of Missouri who recommended him to head the EEOC. As the EEOC director, Thomas angered progressive African Americans by eliminating timetables and goals required by companies to meet nondiscriminatory standards. Thomas also made class-action suits more difficult by dismissing statistical evidence traditionally used to reveal discriminatory behavior displayed by corporations.

The organizations expected to protect all African Americans and challenge any forces that restricted black progress became moribund and ineffective. Attendees at the Fairmont Hotel chose a most propitious time to assert support for a conservative agenda. Indeed, the National Urban League behaved as though the African American struggle for civil rights never occurred. League members endorsed the belief that liberal programs like affirmative action, special training programs, subsidies, and welfare contributed to black dependence on federal handouts.[28] NUL leaders essentially ignored the plight of the black masses, a puzzling stance since the Urban League held the primary responsibility for performing research on the African American condition that proved low-income blacks constantly functioned in the throes of economic crisis. While the league's apparent indifference to black poverty may in part be attributed to Vernon Jordan's convalescence from an assassination attempt that left the NUL momentarily rudderless, underprivileged blacks should not have been forgotten.

Like the National Urban League, the NAACP also appeared in disarray. In the late 1970s, membership declined from an estimated high of 500,000 during the height of the civil rights movement to a paltry 200,000. Middle class blacks who believed equality had been achieved had little cause for remaining in the organization. Furthermore, internal discord among the association's leading personalities enabled the conservative agenda to flourish unchallenged. Soon after long-time NAACP executive director Roy Wilkins resigned, board president Margaret Wilson engaged in a donnybrook with his replacement, an attorney and minister named Benjamin Hooks. The Wilson-Hooks fight consumed the organization and rendered the association ineffective as a champion for African Americans generally, and low-income blacks in particular.

Factors external to the black community also contributed to the lowly condition of many African Americans. Political forces shaped by continuous demographic shifts of whites to suburbia, for example, had a negative effect on inner-city black residents. With the declining influence of cities and the concomitant augmentation of suburban voters, federal and state governments directed more funds to locales containing the largest and most influential electorate.[29]

Economic forces beyond the control of beneficent public servants and civil rights activists likewise facilitated the declining fortunes of impoverished blacks. The trend toward automation that commenced during the 1950s continued. Innovative, labor-saving techniques meant that those without requisite skills in postindustrial America could not find work. Moreover, the American economy quickly moved from manufacturing to high tech service industries. During the 1970s, for example, two of every three adult male workers with less than a high school diploma worked as full-time employees. During the 1980s, however, only half of the unskilled workers acquired gainful employment. As mass production in the United States declined, manufacturing jobs that previously used unskilled laborers in the steel and automotive industries began disappearing in the new postindustrial age. The only guaranteed work for an unskilled black cadre existed in low paying domestic service jobs that characteristically hired more women than men.[30]

Life for inner-city blacks also became increasingly dire as jobs shifted to the suburbs. Between 1977 and 1982 suburban service jobs nearly doubled, comprising approximately four times the growth of job opportunities in central cities.[31] At the same time, inner-city jobs disappeared or moved to the suburbs. Given the federal government's role in reducing subsidized housing during the Reagan administration, the ability of low-income blacks finding homes in proximity to relocated jobs became nearly impossible.[32] While the Carter administration constructed a large number of housing units, new construction trailed off significantly under Reagan. By 1981, Reagan's people reduced funding for Section 8 subsidized housing for low-income families from $30 to 17.5 billion. And by 1985 the HUD budget suffered a two-thirds reduction.[33] When decidedly new jobs evolved as evidenced in the enormous increase of office space, inner-city blacks lacked the experience or expertise to acquire employment.[34]

Without some sense of irony, the removal of inner-city jobs to suburbia occurred simultaneously with the inability of low-income blacks to acquire satisfactory housing. A long-standing policy existed, declaring that for every new unit of public housing created, an unsafe or unsanitary unit must be destroyed. This worked to the disadvantage of inner-city blacks because white suburbanites refused to allow public housing to be erected in their communities. Consequently, blacks evicted from an inner-city tenement failed to acquire comparable lodging in the suburbs.[35] Low-income blacks who migrated from the rural South to the Northeast and Midwest, therefore, had little recourse but to reside in increasingly segregated inner-city slums.[36] Sensing the administration's indifference toward the black poor, between 1985 to 1986 mortgage brokers extended even fewer loans to prospective African American borrowers.[37] As late as 1989, therefore, only 7 percent of the black population lived in suburbia, comprising 2.7 million of a 30 million African American population. Consequently, only the poorest urban areas received public housing units, adding to the segregation, joblessness, and dissolution of the black urban poor.[38]

Prospects for employment became particularly daunting for inner-city black men willing to commute to work. Unfortunately, the distance from jobs and necessary transportation costs created problems for impecunious workers. First, the unemployed must look for work, and meager funds suggested that prospects for an extensive long-term search could prove financially disastrous. Second, the lack of automobile ownership among low-income blacks, combined with the amount of time and money spent on commuting, caused impoverished African Americans easily to become discouraged.[39] Third, as the economy moved from manufacturing to service industries, blacks lacked the requisite skills employers sought to meet consumers' needs. And finally, evidence of racism appeared in several suburban locales outside Chicago, Detroit, and Philadelphia. In these metropolitan areas where black suburbanites resided, African Americans experienced greater difficulties securing work than whites.[40]

Additional evidence that explained the declining fortunes of low-income blacks appeared in the correlation between minimal and higher levels of education. A study prepared for the National Research Committee on National Urban Policy in 1986 found that between 1970 and 1984, the number of jobs available for people with less than a high school education in New York, Philadelphia, Boston, Baltimore, St. Louis, and Atlanta diminished drastically. Those most adversely impacted by job losses comprised boys and young men between sixteen and thirty-four.[41] Meanwhile, a corresponding increase in jobs occurred that required a high school education, a factor that explained the numerical and percentile increase of middle-class blacks in urban America.

Lower-income black men who failed to acquire training and education would eventually experience their inability to meet employer demands. In addition to the declining availability of service-worker jobs, unskilled black men suffered from the aforementioned internationalization of the United States economy. As production, clerical, and unskilled tasks were shipped abroad, undereducated African American males experienced hardships. In nine major cities (Philadelphia, Chicago, Detroit, New York, Los Angeles, Boston, Baltimore, St. Louis, and Houston), for example, jobs traditionally held by high school dropouts declined appreciably.[42] Because education and training became increasingly essential in the international economy, those devoid of the educational background to master new technology and find work joined the ranks of the unemployed. As manual, assembly-line work became passé, the gap between educated and undereducated black men increased exponentially.

Continuing circumstances associated with poverty that kept low-income blacks on the periphery of mainstream America also contributed to a dismally low employment record among impoverished African American men. With a limited work experience and lack of familiarity with the white world, unskilled blacks undergoing job interviews felt inadequate and projected a lack of qualifications to prospective employers. Poor blacks, consequently, failed the subjective tests essential for job placement. Additionally, an understated factor—being external to the network system where jobs became available by word of mouth for white blue-collar workers—kept blacks seeking work outside the traditional employment circuit.[43]

Problems associated with race and class provided a most limiting factor for employing the black masses. Reasons for the disinclination of white employers hiring black men, for instance, ranged from their concern about individual thievery, to indolence, inept language skills, improper character, limited education, failure to pass drug-screening tests, and insolence. If a prospective employee from the inner-city could venture to suburbia for work, a home address located in the ghetto continued to be sufficient for an employer to decline an application.[44]

White employers hardly represented the only people harboring negative views about hiring black men. Even African American employers held misgivings about employing low-income black men. In a candid appraisal of black workers, one African American employer said, "Attitude. Poor attitude . . . . They lazy, a lot of them . . . . I been around them. I know what's happening."[45] Another recognized that poor black men lacked skills, being unable to speak or write properly or dress appropriately. And still others concurred with the negative factors—procrastination, belligerence, indolence, tardiness, absenteeism, and use of illicit drugs—attributed to low-income black men. Indeed, those who witnessed black men hanging on the corner during the work day concluded that black males "don't wanna work" and "don't even try."[46]

Black males even suffered from gender discrimination because prospective employers preferred hiring African American women to men. Black females had better opportunities for finding and retaining jobs because of a perceived constructive work ethic and sense of responsibility. For example, a general manager of a suburban luggage retail store located outside Chicago said, "I think that probably [inner-city black females] are much more responsible . . . they're working two jobs trying to support a family . . . . In many, many cases they're the one that are supporting their four kids and the husband's whereabouts are unknown." Another employer agreed, adding it "has been better with black females . . . than with minority males in terms of the basics—attendance, productivity, [and] work ethic . . . ."[47] Even misgivings about the black female's additional burdens—single-parent child rearing that could detract from work—failed to advantage black males seeking employment.

An additional disadvantage an African American man faced may be attributed to the uneasy relationship between black males and males of different races. White men invariably feared their black counterparts. One white man suggested, "Black men present a particularly menacing demeanor to white men. I think they are frightened by them." Another employer declared, "People are afraid of black men. I would be less afraid of a black woman. I would say . . . maybe he's got a criminal record . . . I would just be a little more apprehensive."[48] And still others suggested that the fear of facing a lawsuit filed by an inept but disgruntled black male employee made white employers wary. Even Latinos and Asians appeared more attractive to white employers than black men.[49]

Employers stigmatized low-income blacks on welfare and dependent upon state employment service programs. Presuming that anyone reduced to the welfare rolls could be deemed indolent and devoid of proper training, employers refrained from acquiring black help. Despite a sincere desire to obtain work, low-income blacks suffered the ignominy of being poor job risks. Consequently, employers seeking workers with literacy, mathematic and basic mechanical ability or amiable personalities, proper grooming, and proper diction would rarely seek low-income black employees.[50]

When white employers hired third-world immigrants to perform unskilled laboring duties, circumstance rather than the fault of African Americans determined who acquired employment. Given the limiting environment of their origins, immigrants retained a greater tolerance for harsh working conditions and lower pay than native-born African Americans. Accustomed to omnipresent poverty, even the most dangerous, boring jobs appeared attractive to immigrants. By contrast, with the endless experience of racial discrimination, blacks felt exploited if they took low-paying, dead-end jobs. Rather than be exploited, African Americans would simply walk off the job and assume providence would provide a means for survival.[51]

When prospects for finding work among the adult-aged population declined, the entire inner-city African American community languished. Those who could move away left behind a young populace who had never worked and possessed few job skills. This, in turn, contributed to the continuous decline in neighborhood institutions—banks, stores, churches, restaurants, gas stations, physicians, legal offices—that traditionally served the black community. But as the lower-class slum expanded, the controls and middle-class value system had been forgotten. Crime and street violence increased, hastening a further demise in the quality of life in black urban America.[52]

The decline in the value of the minimum wage became another unfortunate circumstance that impinged severely upon lower-income blacks. When the federal minimum wage rose from $3.35 in 1981 to $3.85 and eventually $4.25 per hour by the decade's end, the situation seemed to augur well for blacks at the lower end of the pay scale. Unfortunately, the value of the dollar simultaneously declined. Because those at the bottom of the economic ladder in the 1980s earned less real dollars as the decade progressed, the black condition further deteriorated.[53] In short, the minimum wage functioned as a "sub poverty" wage, offering funds far below the economic scale that would enable underprivileged blacks to attain middle-class status.[54]

Restricted job searches that skirted the inner-city also hampered the ability of low-income blacks to find work. By placing advertisements only in mainstream newspapers, blacks became less aware of available jobs. Moreover, public schools responsible for educating inner-city black youths utterly failed to provide the necessary tools that enabled students to find work. Realizing that children of middle-class African Americans who attended private or parochial schools possessed markedly more skills than black public school students, opportunities associated with class rather than race determined who employers would hire.[55]

With suburbia inhospitable and expensive, low-income blacks continued moving into cities. During the 1980s the black urban population increased by at least one-third, comprising nearly six million African Americans. Most of these migrants, however, were poor and became more isolated from the better classes who resided in gentrified communities or on the periphery of the cities.[56] But despite the influx of blacks to metropolitan areas, the population density ironically decreased. While a less dense urban population would suggest a better quality of life, the lower population density resulted in abandoned buildings that housed crack dens and enhanced prospects for a flourishing criminal element.[57]

Black poverty in urban America appeared omnipresent, debilitating cities in the Northeast (Boston, New York, Newark, Philadelphia), Midwest (Cleveland, Detroit, Chicago, Gary), South (Atlanta, New Orleans, Birmingham, Houston), and West (Oakland, Los Angeles). Regardless of region, a consistent urban pathology existed. Augmented crack addiction, homeless people roaming the streets of large cities, and increasing incidences of violent crime rendered inner-city black residential neighborhoods inhospitable.[58] Evidence of the resultant effects of poverty appeared in the daily media. Social scientists Joel Devine and James Wright reported,

> Accounts of well-armed youth gangs shooting it out on the streets without regard for bystanders, assaults perpetrated against students and teachers in their schools, apparently random violence committed by youth "just having fun," street corner murders for Air Jordans or a sports team jacket—all this has become commonplace in the contemporary urban experience and suggests a fundamental erosion of the value of life itself.[59]

This black underclass specifically caused intra-racial class differences to escalate, creating a profound sense of "them" versus "us." Middle-class norms, values, and expectations prescribed that impoverished fathers should pay for their offspring or face incarceration, mothers should work or attend school or lose welfare benefits, and adolescents should study and say no to drugs and unprotected sex.[60] But far more than any previous decade since the civil rights movement of the 1960s, the black poor lost hope and seemed resigned to their lowly status.

The burgeoning crack epidemic of the 1980s proved particularly onerous to inner-city African Americans. In 1974 a coke smuggler based in San Francisco developed the freebase technique of converting powder into rock crystals subsequently known as crack. Easily acquired, distributed, highly addictive, and a means for ambitious but alienated young men to acquire money as drug dealers, crack became a lucrative product sold throughout inner-city America. As crack dealers acquired guns for self-production, life for inner-city blacks became more dangerous. Rising crime and arrests accompanied the crack epidemic, and innocent people sought sanctuary by remaining at home. Consequently, impoverished African Americans became more isolated, and the inner-city black community became increasingly dysfunctional.[61] Problems within urban black communities became a convenient apparatus for conservative whites as Reagan's rhetoric about crime and welfare, and the War on Drugs created ground work for the prison-industrial complex.

Michelle Alexander's insightful book, *The New Jim Crow*, revealed how the Reagan administration used the politics of race—targeting the indigent black community—to denigrate African Americans, minimize the focus on white-collar crime, and increasing expenditures by millions on capturing and imprisoning drug offenders. The not so subtle War on Drugs specifically targeted low-income African Americans who bought and sold crack rather than powdered cocaine. Crack offenders, usually poor and black, received far harsher sentences than white counterparts who indulged in powder cocaine. The hostile view poor whites had toward civil rights, coupled with the need to find work in a struggling economy for whites who could build and man prisons, created a perfect political storm for white conservatives. The American public fixated on black drug users and crime rather than failed inner-city schools, desolate neighborhoods, and avaricious capitalists who fleeced the American public.[62]

In addition to a marked increase of crack cocaine addiction, an escalation of the AIDS epidemic and a sharp rise in the homeless population occurred. Young black women became particularly vulnerable to AIDS as irresponsible men engaged in unprotected sex. Children also became victimized, as single mothers lacked the ability and resources to care for dependent children. While the social malaise attributed to drugs appeared throughout urban America, inner-city blacks found themselves less capable of dealing with the problems that threatened daily survival. Thus, the newly transformed slum became increasingly inhospitable, dangerous, and draining for black people trapped in the tenderloin areas of urban America.[63]

The pejorative aspect of the drug culture contributed indirectly to other asocial manifestations that worked to the disadvantage of black youth. While young men interacted socially as gang members and embraced other pejorative norms disadvantageous to the black community, actions that produced positive outcomes proved conspicuously absent. A disproportionate number of black youths exhibited disdain for a strong work ethic, academic success, authority, filial piety, and other acceptable middle-class norms. Rather, street culture endorsed the avoidance of eye contact, dictated a tough façade and reveled in a misguided pride of anti-intellectualism. While these norms existed as an acceptable means for survival in the so-called hood, in the broader middle-class society, street culture guaranteed failure.[64] Consequently, young black men proved more than three times likely to be on probation or in prison than in college.[65]

A myriad of additional factors kept disadvantaged blacks poor. Collectively, these forces created another perfect storm with human dimensions that caused the black masses to react in an untoward, negative manner.

The lack of equal access to education, employment, and occupational training, coupled with structural, social, and psychological problems, meant that issues negatively affecting the black underclass would persist. Family disorganization, joblessness, drug abuse, and self-hatred represented the low-income black condition within an era comprising the "New American Poverty."[66] Furthermore, the United States military became more selective and no longer existed as a viable option for wayward young black men who required discipline, sought dignity, and longed for a sense of purpose.

The ever-increasing dysfunctional black family contributed to the woeful condition of low-income African Americans. When Daniel Patrick Moynihan published his critique of the black family in 1965, approximately 25 percent of African American births occurred outside the family. By 1980, however, the corresponding percentage of births rose to 43 percent. Equally significant, the numbers of welfare recipients increased, as did unemployment and violent crime.[67] One decade after the demise of the relatively successful civil rights movement, family life for inner-city blacks at once appeared more onerous, feeble, and negligible.

The asocial behavior exhibited by low-income African Americans provided further evidence of the deteriorating family structure. By the mid-1980s, for example, nearly half of all Americans arrested for murder, as well as individuals murdered or who died because of negligent manslaughter, were black. Nearly two of every three persons arrested for robbery were also black. Understandably, incarceration for African Americans proved more than 6 percent higher than for whites. While blacks comprised only 13 percent of the urban population, the race accounted for more than half of the arrests for violent crime and nearly two-thirds of all arrests for robbery.[68]

Violence became particularly problematic when African American males reached adulthood. A large portion of unemployed blacks not only failed to assume adult roles and responsibilities but also exhibited symptoms of juvenile immaturity by engaging in violent crime.[69] And yet, holding legitimate jobs hardly served as a panacea for violence. A survey conducted on young African American males in 1989 found that by a three-to-one ratio, inner-city black men believed they could make more money on the street than engaging in a socially acceptable line of work.[70]

Greatly disturbed by the violence and declining fortunes of the black masses, civil rights leaders blamed the Reagan administration for the race's despicable condition. Urban League director Vernon Jordan professed misgivings about Reagan's conservative agenda, which promised better times but failed to produce the anticipated prosperity. In his keynote address, Jordan "asked the Administration how blacks and the poor were to survive until the President's program produced the prosperity he promised."[71] Executive Director Benjamin Hooks of the NAACP also blamed the president for permitting wide-scale unemployment among blacks and for fomenting a hostile racial environment.[72] Obviously, the trickle-down theory in regard to low-income African Americans or others destabilized by unremitting poverty never worked.

Although the Reagan Republicans provided a convenient target for disgruntled African Americans, black leadership and civil rights organizations could hardly be exempted from blame. Just as Reagan Republicans acted in the best interest of wealthy whites, black leaders correspondingly focused exclusively on the black middle class.[73] Therefore, the *New York Times* could report with confidence that "community activists and others have characterized their national leaders as being out of touch with the masses of blacks and afraid to wage a real fight against injustices for fear of alienating white businesses that provide financial support."[74] Strategies designed to address unemployment, inflation, and narrow the widening fissures between underprivileged African Americans and the black bourgeoisie never materialized.

Influential citizens and institutions failed to pay sufficient attention to the welfare of low-income African American youth. For teenaged girls who had babies, no concerted effort had been made to offer child-rearing training. Moreover, young men who produced children had been given little, if any, sense of responsibility for producing a son or daughter. But perhaps the most insidious and heartless example of indifference toward youth existed in the utilitarian use of black school-age children. Some foster care parents and pharmaceutical companies engaged in practices that placed profit before child welfare. Those who participated in the foster care program and cared primarily for economic gain conceivably created irreparable damage to all children who became experimental guinea pigs. Included among the avaricious foster parents would be those willing to increase their larder by allowing pharmaceutical companies to test new medicines on foster children to receive a financial reward.

A consensus existed regarding flaws in the welfare system that served African Americans. A commissioned study known as the Family Support Act of 1988 declared that welfare should be predicated on reciprocal responsibilities—society is obligated to provide assistance to welfare applicants who, in turn, are obligated to behave in socially endorsed ways—and able-bodied adult welfare recipients should be required to prepare themselves for work.[75] Unfortunately children and dependent mothers suffered grievously as state contributions to AFDC programs declined, rendering the concept of "able-bodied adult welfare" irrelevant.[76]

Budget cuts failed to resolve the problems visited upon underprivileged African Americans. Without money, inner-city black neighborhoods lacked the resource base and necessary institutions required for a self-respecting, productive community. Dysfunctional schools and churches, weak civic clubs, irresponsible political associations, inappropriate business establishments, an absented middle class, and nonexistent mutual-supporting institutions kept low-income people mired in an unhealthy environment. Children and young adults specifically suffered from the lack of facilities that could provide constructive outlets for energetic youths. Concerned parents encountered difficulties when trying to protect their children from the negative aspects of slum life. An inner-city Chicago resident mournfully declared, "Our children . . . seems [sic] to be more at risk than any other children there is, because there's no library for them to go to. There's not a center they can go to, there's no field house that they can go into. There's nothing. There's nothing at all."[77]

Given the accomplishments blacks achieved because of the civil rights movement, the existence of a significantly large African American underclass might appear puzzling. Intractable factors associated with poor people, like geographical concentration, asocial behavior, and chronic dependency, however, meant that class superseded race as an explanation for the downtrodden urban masses.[78] In addition to aforementioned causes for African American poverty, another new element became added to the ranks of the impoverished. The new, more deeply entrenched poverty became localized in inner cities with a pathological bent unlike any previous era. Divine and Wright placed the black underclass of the 1980s in the proper historical perspective by stating,

> The poverty of decades past seems to have been less deeply rooted, less self-destructive, and less socially catastrophic than the poverty of today. It was seemingly more tractable and arose more from the lack of opportunity than from the lack of determination to succeed in socially acceptable terms. The labor market and familial dislocations associated with the old poverty were more understandable, if no less invidious, than the forces at work today. The old poverty seemed more temporary, more amenable to intervention, and less likely to lead to personal and social devastation.[79]

Only low-income blacks who acquired some experiences outside the confining slum could explain their plight on conditions fostered by the larger outside society. But those who had difficulty finding steady work—victims of chronic unemployment—had only a partial understanding of delimiting forces at work that shaped their lives. Additionally, when blacks found low-paying jobs, dissatisfaction invariably resulted. Men erroneously decided that dignity trumped work and refused to accept low-paying jobs. For some hardened people, risking incarceration seemed preferable to working on demeaning jobs without sufficient recompense.[80]

Lacking proper black institutional support, underprivileged African Americans became more engaged in self-defeating behavior. Since inner-city blacks had little contact with white people, whites had no direct responsibility for the dire situation of the African American masses. Many discerning African Americans blamed their sordid circumstances on their own race. Believing upward mobility to be a personal matter, a segment of the black population in inner-city Chicago, for example, failed to understand the concept of racial inequality or other limiting factors that rendered blacks destitute.[81]

As late as the 1980s the Southern, rural or small-town American lifestyle failed to prepare children for the mean streets of the inner city. Parents and grandparents rooted in the South held perceptions on the value of education and religion that proved limiting to boys and girls who functioned in urban slums. While ambitious blacks from older generations sincerely believed upward mobility could be achieved through education and religion, disadvantages inherent in inner-city schools inhibited prospects for success.[82] Parents and grandparents failed to transcend the obstacles that prevented children from attaining success in schools. Parents who embraced the church as an institution that enhanced their child's prospects for success failed to recognize the allure of the streets transcended choir practice and the admonitions of a preacher's message.

Another factor that resulted in limited advancement during the 1980s (but could be applicable to any decade) occurred with the reluctance of impoverished youngsters to attend school or church because of threadbare clothing. An embarrassing appearance meant that self-respecting but unkempt young people chose not to attend school or church. This problem, added to the aforementioned delimiting issues with religious and educational institutions, prevented black youth from securing a proper educational and moral compass. Understandably, four large inner-city public high schools in 1980s Chicago graduated only 15 to 30 percent of their students.[83] The quest for money caused concerned but imperfect parents to engage in questionable activities inimical to family life. If poverty caused parents to steal, fence items, sell drugs, or engage in other nefarious acts, arrests and incarceration seemed inevitable. Given the omnipresence of poverty and the accompanying malaise endemic in downtrodden people, even responsible parents could resort to crime to provide for their family. Parents who took extreme risks on behalf of their family invariably failed because incarceration rendered caring for children impossible.[84]

If parents engaged in nefarious activities, adolescents found credence for asocial behavior in gangsta rap lyrics. By the 1980s, gagsta rap became incorporated into the hip-hop culture. This West Coast musical expression emerged as a medium that disparaged women, promoted male bravado, spewed hatred toward law enforcement, and offered utter contempt for mainstream society. In 1984 KDAY of Los Angeles became the first recognized rap radio station.[85] Songs like "Batter Ram" and "Cabbage Patch," and a fledgling group from Compton, California, that adopted the name Niggaz With Attitudes (NWA) provided lyrics on police brutality, joblessness, and other societal ills associated with poverty.[86]

Emboldened black youths acted out rap lyrics, evidenced by increased incidences of illegitimate children, continuous gang warfare, and constant run-ins with the police.[87] Los Angles in particular witnessed an augmentation of negative gang activity. Gang deaths increased from 168 in 1977 to 515 in 1989, with robberies, assaults, and murders up 12, 25, and 50 percent respectively.[88]

Unfortunately, low-income hip-hop artists who spoke on behalf of disadvantaged blacks failed to generate national enthusiasm for addressing the plight inherent in inner-city slums. While rappers like Ice-T, Ice Cube, Dr. Dre, and others gained fame and fortune, the black masses remained poor and dissolute. Rappers spoke angrily of black degradation to a welcome audience that appreciated the rhymes and lyrics projected through hip-hop. Those in decision-making capacities, however, failed to hear the messages. A destitute, frustrated, and irrelevant underprivileged black populace not only remained inviolate but also became more isolated in ever-increasing, sprawling, impoverished, segregated neighborhoods.[89]

The New Federalism instituted by President Reagan and continued under the newly elected George Herbert Walker Bush sharply diminished federal aid to cities. General revenue sharing, urban mass transit, job training, public service employment, local public works, economic development assistance, compensatory education, and other altruistic endeavors were reduced or eliminated. Unfortunately for the inner-city masses, the federal contribution to urban budgets declined from 18 percent in 1980 to 6.4 percent by 1990. The devastating impact of Reagan and Bush policies created an urban fiscal crisis and caused major cities to become severely underserved. Consequently, the financial well-being of low-income blacks declined significantly, and the level of family poverty increased. Approximately half of all low-income African Americans fell below the poverty line.[90]

While the presidencies of Reagan and Bush proved inimical to Northern black urbanites, the condition of African Americans in the urban South appeared equally egregious. Rooted in historical racism and a meager industrial base, low-income black Southerners experienced endemic regional poverty that engulfed a higher percentage of African Americans. Equally distressing, impoverished Southern blacks functioned under a less developed welfare system and suffered accordingly from insurmountable problems.[91] Reductions in municipal services and programs severely hurt those in most need of assistance. No longer interested in finding solutions to urban poverty, policy makers focused on isolating the black poor at the minimal cost to the public.[92]

The conservative Reagan and Bush administrations severely damaged low-income African Americans and did little to address the revenue crises devastating institutions that served the urban black poor. Their collective actions undermined service agencies designed to improve the quality of life for disadvantaged blacks and limited any chance for the impoverished masses to benefit from gains achieved during the civil rights movement.[93]

Chapter 11

Lost and Forlorn: The 1990s

At the close of the twentieth century, a confluence of negative factors impacted the lowest level of African American society. Racism had spawned generations of continuous poverty that wreaked havoc on black people reduced to living in urban slums. Prospects of returning to the hospitable, familial comforts of the rural South became severely eroded as discriminatory practices of the United States Department of Agriculture enabled avaricious whites to seize land owned by African American farmers.[1] Additionally, insensitivity toward African Americans promulgated by Newt Gingrich through the Republican Party's Contract with America excluded impoverished blacks from receiving any ameliorative consideration from economic policies instituted by Congress.[2] Low-income blacks were also excluded from the booming economy of the 1990s because postindustrial America had few jobs for unskilled and undertrained workers.[3] Scores of marginally skilled men and women unfamiliar with work and the work ethic, and already irrelevant in the new global economy, faced diminishing options for survival. Once again, omnipresent poverty caused many counted among the black masses—those comprising the designated underclass—to make illogical decisions detrimental to their self-interests.[4]

Poverty within the United States transcended race and impacted blacks and whites alike. Both races experienced the pangs of indebtedness, dysfunctional families, physical abuse, alcoholism, and the absence of resources essential for a middle-class lifestyle. Initial reflections on the demographic locale of impoverished Americans suggested that low-income blacks could fare better than white counterparts. African American poverty existed in the more urbane sophisticated metropolitan communities while impoverished whites resided in relatively backward rural areas. Logically, poor blacks should have been better capable of meeting job demands inherent in postindustrial America. And yet, pronounced differences existed between the races that placed blacks at a disadvantage. While poor white men maintained constant concerns about being laid off from jobs, many comparable blacks never experienced work.[5]

Ironically the black underclass's economic nadir occurred when the United States became the world's sole superpower. Propitious prospects appeared to await average Americans. The Soviet Union collapsed. The national economy of the United States increased exponentially. Rising family incomes, low unemployment, a shrinking federal deficit, and state budget surpluses represented unprecedented economic successes that fostered a strong sense of nationalism.[6] However, excesses of the 1990s—evident in the growth of high-tech industries, the policies of market extremism, politics dominated through the use of campaign contributions, and unbridled speculation—enabled enterprising and ruthless individuals to make fortunes.[7] The prosperity concentrated among the elite, unfortunately, never trickled down to the black masses. The focus on wealth rather than poverty would have ominous consequences for marginalized African Americans.

In part, economic problems African Americans encountered could be traced directly to the administrations of Ronald Regan and George Herbert Walker Bush. Because economic programs initiated by President Nixon continued under Presidents Reagan and Bush, corporations engaged in multinational thinking instead of acting in the interest of average Americans. Jobs would be shipped overseas to take advantage of reduced laboring costs. This, in turn, reduced employment in the United States and lowered the tax base necessary to provide services for impoverished American citizens. In addition to corporations, banks also acted with avaricious independence. Bankers demonstrated little concern for downtrodden people who struggled to survive during President George H. W. Bush's term in office. Rather than being accountable to the people or elected representatives, central bankers answered solely to boards of directors dominated by wealthy elites who dominated the political and economic landscape.

Republicans ignored the damage Reaganomics inflicted upon the poor and depicted President Reagan as the paragon of strong, dedicated leadership that Bush would emulate. Moreover, George H. W. Bush ran on the coattails of the Great Communicator. When campaigning as the Republican candidate for president, Bush, like Reagan, presented African Americans in a sinister light. Bush used Willie Horton, a released parolee who committed a murder, for an infamous advertisement that implied African Americans were lawless, vicious, and must be controlled by a stern, no-nonsense administration.

But while Presidents Reagan and Bush successfully typecast black men as public villains, impoverished, defenseless members of the race languish. African American children in particular suffered inconspicuously. By 1990 black children were three times more inclined to be impoverished than white peers, and two of three were born to single mothers.[8] Political expediency suggested that sympathy would not be accorded downtrodden blacks during the administrations of Ronald Reagan and George H. W. Bush.[9]

President Clinton never deviated from the conservative mantra established by the Reagan administration that focused more on augmenting wealth than mitigating poverty.[10] Clinton accepted the concept that people have low incomes because of insufficient training and skills. Unfortunately, the president failed to address the long-existing reality that women and minorities performing comparable work received lower wages than white men engaged in identical tasks. No Clintonites in the administration worked assiduously to achieve gender and racial equity for low-income African American men and women.[11]

Indeed, an unspoken theory evolved that suggested Presidents Reagan, George H.W. Bush, and Clinton believed unemployed people aided the economy.[12] During Clinton's presidency Alan Greenspan, head of the Federal Reserve Board, contended that limited inflation helped the economy and served the interests of corporate America. Equally significant, Greenspan also sought to maintain sufficient numbers of unemployed people to limit the ability of labor to bargain effectively with management. Because jobless people eagerly accepted low salaries to acquire work, business interests remained hegemonic.

Ever the political pragmatist, Clinton introduced government-sponsored social programs to recapture Reagan Democrats after the 1992 presidential election. After gaining the White House, the following year Clinton endeavored to institute a health care program. He also supported the expansion of the Earned Income Tax Credit to provide more money for low-income workers. But as Clinton supported progressive tax hikes for the wealthiest Americans, he failed to achieve health reform. Clinton's policies fell far short of goals designed to help the downtrodden. Furthermore, Clinton and his Council of Economic advisors believed that the United States needed to keep seven to eight million people unemployed to maintain a solvent economy.

Further evidence of the Reagan administration's influence on the Clinton presidency appeared when Clinton failed to ridicule the Great Communicator's concept of poverty. Reagan believed that poverty stemmed from cultural and social flaws inherent in poor people rather than low wages, unemployment, or demeaning factors comprising classism, sexism, and racism.[13] Reagan conservatives ignored the lifesaving benefits of welfare programs and, instead, exaggerated the weaknesses of welfare and contended that public assistance contributed to absentee fathers, indolence, and irresponsibility. By inadequately addressing and refuting welfare critics, Clinton appeared more an enabler for the conservative agenda than as an altruistic, progressive leader seeking to enhance opportunities for downtrodden Americans.

Despite his conservative inclinations, Clinton arguably became the African American community's most popular United States president since Franklin Delano Roosevelt. As a native-born Arkansan, Rhodes Scholar, and with experience in the governor's office, Clinton ran on a platform of welfare reform. His position compared favorably with the tax-adverse middle class who bristled at the thought that their hard-earned capital supported the unemployed, indolent, irresponsible adults who gave birth to numerous children and survived on welfare.[14] Despite evidence that the military industrial complex engaged in excessive spending, the media and political leaders focused on the perception that able-bodied unwed black women received money to stay home, care for their children, and bask in luxury provided by the federal dole.[15]

Unlike his predecessors, President Clinton's strong identification with African Americans suggested prospects for economic assistance would be rendered to downtrodden blacks. Clinton played the saxophone, claimed former Urban League director Vernon Jordan as one of his best friends, and projected serenity and comfort when photographed attending services in black churches. Despite Southern roots as an Arkansan raised under modest circumstances, Clinton presented a unique identification with the black masses that appeared unparalleled in the annals of the United States presidency. Moreover, President Clinton gained popularity from the economic boom that occurred during his first term in office. Bolstered by a soaring stock market, consumer confidence increased. Technological developments in the Silicon Valley of California and optimism promulgated by the Federal Reserve Board added to Clinton's mystique as a popular leader. Blacks, therefore, felt comfortable designating Clinton as the first "black president."

Unfortunately for low-income blacks, Clinton's embrace of late-twentieth-century negritude provided little succor for downtrodden African Americans. Blacks simply failed to benefit from the good fortunes of the national economy. The economic distinction between the wealthy and the poor of the 1990s differed little from the class and race differences that prevailed during the Great Society of the 1960s. Deeply entrenched inequities in regard to privilege and class remained. Civil rights activists, political leaders, the courts, and unions charged with enhancing prospects for African American employment failed to alter the prevailing poverty that existed in black slums. As before, wealth remained concentrated within the hands of plutocratic elites. Unemployment and residence in depressed areas, coupled with an increasing number of female-headed households, spelled economic disaster for underprivileged African Americans.[16]

Clinton alone could hardly be blamed for the continuing plight of African Americans. Even before he became president, Congress decided to abdicate its responsibility for assisting impoverished Americans. Although Congress overwhelmingly supported the Family Support Act of 1988 that provided the illusion of welfare reform, sufficient funding never reached job-training centers. Problems associated with public assistance continued into Clinton's first term in office. Conservative, hard-working Americans still resented tax money going to "lazy" people who acquired assistance through the AFDC. Republicans and Democrats alike agreed to limit six decades of federal funding for downtrodden single-parent households, enabling Clinton to reduce welfare expenditures.[17] But again, the intended goal of moving people from welfare to work failed. Blacks specifically suffered from governmental policies that cut assistance programs to the extreme detriment of dependent people.[18] The customary reluctance of wealthier people to pay taxes and use funds to ameliorate the condition of the downtrodden persisted.

By 1994 the dire situation low-income blacks encountered became abundantly clear through the proceedings of an international conference. In that year Detroit hosted the Group Seven (G-7) conference, an international gathering that focused on job procurement. Attendees from the United States, United Kingdom, Germany, Canada, France, Italy, and Japan recognized the necessity for finding work for the least-skilled members of their respective countries. Group Seven leaders also understood that a widening gap existed between skilled and unskilled workers, and that a strong relationship existed between low paying jobs, unemployment, and low levels of education.[19]

Three fundamental differences, however, appeared in the conference involving G-7 nations and the United States. First, other countries placed a higher premium on educating their populace to meet national standards. Second, the United States allowed for an unequal distribution of funds and resources between schools located in wealthy, as opposed to poor, areas. And third, African Americans who comprised the largest per capita percentage of a young, marginally educated potential work force, displayed—by personal choice or circumstance—a general disdain for education.[20] Collectively, the United States government and African Americans disinclined to embrace education ensured that a large segment of the black population would remain economically disadvantaged. Without obtaining a proper education, unemployment among low-income African Americans at the dawn of the twenty-first century would continue.

Although the most prominent leader at the G-7 Conference, Clinton proved reticent to make suggestions to other nations given the economic problems associated with impoverished African Americans at home. Rather than presenting a sweeping educational program targeting the least employable members of society, the president decided to appease welfare critics. On August 22, 1996, Clinton signed into law the Personal Responsibility and Work Opportunity Reconciliation Act (PRWORA). Using the Temporary Assistance for Needy Families (TANF) as a foundation, PRWORA replaced Aid to Families with Dependent Children, the federally funded block grant program designed to aid indigent parents. The new program limited the federal government's financial assistance program for families to five years and required that 80 percent of the families receiving welfare must find employment.[21] African Americans mired in poverty for generations became accustomed to cashing welfare checks without being required to perform some kind of compensatory work. Presidential sensitivity toward the indigent no longer applied. Without a sense of responsibility, the future looked dim for those who failed to adjust to new government strictures.

President Clinton's solution for resolving problems associated with welfare encountered difficulties from both the public and private sectors. Public challenges existed with state administrators who had to devise plans to help the working poor make progress in the labor market. Public officials also needed to make concerted efforts to help the "hard to employ" left behind by stringent welfare reform find and retain work.[22] In the private sector, a serious flaw surfaced in the aforementioned TANF program. Businesses insisted paying their unskilled employees low wages. Employers, therefore, appeared loath to pay more money to TANF recipients than for undocumented aliens. Businesses, moreover, existed to procure high profit margins rather than engaging in altruistic policies designed to provide wage earners in destitute families with a bountiful income.

Unwittingly President Clinton signed a flawed document. Full-time minimum-wage incomes earned by families under TANF stipulations failed to provide sufficient funds to care for a parent with two children.[23] Those who had administrative responsibility for TANF also failed to recognize that some parents could not acquire gainful employment because of extenuating circumstances. Parents with physical, emotional, or mental disabilities experienced continuous unemployment. Similarly, those with drug problems and prison records would have difficulty qualifying for job programs. Other challenging factors including transportation difficulties, the needs of special children, low basic skills, learning disabilities, and other problems meant some parents simply proved unemployable. Obviously, if the fortunes of parents with children had been sound, the family would hardly experience penury and be forced to rely on public assistance. Destitute parents with children on the edge of survival remained vulnerable to the capricious actions of federal and state administrators.

Given the problems that accrued for administering TANF policies, at best, welfare reform seemed feasible only when the nation experienced a bullish economy. When an economic recession occurred, local and state governments lacked sufficient resources to sustain destitute families. Again, African Americans would have cause to believe the impersonality of the welfare system worked to the disadvantage of their race. Unlike the Great Depression refrain that lamented "blacks were the last hired and first fired," a more contemporary slogan would proclaim that during the 1990s, impoverished "blacks were not hired at all."

With the focus on lowering taxes while simultaneously maintaining and generating wealth, an unfortunate misconception occurred that equated a booming economy with eliminating poverty. When the economy entered a recession, the government focused on protecting corporate America rather than the general public. While corporations received tax breaks and subsidies and executives benefited from inflated salaries, low-end employees experienced layoffs and faced permanent dismissals. Every person who lost a job meant a reduction in tax dollars essential to the survival of desperate African Americans.[24] In 1990, for example, six hundred thousand families declared bankruptcy while corporate executives took the opportunity to make additional cutbacks known as downsizing. Thus, when managers, technicians, and other professionals lost jobs, the plight of marginal workers and impoverished Americans would certainly be ignored.[25] Republicans and Democrats alike focused on stock market successes on Wall Street and the effect of rising interest rates and its impact on the economy rather than concentrate on disseminating some wealth among the poor.

The booming economy that occurred during the closing years of Clinton's administration had little impact on low-income African Americans. Without jobs or prospects for work, the pattern of black unemployment continued without pause. At least two of every three jobs in this decade required computer knowledge. Since only 35 percent of African American youths had access to computers at school, employment prospects for low-income blacks appeared worse than bleak.[26] Even blacks who remained in school and obtained a high school diploma experienced difficulty finding work. Few Fortune 500 companies hired high school graduates in entry-level jobs with growth opportunities. Youths of all races faced the problem of transitioning from school to work. Young blacks suffered most severely, however, from joblessness regardless of educational successes in school.[27]

Perhaps one of the most important factors derived from poverty within the young, black urban lower class existed in what may be deemed an irrational, oppositional, cultural mind-set. Young, inner-city African Americans still appeared profoundly irresponsible, demonstrating little concern for themselves or anyone else. And some self-indulgent low-income black males continued behaving irresponsibly in regard to young women. Boasting a legendary but unsavory reputation for impregnating females—and demonstrating little concern for the child—these males garnered self-esteem by demonstrating their ability to procreate. This pattern became particularly disturbing when a man would impregnate several different women. Committing a manly act without heeding the responsibilities of fatherhood could be deemed primitive, selfish, and unwarranted.[28] Girls of child-producing age who became pregn. also seemed reckless. Rather than obtain proper medical care or seek abortions, the overwhelming need for unconditional love propelled young women to carry children to full term.[29] Since the 1990s, moreover, black females registered the greatest incidence of AIDS than any other race or gender in the nation and became victimized by male partners.[30] Although most black women invariably gave birth to healthy children, an impoverished mother often lacked proper prenatal care and had limited opportunities to provide for a child born into disadvantageous circumstances.

Although the proclivity of black males to disseminate their seed epitomized self-aggrandizement, these actions also resulted in personal self-destruction. More young black men between eighteen and twenty-four died from violence than accidents, disease, or suicide.[31] Teen aged males engaged in mutual killing over drug trafficking, perceived slights, women, and other factors that promoted a singularly mean and selfish disposition. Young black males, unfortunately, became recognized as predators of the inner cities that would victimize people regardless of race, gender, age, creed, or color.[32]

Low-income black neighborhoods lacked sufficient numbers of ameliorative institutions to move impoverished African Americans in a positive direction. Concomitant with the breakdown of the impoverished black nuclear family, service institutions became more irrelevant. Dysfunctional schools, the declining significance of black churches, the decreasing importance of the YMCAs and YWCAs, and limited space for constructive recreational activities caused youthful African Americans to gravitate toward entities providing excitement and escape from a desultory existence.

Failed institutions contributed to scores of impressionistic young men joining gangs.[33] Gangs and gang warfare embodied by the Crips, for example, represented one of most violent functioning gangs in the United States. Founded in Los Angeles in 1969 by fifteen- and sixteen-year-old adolescents Raymond Washington and Stanley "Tookei" Williams, the group became originally known as the Avenues. Names later ascribed to the organization included Baby Avenues and Avenue Crips until finally the club settled on the name Crips. Initially, the gang served as a safety unit designed to protect members from the harsh aspects of slum life. Modeled after the Black Panthers of the 1960s, the fledgling organization evolved from a socially conscious club and protective entity to a drug-dealing, corrupt, underworld-extortion-oriented band that used violence to intimidate and promote the organization's interests.[33]

By the late 1990s, in Los Angeles County alone, nearly two hundred Crips and Crips affiliates existed. Eventually, cells evolved in New York, New Jersey, North Carolina, Georgia, Connecticut, Florida, Pennsylvania, and even extended to foreign countries like Belize.[35] The organization boasted between thirty thousand and thirty-five thousand members nationwide who acquired ng crack cocaine and participating in other illicit activities. urly disposition, intimidating presence, participating in wanton having a callous indifference toward taking a life, the Crips w socially redeeming qualities.

Wh... ome who joined gangs were coerced into becoming members for reasons of personal safety, others volunteered for membership because of an aberration known as the Antisocial Personality Disorder (APD).

Someone with APD—defined by the American Psychiatric Association as an individual with a pervasive pattern of disregard for, and violation of, the rights of others—easily became incorporated into the brutal gang lifestyle. Because only three of the seven diagnosed symptoms of APD identified an individual as being psychologically unbalanced, many members of violent gangs easily qualified as having the disorder. Discernable symptoms of APD comprised the following:

1. Failure to conform to social norms with respect to lawful behaviors as indicated by repeatedly performing acts determining grounds for arrest
2. Deceitfulness, as indicated by repeatedly lying, use of aliases, or conning others for personal profit or pleasure
3. Impulsivity or failure to plan ahead
4. Irritability and aggressiveness, as indicated by repeated physical fights or assaults
5. Reckless disregard for the safety of self or others
6. Consistent irresponsibility, as indicated by repeated failure to sustain consistent work behavior or honor financial obligations
7. Lack of remorse as indicated by being indifferent to or rationalizing having hurt, mistreated, or stolen from another[35]

If youth with gang affiliations failed to extract themselves from the destructive aspects of a delimiting environment replete with asocial norms, few prospects for a propitious future existed. Without the skills, training, and the ability to obtain a respectable job, gang members sought immediate gratification by taking risks to obtain easy money. Positive influences acquired through education and obtaining entry-level jobs offering the necessary experience to garner better positions and higher wages had no meaning for those with APD.[37] Instead, gang members derived pleasure by using drugs and alcohol, engaging in vandalism, and warring against rivals rather than enjoying satisfaction derived from endeavoring to acquire a useful education and obtaining gainful but legal employment. While biological or genetic factors may be deemed responsible for the asocial norms evident among some black youths, environmental factors also caused aberrant behavior. A dysfunctional home life and a sordid lifestyle caused many young men to be drawn into questionable and devious acts.[38] Circumstances far beyond the comprehension of middle-class Americans created monsters that dwelled in the squalor of inner-city slums.

Meanwhile the Clinton administration perpetuated the prison-industrial complex, a policy designed to supply prisons with low-income blacks to fuel the economy. Federal expenditures on prisons increased on Clinton's watch, rising from $4 billion in 1975 to $50 billion by 1996.[39]

The tragic life and brutality evident in Willie Bosket, the most heinous criminal in the history of New York provided evidence that exemplified the extreme behavior of a family beyond redemption and provided evidence for a need to incarcerate felons with APD. Having been incarcerated several times, Willie's father, Butch Bosket, craved excitement, took risks, killed several people, and subsequently avoided imprisonment by committing suicide.[40] Willie Bosket's highly stressed mother was five months pregnant and jobless when the police initially arrested her husband. Depressed and lonely, she demonstrated coolness toward her unborn child that might have injected harmful chemicals to the unborn fetus that would have damaging consequences for the baby.[41] Almost immediately, the newly born child displayed an active mind and, soon, would demonstrate a penchant for impulsive behavior that would classify him as APD. Consequently, as an adult the extremely compulsive Willie Boskett committed mayhem and eventually murder. After being incarcerated, he purposely clashed with guards and intended to martyr himself as a victim of the system. Willie Bosket received a sentence that confined him to prison for the remainder of his natural life.[42]

Although the Rosa Lee Cunningham family of Washington, DC, never displayed the propensity for violence comparable to the Bosketts, their story represented a sorrowful example of African American destitution. Three generations of poverty, drug use, and an array of welfare-dependent criminals reinforced, in middle-class society, the unfortunate folkways and mores of the black underclass. Born into a North Carolina sharecropping family and illiterate, Rosa Lee Cunningham had eight children by five different men. She raised the children by herself and survived by selling drugs, shoplifting, and working as a prostitute. Despite noble efforts to care for her children, six had prison records, five became addicted to heroin or cocaine, and two contracted AIDS. Rosa Lee taught her children to steal, permitted an eleven-year-old daughter to sell her body, and engaged in parental drug abuse. And to complete the level of degradation experienced by the family, the older son succumbs to AIDS, the elder daughter served time for conspiracy in a murder, a grandson received imprisonment for armed robbery, and Rose Lee Cunningham died at fifty-eight for engaging in a dissipated lifestyle.[43]

The Caples family of Chicago and Milwaukee represented another sad saga that represented African American misfortunes attributed to poverty, a dysfunctional family life, and the constant quest for survival. This family comprised ten children and three adult women who left Chicago for Milwaukee in order to benefit from the lower cost of living and more generous welfare benefits offered in the Badger State. Cousins Angie Jobe and Jewell Reed bluntly stated, "We came up here [Milwaukee] because the aid in Chicago wasn't nowhere as much as it was up here . . . . We were figuring out how we were gonna pay our bills." Opal Caples had six children by several different men. And because of a ten-year crack habit, the fifth and sixth children tested positive for cocaine. Eventually the state severed Opal Caples's parental rights. Unfortunately the usual pitfalls that confined destitute families to poverty—teenage girls producing babies, drug and alcohol abuse, constant fights, unemployment, the absence of a father figure—meant that this family comprised primarily of women survived by any means necessary. Even those who worked remained poor. As a mother, Angie Job found a job that enabled her to leave the welfare rolls. Financial independence, however, resulted in higher expenses, a loss of health insurance, and, when illness occurred, greater indebtedness to doctors and hospitals that resulted in garnished wages that plunged the family into greater debt.[44] The family shoveled sand from the pit only to be inundated by granules returning to the original, excavated hole.

While African American women and children suffered egregiously from poverty, psychologically the disillusion of black men devoid of hope might have been even more severe. Several measures of true disadvantage impacted black males that contributed to higher homicide rates than for white and Latino counterparts. Negativity in regard to family structure, unemployment, poverty, and unequal income distribution, young black men participated in callous indifference toward others and displayed anger impossible to contain. In 1990 the average black homicide rate was listed at 33.7 per 100,000, eight times that of whites (4.3 per 100,000) and nearly three times greater than Latinos (12.4 per 100,000).[45] By 1996, when 1.5 million people were incarcerated in federal, state, and municipal prisons throughout the United States, African American males represented a disproportionate number of inmates. Harsh legacies inherent in African American life that comprised slavery, sharecropping, racial discrimination, and poverty continued unabated at the dawn of the new millennium.[46]

In addition to the omnipresence of violence, black slum residents also became victimized by black and white leaders who failed to address the mundane needs of impoverished African Americans. White racism persisted, evidenced by meager resources being directed to needy inner-city black residents. Virtually every major city in the United States, however, had recently been headed by an African American mayor. Nevertheless, municipal leaders regardless of race permitted run-down schools to exist. In addition, the so-called tenderloin neighborhoods had less than satisfactory trash collection and street-cleaning services. These shortcomings, coupled with the proliferation of low quality store-front businesses and liquor stores, suggested that long-standing practices inimical to impoverished blacks residing in low-income neighborhoods continued uninterrupted.

Race-conscious African Americans who lamented the dissolute condition of the black masses had justifiable cause for concern. An African American community developer from Chicago's South Side said, "It's hard to maintain the high lofty goals you have for yourself when this abject poverty is all around you." Social scientist William Julius Wilson underscored problems associated with poverty, noting that "the middle-class residents of the South Side are much more likely to be exposed to crime and other manifestations of social dislocation and social problems." But perhaps the most candid declaration of urban pathos came from a twenty-eight-year-old former gang member from the Woodlawn section of Chicago who discussed the fragility of life in the low-income black community by stating, "Everybody in d'ghetto frustrated . . . nigga, I'mma kill ya" existed as a common phrase.[47]

African American poverty also existed in the rural reaches of society where blacks were disadvantaged when compared with white peers. In 1990 only 6 percent of farm laborers were African American, but the incidence of poverty among black farmers reached 33.9 percent as opposed to 22.4 percent for whites.[48] Older established blacks, moreover, proved three times more likely to be impoverished than whites. Of course, unemployment statistics for young black men proved outrageously high when compared with white peers.[49]

Some challenges the black underclass experienced, particularly in the area of health, could be attributed to both innocence and ignorance. Low-income African Americans unconsciously engaged in unhealthy dietary practices. Those who failed to complete high school had less access to nutritional information. A correlation, therefore, existed between the number of years in school completed and the health and nutritional status of impoverished African Americans. Consequently, a disproportionately high number of low-income African Americans appeared more prone to consume foods high in calories.[50] Fruits, leafy vegetables, and whole grains seldom replaced fried foods and starches as staple diets in African American households. Moreover, Southern-based soul food like fried chicken, mashed potatoes, grits, pork, fruit cobblers, and other sugar-laden desserts—tasty but high in cholesterol—appeared as standard fare in scores of low-income African American households.[51]

Equally problematic, a disproportionately high number of popular fast-food chains existed in black neighborhoods. The easy accessibility and convenience of fast foods, combined with relatively inexpensive costs of this popular, tasty fare, enabled the black populace to consume food responsible for creating excessive obesity. While commercial retailers could hardly be blamed for generating wealth by making fast food available to the public, these retail outlets undermined the health of low-income African Americans.[52] Unfortunately black leaders failed to make a concerted effort to enlighten and alter the dietary practices of low-income blacks.

Within the impoverished black community a relationship existed between diet, poverty, and high mortality rates. Indeed, between 1990 and 2000, African Americans, more than any other race, consistently lived below the poverty line, a factor that had a deleterious impact on the race's health.[53] During the 1990s, African American mortality proved 30 percent higher than deaths among whites. Deaths attributed to obesity, heart disease, cancer, high blood pressure, strokes, kidney disease, and diabetes impacted impoverished black communities throughout the nation.

An additional factor that endangered the health of dissolute blacks appeared in the dearth of exercise. The paucity of parks, playgrounds, and recreational facilities in black slums heightened prospects for an increase in obesity, a scourge particularly visited among black women. Disinclined to exercise and addicted to consuming fast foods, more black women displayed a propensity to become obese than any other race or gender in the nation.[54] Since black women headed many low-income households, improper dietary habits and the inability to secure proper health care impacted an entire family.

Given the difficulty black mothers experienced in obtaining proper health care, high rates of black infant mortality occurred. In 1986, for example, a black infant proved more likely to die within the year than a white child. Similar findings appeared in regard to black and white infants in birth weight. During the 1990s, black mothers remained less likely to receive prenatal care and often failed to initiate care procedures until the last trimester, if at all. Understandably, black infant mortality rates remained higher than for whites through the end of the century.[55]

The unhealthy status of impoverished African Americans could also be attributed to insufficient access to clinics, hospitals, nurses, physicians, and other health providers. Although the civil rights movement of the 1960s removed visible racial and ethnic barriers, the movement had far less bearing upon black health conditions. Anti-affirmative action dictums enforced in California, for example, resulted in a lower number of trained black physicians to cater to the health needs of marginalized African American communities.[56] Impoverished African Americans residing in cities throughout the United States, as well as those who resided in the rural South, also suffered grievously because of inadequate health care. Former surgeon-general David Hatcher lamented that eighty-five thousand fewer blacks would have died if access to proper health care for the race existed.[57]

The difficulty in securing health insurance became particularly problematic for African Americans. Quests to obtain proper health insurance became the new civil rights struggle. Decidedly fewer blacks than whites had health insurance, and far fewer African Americans than whites visited physicians with any regularity. Only 58 percent of blacks under sixty-five had private health insurance as opposed to 79 percent for whites. Nearly one-fourth of African Americans as opposed to 12 percent of European Americans failed to carry health insurance.[58] Because the health-care system functioned primarily for privileged citizens, impoverished Americans generally, and blacks in particular, placed themselves and their families at risk. In 1984, for instance, thirty-five million Americans lacked insurance, one-third of who were children. Of this number, black children comprised approximately one-fourth or 2.5 million of the uninsured citizens. As years passed the numbers of uninsured Americans under age sixty-five increased, climbing to forty-four million and comprising 43 percent of the African American population by the close of the century.[59] Few among the African American poor held jobs, and even less worked for companies that provided health insurance packages to employees.

Because the health-care system determined the quality of service based on race, socioeconomic status, and geographical location, a significant number of low-income African Americans died prematurely. Heart disease killed one hundred thousand blacks annually four years into the first millennium. At least 41 percent of black men and 40 percent of black women, as opposed to 30 and 24 percent respectively for white men and women, succumbed to heart failure.[60] Similar foreboding statistics existed regarding black deaths attributed to cancer. African Americans who succumbed to lung, breast, and prostate cancer far outpaced the percentages of deaths registered for whites. Several factors contributed to high black mortality rates. Dangerous, air-polluted jobs, high-fat / low-fiber diets, late diagnosis, disparities in medical treatment, unrestricted tobacco advertisements in black neighborhoods, and obesity caused impoverished blacks to die at an increased rate from cancer.[61] Likewise, insufficient information about AIDS prevention impacted the black community. While African Americans comprised only 13 percent of the population on the eve of the twenty-first century, AIDS infection among blacks was diagnosed as being ten times higher than for whites.[62]

In part, the abnormally high African American rates of death to cancer and AIDS may be attributed to self-hatred and/or purposeful denial. Southern blacks particularly suffered from high incidences of AIDS because of poverty and cultural norms.[63] Strong religious principles prevented Southerners from openly discussing sexual practices. This lack of communication, consequently, resulted in one of six black Southerners living below the poverty line being infected with AIDS. In addition, seven of the fifteen Southern states experienced the highest rate of unemployment in the nation, and nine of the states had the fewest number of high school graduates. In many respects, Southern poverty and pride prevented black Southerners from dealing effectively with AIDS, other communicable diseases, and mental illness.[64]

Despite the lowly condition of disadvantaged African Americans, Clinton's popularity with black people during the 1990s became legendary. Given the limited effort of his administration to help impoverished blacks, the positive Clinton mystique seemed surprising. Clinton not only failed to advocate on behalf of a poverty program, but, more significantly, also presided during a time when low-income blacks fared worse than at any time since the post–civil rights era. According to a United Nations report, "the life expectancy for a black man in Harlem was forty-six years, less than that in Cambodia or the Sudan."[65] Economic inequalities certainly existed. Nevertheless, Clinton's positive relationship with black leaders proved more an asset than detriment to the American psyche. Middle-class African Americans enjoyed a president with whom they could identify, and white Americans had less reason to feel guilty about past wrongs inflicted upon blacks. The customary thinking persisted in America that connoted a disproportionate number of impoverished blacks remained poor because of indolence rather than being undermined by a racist heritage.[66]

Unfortunately, political decisions enacted during the administrations of George H.W. Bush and Clinton had an inimical impact on African Americans during a critical period of the race's history. When comparing the status of the underserved black population with whites, African Americans fared miserably. Rising incidences of communicable diseases, higher death rates, the prevalence of crime and unemployment, coupled with disastrously low levels of academic performance in public schools, suggest the Bush and Clinton years hardly proved bountiful for the black masses. While black leaders basked in the light of Clinton affability, little accrued to the masses that lightened the burden of poverty, frustration, and dissolution.

Despite good intentions of welfare reformers and concern for aiding destitute blacks, a daunting task awaited anyone eager to enhance living conditions for low-income African Americans. Given the challenges faced by impoverished blacks, satisfactory welfare reform and prospects for favorable job procurement for unskilled blacks appeared virtually impossible.[67] Destitute African Americans had little in reserve to provide protection against unforeseen eventualities. An unexpected illness, injury, family dispute, or economic recession stood to undermine the most sincere efforts of both altruistic reformers and ambitious blacks who comprised the working poor.

While federally funded programs like welfare and Medicare enabled low-income African Americans to survive, government funds allocated to housing negated documented success. Nicholas Lemann spoke accurately about the realities encountered by the black poor in the 1990s when he said, "The atmosphere of these federally funded [housing] projects—the rampant crime, the drugs, the sense of absolute apartness from the rest of American society, the emphasis on an exaggerated and misguided version of masculinity that glorifies gang membership and sexual conquest . . ." keeps the black underclass downtrodden.[68] Given the overwhelming challenges underprivileged African Americans encountered during the 1990s, the twentieth century would close with the black masses faring no better than in 1900.

Epilogue

During the previous century, few positive changes occurred that enhanced the quality of life for impoverished African Americans. The historical aspects of American racism instituted during slavery and continued with advent of sharecropping, the evolution of ghettos that degenerated into slums denied scores of blacks an equal opportunity to attain the American Dream. Without access to means for creating wealth, obtaining a meaningful education, and residing in a pristine environment, truly disadvantaged African Americans remained in abject poverty. Other adverse factors limited black prospects for upward mobility. Police departments nationwide arrested blacks with impunity, presenting captured souls before a harsh, unfair judicial system that stigmatized African Americans as a criminal race. With a disproportionate number of African Americans being incarcerated and having a record, jobs became difficult to acquire, families disintegrated, and an oppositional black culture evolved. Outside of creating rap music, the only viable role young, undereducated African American males provided the nation existed in being arrested, incarcerated, and contributors to the prison-industrial complex.

Just as the themes of this book are multifaceted, finding resolutions for problems inherent within the impoverished black masses require multiple approaches. Head Start, public works programs, constructive community action efforts, and other government attempts to encourage success among disadvantaged African Americans were attempted.[1] Thus far, however, every attempt to eradicate African American poverty failed. Of course full employment, rising wages, and acquiring sufficient education to enable the ambitious poor to obtain work could be found to provide the necessary panaceas for upward mobility. But perhaps the most simplistic means for mitigating poverty among the ambitious working poor would exit in the ability to make a decent wage. As powerless people, however, impoverished blacks were incapable of making demands on employers. Instead, the working poor who escaped welfare earned proportionally lower and lower wages during the initial years of the twenty-first-century economy.[2]

Urbanologist Helene Slessarav contended that low-income African Americans established the parameters of debate, but issues of concern that needed to be addressed on behalf of the poor never became part of the political discussion.[3] Since the implementation of President Johnson's Great Society, conservative forces shaped public debate. The concerted conservative interests of the business community, combined with the antigovernment and tax stance embraced by the white middle class, garnered only a weak rebuttal from progressive and liberal forces expected to aid the disadvantaged. The poor rarely received consideration because a diversion of resources would be inimical to the major political parties' influential constituencies. When the poor failed to vote, policy makers sacrificed the need of impoverished blacks—whether rural farmers or residents in urban slums—to advantage more powerful entities in society.[4]

Leaders of both political parties in this new millennium focus on protecting the middle class rather than helping the poor. Today, the War on Poverty hardly exists as a distant memory. President Johnson's endeavors not only failed to achieve a resounding success but politically created enemies among local politicians intent on providing services directly to middle-class constituents. The unheralded domestic war against black poverty required an enormous influx of funds and training. Moreover, the needs of impoverished African Americans exceeded the nation's willingness to pay for beneficiaries who refused to acclimate and accede to middle-class norms.

Fiscal conservatives embraced the hard-line assumption that all poverty programs were wasteful. This logic suggested blacks in a desultory position lacked ambition, and thereby contentedly and willfully accepted a servile existence. Doctrinaire conservatives ignored success stories that revealed many African Americans benefited from public largess, escaped poverty, found jobs, and joined the ranks of the middle class. Rather, conservative ideology focused on areas where federal oversight was lacking or misguided. But more significantly, these same conservatives failed to provide evidence that state and local governments offered better direction and used resources more effectively to eliminate poverty and elevate the standard of living among low-income African Americans than the federal government.

The public fixation on impoverished, ghetto dwelling African Americans created the illusion that the overwhelming majority of poor people in the United States were people of color rather than white. By devoting attention to racial issues related to civil rights, school integration, busing, public housing, and affirmative action, mainstream Americans ignored class differences that divided the nation between the haves and have-nots. If and when discussions regarding poverty arose, the subjects envisioned would appear primarily, if not entirely, in blackface. In order to obfuscate deeply entrenched racism that caused a disproportionate number of blacks to be ensconced in poverty, savvy politicians subtlety used the race card and insignificant wedge issues to garner votes from an unsophisticated white electorate. To keep African Americans subservient, white Southerners particularly voted contrary to the interest of poor people like themselves. Since the civil rights movement, conservative politicians and pundits have been able to convince low-income whites of two "indisputable" truths: the federal government focused primary attention to assisting blacks, and small government should be perceived as the panacea for eradicating poverty.

Focusing on inner-city blacks as those who filled welfare rolls, the Reagan administration publicized the need to create Enterprise Zones in the nation's depressed cities to stimulate a new economic paradigm. Reaganites contended that "it is quite possible that some entrepreneurs" would consider locating new facilities within the zones and thereby bring economic development to depressed areas of major cities.[5] Reagan administrators, however, failed to address those problems associated with poverty—crime, defeatism, a failing infrastructure, substandard education, and depressed housing conditions. Moreover, the likelihood that prospective investors and firms would have the capacity and interest to tackle urban problems better than the federal government would be an unrealistic pipe dream. The spirit of entrepreneurship encouraged by platitudes that evoke low taxes and self-help bootstrap policies appealed to those successful people who embraced rugged individualism.

Rather than spending money on schools to create better opportunities for disadvantaged blacks, state governments allocated funds to build prisons without significant fanfare, dissension, or debate. Ironically, the American public appeared more inclined to use tax money and pay for past indiscretions than invest in the future by providing students with a useful education. And yet, few fiscally conscious conservatives publicly address the efficacy of raising taxes to invest in children. Rather, wedge issues comprising abortion, same-sex marriage, stem-cell research, creationism, gun control—added to sweeping concerns that involve lower taxes and small government—cause people to overlook the prison-industrial complex and costs that rival, or exceed, monetary investments for public education.

Although deeply entrenched racism contributed primarily to the lowly status of impoverished African Americans, the self-serving objectives of post–civil rights leadership also contributed to the debased black condition. Like white counterparts, black politicians have a limited interest in poverty programs. Black politicos focused on providing largess to the middle class rather than meeting the explicit needs of the poor.[6] Consequently, some black mayors, ministers, social service directors, school principals, and others holding influential public positions invariably demonstrate little concern for their African American clientele. These people received high salaries and perks at the expense of subordinate workers and the low-income masses. Impoverished African Americans remained dependent upon leaders who appeared indifferent to programs designed to assist the working poor.

In many respects the plight of low-income African Americans appears greater today than during the civil rights era. White guilt no longer exists. Overt racial discrimination of yesteryear that limited black success could no longer be blamed exclusively on "the man." After experiencing centuries of degradation caused by American racism, the black masses invariably turn on each other and engage in singular or mutual self-destruction. Rather than envisioning successful middle-class African Americans as positive role models, impoverished black males appeared to embrace the gritty, angry lyrics in rap music that glorified some form of asocial behavior. Moreover, the black masses appeared to eschew African Americans who acquired middle-class status, labeling successful blacks as sellouts. Those who proposed remaining "ethnic" and "keeping it real" acted like crabs in a barrel. They used the derogatory "acting white" shibboleth to stunt intellectual growth, minimize prospects for gainful employment, and shame advocates who championed the need to embrace middle-class conformity. In truth, oppositionists—the criminals, deadbeat fathers, young hoodlums, and those who fail to voice outrage at self-destructive tendencies—function as the true sellouts in African American society.[7]

Even those who profess to be supportive of the masses fell short in articulating black plight. Professors Cornel West of Princeton and Eric Michel Dyson of Georgetown seized Martin Luther King Jr.'s mandate as a voice for the poor. Moreover, these African American intellectuals placed primary blame on other black leaders. Dyson excoriated Bill Cosby in print (*Is Bill Cosby Right?*), and West targets President Obama with abuse at virtually every opportunity for not devoting more time and resources to help downtrodden African Americans. And yet West and Dyson also have detractors who sense their views are more self-aggrandizing than helpful to disadvantaged blacks. An African American scholar like Houston A. Baker Jr. of Vanderbilt derided West and Dyson as intellectual pamphleteers who presented poorly researched work and engaged in silly polemics.[8] Baker reasons that lowly African Americans remain without a relevant voice that speaks and acts constructively to enhance the lot of the disadvantaged.

In addition to the aforementioned circumstances that undermined and curtailed black progress, the eradication of poverty and educating black youth appear as the only real plausible hope for relieving African American plight. The monumental challenges facing impoverished black children almost defy comprehension. Even the most ambitious young African Americans from low-income families who aspire to attend college face a near-impossible task. Evidence of the challenges striving African American students faced could be gleaned from a survey of one hundred graduating seniors from five counties in Southern California (Los Angeles, Orange, Riverside, San Bernardino, and Ventura Counties) who competed for thirty scholarships offered through the

McDonald's Future Achiever Scholarship Program.[9] Despite their academic prowess, these students represented the problems and pathos encountered by many impoverished African American students.

Black academic adversity could be related directly to the substandard income generated by single-parent, female-headed households. The survey found fifty-eight of the one hundred families had single parents; only one male served as the head of household. And customarily, more females (68) than males (32) submitted funding applications, as girls demonstrated more proclivity to use academics as a means toward upper mobility than boys. Virtually all female parents and their progeny faced overwhelming challenges. One girl specifically transcended enormous obstacles to achieve success. Speaking on behalf of scores of black children who faced almost insurmountable odds, the girl said,

> Living with my mother was very unstable and stressful. We moved from place to place, to place, and we never had much space. We had no table, desk, or any furniture for that matter, so I usually did my homework on the floor . . . . I always try to take advantage of the academic opportunities available to me, but my mother does not understand why I am always so busy . . . . She began to put restrictions on the time I spent on homework. I had to be done with my chores, dinner, and ready for bed by 8:00 p.m. I was not allowed to do homework after this time. Since I do not have family support, I have to motivate myself to be successful.

Despite her irresponsible, delimiting, ignorant mother, this young lady boasted sufficiently high grade point averages and test scores to gain admission into the University of Southern California.

Other students spoke of harsh experiences associated with poverty. The personal story of a male student read, "My father, in his absence, showed me what I did not want to become . . . . I cannot say that I miss my father because I never knew him." A girl intending to major in civil engineering at San Diego State University related her plight to scholarship evaluators by saying, "When I was born my father was in prison, so my mother was forced to live with my grandmother. It was extremely difficult for her because she was the first one in our family not to receive federal aid." And still another girl, expressing a tinge of self-hatred, declared, "I struggle with the racial label of being 'African-American . . . .' My mother is a prime example of the stereotypes that are perpetuated in our community. My mother was a convicted felon serving time in prison and as her child I struggle with this situation on a daily basis." One may only hope that the college experience can mitigate her pain.

The grit and determination of these young people nearly defied reality. An African American boy ranked eighth in a class of eight hundred with a 3.9 grade-point average said, "At many points in my life I had wished to have a 'traditional' family, one with both parents, just to make life easier to live, but that hasn't been a reality. Since my mother was a single African American woman, she had to work forty hours a week just to put food on the table." Death and illness created additional pressures for black children. A girl intent on continuing her education and obtaining a doctorate in psychology shared a sorrowful experience and said,

> August 1, 2004, 9:18 p.m.: the day my life was turned upside down. I can still hear the sounds of the sad sobs and the sight of tearful eyes as I watched my grandmother die . . . . I was born to a single African American woman who struggles to provide for me . . . . My mother is unable to work due to carpel tunnel syndrome and severe thoracic outlet syndrome . . . . She was told she could not work a normal "9–5" job . . . [and] was forced to retire . . . . Our income is very limited . . . .

Finally, a boy who overcame enormous adversity living as a ward of the courts reported,

> I went through a difficult childhood, growing up separated from my brothers and sisters with neither mother nor father, both having died when I was an infant. I lived in a foster home with a bitter, old woman whose neglect left me with a bad attitude and no motivation in life. I would constantly be in trouble and did very poorly in school . . . . I was placed in Special Education classes . . . . I . . . was headed down a path of self-destruction just as any African American male without parents . . . .

Fortunately, an older sister—a single mother with two children who worked as a mail carrier—rescued him along with two additional siblings. The woeful youth changed his behavior, became studious, earned a 3.9 grade-point average, and prepared to enter the University of San Diego to major in engineering.

Since at best only thirty scholarships were awarded, most of these exceptional student applicants failed to receive money. Given the realization that no more than two hundred African American seniors in a five-county area containing thousands of low-income black students applied for money, the number of qualified black applicants who sought a college education appears to be appallingly low. Therefore, future prospects for elevating the severely disadvantaged appear extremely dismal. Students with learning disabilities, joined by delinquent dropouts and graduates who function far below the twelve-grade level, suggest that most impoverished African Americans will continue a lowly existence far into the future.

A factor that sheds light on the pejorative view toward low-income blacks may be related to the origins of the United States. Excluding Native Americans, the original inhabitants, and Africans brought forcefully to the New World, all others took risks and voluntarily ventured to America. These risk-adverse settlers, classified as individuals with ADHD or adventurous by psychologists, were industrious, confident, and, in turn, largely successful. These traits represent the ethos of American society. Another principle attributed directly to the ethos of the Founding Fathers who proclaimed that all men are created equal also explains the competitive Social Darwinian spirit that encouraged Americans to achieve, excel, and become more equal than others. For enslaved African Americans and their progeny, this eighteenth-century platitude regarding equality rests on an extremely faulty premise. For many black Americans, inequality remains omnipresent and irrefutable. And regrettably for most black children born into dire circumstances, a child's mental acuity, physical appearance, gender, health condition, class status, and limited potential for greatness are already preconditioned at birth.

The Founding Fathers declared that citizens in the United States should enjoy unfettered opportunities to succeed. This concept proclaiming equality for everyone remains a commendable ideal. Unfortunately, for scores of African Americans life has been unequal, extremely unfair, and devoid of equal opportunity. For a large segment of African American population, past wrongs have never been properly addressed. Disadvantage attributed to race should be addressed and debated by a reluctant American public. Any child born in the United States should be given the opportunity to reach his/her potential. For a significant contingent of African Americans whose heritage after slavery was influenced by sharecropping, ghettos, and slums, equally opportunity only exists as a "Dream Deferred."

NOTES

Chapter 1

1. Leon F. Litwak, Trouble in Mind: Black Southerners in the Age of Jim Crow (New York: Alfred A. Knopf, 1998), 303–304. Also see Hortense Powdermaker, After Freedom: A Cultural Study of the Deep South (New York: Atheneum, 1968), 358.

2. See William F. Pinar, *The Gender of Racial Politics and Violence in America: Lynching, Prison, Rape, and the Crisis of Masculinity* (New York: Peter Lang, 2001), 52. Also see Omar H. Ali, *In the Lion's Mouth: Black Populism in the New South, 1886–1900* (Jackson: University of Mississippi Press, 2010), 18; Charles S. Aiken, *The Cotton Plantation South: Since the Civil War* (Baltimore: Johns Hopkins University Press, 1998), 17; and Leon Litwack, *Trouble in Mind: Black Southerners in the Age of Jim Crow* (New York: Alfred A. Knopf, 1998), xiv–xvi.

3. Gerald David Jaynes, *Branches Without Roots: Genesis of the Black Working Class in the American South, 1862–1882* (New York: Oxford University Press, 1989), 58–59.

4. Jaynes, *Branches,* 59–61, 74.

5. John Hope Franklin, *From Slavery to Freedom* (New York: Alfred A. Knopf, 1967), 397–398.

6. Gunnar Myrdal, *An American Dilemma,* Vol. I (New York: McGraw-Hill Book Company, 1964), 228; Michelle Alexander, *The New Jim Crow: Mass Incarceration in the Age of Color Blindness* (New York: The New Press, 2012), 28.

7. Although recent scholarship suggests that the idea of tenant farming originated with freedmen, the white planter and business class soon

took advantage of landless blacks. Franklin, *From Slavery to Freedom*, 303, 310–311; Ali, *In the Lion's Mouth*, 17–19. See Claud Anderson, *Black Labor White Wealth: The Search for Power and Economic Justice* (Bethesda, Maryland: PowerNomics Corporation of America, 1994), 161; Robert H. Zieger, *For Jobs and Freedom: Race and Labor in America since 1865* (Lexington: University of Kentucky Press, 2007), 19. Also see Aiken, *Cotton Plantation South*, 19.

8. Although the terms *tenant* and *sharecropper* were used interchangeably, a distinction existed between tenants and "croppers" in their relationship with landlords. Fortunate blacks who became tenants occupied a more advantageous position. Douglas A. Blackmon, *Slavery by Another Name: The Re-Enslavement of Black Americans from the Civil War to World War II* (New York: Doubleday, 2008), 377–379. See Leon F. Litwack, *Trouble in Mind, Black Southerners in the Age of Jim Crow* (New York: Alfred A. Knopf, 1998), 129. Also see Jaynes, *Branches Without Roots*, 313.

9. W. E. B. Du Bois, *The Souls of Black Folk* (New York: Vintage Books, 1990), 96.

10. Jaynes, *Branches*, 159–163.

11. Jaynes, *Branches*, 291.

12. Ibid.

13. Litwak, *Trouble in Mind*, 131–132. Also see Zieger, *For Jobs and Freedom*, 16–17.

14. Litwack, *Trouble in Mind*, 120.

15. Litwack, *Trouble in Mind*, 119.

16. Ali, *In the Lion's Mouth*, 72–76.

17. Willard B. Gatewood, *Aristocrats of Color: The Black Elite, 1880–1920* (Bloomington: Indiana University Press, 1993), 37–38, 50–51, 82, 161–162.

18. John Hope Franklin, *From Slavery to Freedom* (New York: Alfred A. Knopf, 1967), 276–277.

19. Christopher M. Span, *From Cotton Field to Schoolhouse: African American Education in Mississippi 1862–1875* (Chapel Hill: The University of North Carolina Press, 2009), 3–5; Aiken, *Cotton Plantation*, 21.

20. Aiken, *Cotton Plantation*, 26.

21. Span, *From Cotton Field,* 10.

22. See Span, *From Cotton Field,* 10–12.

23. Litwack, *Trouble in Mind,* 101.

24. Litwack, *Trouble in Mind,* 17.

25. See Span, *Cotton Field to Schoolhouse,* 107–108.

26. This ambitious, literate group formed the black aristocracy. See Gatewood, *Aristocrats of Color,* 1-17 passim.

27. Robin D. G. Kelley and Earl Lewis, eds., *A History of African Americans from 1880*; Barbara Blair, *Through Justice Sleeps, 1880–1900* (New York: Oxford University Press, 2000), 3.

28. Charles E. Hall, *Negroes in the United States 1920–1932* (New York: Arno Press and the New York Times, 1969), 231. Also see Litwack, *Trouble in Mind,* 125–126.

29. Litwack, *Trouble in Mind,* 57, 59–60.

30. Litwack, *Trouble in Mind,* 70–71.

31. The white Populist leader Tom Watson, for example, voted against funding for black education. See Ali, *In the Lion's Mouth,* 80.

32. Jaynes, *Branches Without Roots,* 248–249.

33. Litwack, *Trouble in Mind,* 122. Also see Jaynes, *Branches,* 308–313.

34. Khalil Gibran Muhammad, *The Condemnation of Blackness: Race, Crime, and the Making of Modern Urban America* (Cambridge, Mass.: Harvard University Press, 2010), 17–18.

35. Blackmon, *Slavery by Another Name,* 7.

36. Blackmon, *Slavery by Another Name,* 7, 99.

37. Blackmon, *Slavery by Another Name,* 96.

38. See Zieger, *For Jobs and Freedom,* 45–47.

39. Blackmon, *Slavery by Another Name*, 7.

40. Gunnar Myrdal, *An American Dilemma*, Vol. II (New York: McGraw-Hill Book Co., 1964), 525–526, 547.

41. See W. E. B. Du Bois, *The Philadelphia Negro: A Social Study* (1899: Reprint, New York: Schocken Press, 1967), 240, 282–285.

42. Muhammad, *Condemnation*, 4–5.

43. Muhammad, *Condemnation*, 1–4, 35, 76.

44. Muhammad, *Condemnation*, 52.

45. Du Bois, *Philadelphia Negro*, 240, 282–285.

46. Seth M. Scheiner, *Negro Mecca: A History of the Negro in New York City, 1865–1920* (New York: New York University Press, 1965), 6–7, 24–26.

47. Paul A. Gidje and Howard B. Rock, "Sweep O, Sweep O: African-American Chimney Sweeps and Citizenship in the New Nation," *William and Mary Quarterly*, 51 (1994), 507–508.

48. Francisco Cordasco, ed., *Jacob Riis Revisited: Poverty and the Slum in Another Era* (Garden City, New York: Anchor Books, 1968), 51.

49. Du Bois, *The Philadelphia Negro*, 126. Also see Scheiner, *Negro Mecca*, 47.

50. David M. Katzman, *Before the Ghetto: Black Detroit in the Nineteenth Century* (Urbana: University of Illinois Press, 1975), 17, 25–27, 70–71, 75.

51. Katzman, *Before the Ghetto*, 61.

52. Katzman, *Before the Ghetto*, 105–106.

53. Allen H. Spear, *Black Chicago: The Making of a Negro Ghetto 1890–1920* (Chicago: University of Chicago Press, 1967), 29–30.

54. Joe William Trotter Jr., *River Jordan: African American Urban Life in the Ohio Valley* (Lexington: University of Kentucky Press, 1998), 73.

55. Trotter, *River Jordan*, 73–74.

56. See Carter G. Woodson, *The Mis-Education of the Negro* (Trenton, NJ: Africa World Press, 1998), 12–14. Also see Harry S. Ashmore, *The Negro and the Schools* (Chapel Hill: University of North Carolina Press, 1954), 21.

57. See Fox Butterfield, *All God's Children: The Bosket Family and the American Tradition of Violence* (New York: Alfred A. Knopf, 1995), xvii, 7–14. Also see Myrdal, *An American Dilemma*, 532.

58. Myrdal, *An American Dilemma*, Vol. II, 560.

59. See Litwack, *Trouble in Mind*, 280–281.

60. Wade, *Slavery in the Cities*, 100–106. Also see Litwack, *Trouble in Mind*, 70–71. For information that provided Southern whites with credibility for black violence, see the discussion about Robert Charles, who resisted arrest in New Orleans in Philip Dray, *At the Hands of Persons Unknown: The Lynching of Black America* (New York: the Modern Library, 2002), 127–137.

61. See Rayford W. Logan, *The Betrayal of the Negro: From Rutherford B. Hayes to Woodrow Wilson* (London: Collier Books, 1969), 224–228.

62. Dray, *At the Hands of Persons Unknown*, 67.

63. Du Bois, *The Philadelphia Negro*, 283–284.

64. See Jaynes, *Branches Without Roots*, 316.

Chapter 2

1. C. Vann Woodward, The Strange Career of Jim Crow (New York: Oxford University Press, 1966), 67–109.

2. David Levering Lewis, *W. E. B. Du Bois, Biography of a Race, 1868–1919* (New York: Henry Holt and Company, 1993), 243–244.

3. Kimberley Johnson, *Reforming Jim Crow: Southern Politics and the State in the Age Before Brown* (New York: Oxford University Press, 2010), 38–39.

4. See Michael Lewis, *The Culture of Inequality* (Amherst: The University of Massachusetts Press, 1978), 4–6.

5. By the 1920s Elwood would become far more liberal in his thinking toward race. Yet in 1906–1907, his views corresponded to the opinions of most sociologists. See book review of George S. Merriam, *The Negro and the Nation: A History of American Slavery and Enfranchisement*, by Charles A. Ellwood, *The American Journal of Sociology* (1906–1907), XII, 275. Also see Philip Dray, *At the Hands of Persons Unknown: The Lynching of Black America* (New York: The Modern Library, 2003), 100–101.

6. Khalil Gibran Muhammad, *The Condemnation of Blackness: Race, Crime, and the Making of Modern America* (Cambridge, Mass.: Harvard University Press, 2010), 35.

7. Muhammad, *Condemnation of Blackness*, 52–54.

8. Muhammad, *Condemnation of Blackness*, 67.

9. Ray Stannard Baker, *Following the Color Line: American Negro Citizenship in the Progressive Era* (New York: Harper and Row, 1964: original printing 1908), 47.

10. Randall Kennedy, *Sellout: The Politics of Racial Betrayal* (New York: Vintage Books, 2008), 40.

11. Kennedy, *Sellout*, 41.

12. Muhammad, *Condemnation of Blackness*, 79.

13. See Muhammad, *Condemnation of Blackness*, 79–81.

14. Philip Dray, *At the Hands of Persons Unknown* (New York: The Modern Library, 2002), 15. Also see Walter White, *Rope and Faggot* (New York: 1929), 97.

15. See Willard B. Gatewood, *Aristocrats of Color: The Black Elite, 1880–1920* (Bloomington: Indiana University Press, 1990), 1-29 passim.

16. See W. E. Burghardt Du Bois, *The Black North in 1901: A Social Study* (New York: Arno Press and the New York Times, 1969), vii–viii.

17. H. Viscount Nelson, *Black Leadership's Response to the Great Depression in Philadelphia* (Lewiston, New York: The Edwin Mellen Press, 2006), 24–25.

18. Gatewood, *Aristocrats*, 72–74, 80, 91, 217–220, 227–228; Katz, *Before the Ghetto*, 155–156, 162–146.

19. W. E. B. Du Bois, *The Philadelphia Negro: A Social Study* (New York: Schocken Books, 1967), 80–81; David M. Katzman, *Before the Ghetto: Black Detroit in the Nineteenth Century* (Champaign, Ill.: University of Illinois Press, 1975), 155–156, 162–164; Robert C. Weaver, *The Negro Ghetto* (New York: Russell and Russell, 1948), 12; George W. Groh, *The Black Migration: The Journey to Urban America* (New York: Weybright and Talley, 1972), 55.

20. Although the *Chicago Defender* urged Southern blacks to move North, the *New York Age*, with former Floridian T. Thomas Fortune serving as editor, encouraged the Southern black rustic to remain in Dixie. Again, with mixed signals emanating from the black press as well as strong differences voiced by leaders like Booker T. Washington and W. E. B. Du Bois, no consensus existed within black leadership that provided the masses with proper direction. Scheiner, *Negro Mecca*, 116. Also see Gunnar Myrdal, *An American Dilemma* (New York: McGraw-Hill Book Company, 1964), 195–196.

21. Robert H. Zieger, *For Jobs and Freedom: Race and Labor in America Since 1865* (Lexington: The University Press of Kentucky, 2007), 52.

22. Rayford W. Logan, *The Betrayal of the Negro: From Rutherford B. Hayes to Woodrow Wilson* (London: Collier Books, 1969), 371.

23. In 1900, more than six million, or 82 percent of the African American population resided in the South. See Baker, *Color Line*, 66.

24. Baker, *Color Line*, 6, 8.

25. Baker, *Color Line*, 58.

26. Du Bois, *Philadelphia Negro*, 138.

27. Litwack, *Trouble in Mind*, 149.

28. Blackmon, *Slavery*, 117-154, 155-180 passim.

29. Monroe N. Work, "Criminality in the South," *Annals of the American Academy of Political and Social Science* XLIX, no. 138 (Sept. 1913): 74. Also see Robert A. Gibson, "The Negro Holocaust: Lynching and Race Riots in the United States, 1880–1950" (Yale-New Haven Teachers Institute, 2010).

30. *Philadelphia Negro*, 97–98; Baker, *Color Line*, 133.

31. Zieger, *Jobs and Freedom*, 60.

32. Zieger, *Jobs and Freedom*, 61–62.

33. Baker, *Color Line*, 132–133.

34. Baker, *Color Line*, 132.

35. Gunnar Myrdal, *An American Dilemma*, Vol. I (New York: McGraw-Hill Book Company, 1964), 29. Also see George W. Groh, *The Black Migration: The Journey to Urban America* (New York: Weybright and Talley, 1972), 21–22.

36. Fox Butterfield, *All God's Children: The Bosket Family and the American Tradition of Violence* (New York: Alfred A. Knopf, 1995), 5–13.

37. Baker, *Color Line*, 49.

38. David Fort Godshalk, *Veiled Visions: The 1906 Atlanta Riot and the Reshaping of American Race Relations* (Chapel Hill: The University of North Carolina Press, 2005), 20–21, 26.

39. Also see Godshalk, *Veiled Visions*, 30–34.

40. Blackmon, *Slavery by Another Name*, 176–180.

41. Baker, *Color Line*, 50.

42. Blackmon, *Slavery by Another Name*, 7–8, 284–285, 356.

43. Myrdal, *An American Dilemma*, 121.

44. Blackmon, *Slavery by Another Name*, 288–289, 331.

45. Litwack, *Trouble in Mind*, 438.

46. See Work, *Criminality*, 76.

47. Philip Dray, *At the Hands of Persons Unknown: The Lynching of Black America* (New York: The Modern Library, 2002), 146.

48. Legal redress for African Americans only became feasible after the establishment of the NAACP in 1909. Dray, *Hands of Persons Unknown*, 176–178. Also see Blackmon, *Slavery by Another Name*, 175–180.

49. Leon Litwack, *Trouble in Mind: Black Southerners in the Age of Jim Crow* (New York: Alfred A. Knopf, 1998), 197–199, 211–214; I. A. Newby, *Jim Crow's Defense: Anti-Negro Thought in America, 1900–1930* (Westport, Connecticut: Greenwood Press, Publishers, 1980), 120–126.

50. Litwack, *Trouble in Mind*, 16, 36–42. Also see Butterfield, *All God's Children*, 58–59.

51. Dray, *Hands of Persons*, 60.

52. Blackmon, *Slavery by Another Name*, 108–109. Also see Aiken, *Cotton Plantation*, 27–28.

53. Isabel Wilkerson, *The Warmth of Other Suns: The Epic Story of America's Great Migration* (New York: Vintage Books, 2010), 39.

54. Baker, *Color Line*, 100.

55. Leon Litwack, *Trouble in Mind: Black Southerners in the Age of Jim Crow* (New York: Alfred A. Knopf, 1998), xiii–xiv.

56. Prior to 1900, only Kentucky required school attendance. In 1907 North Carolina became the first state in the Deep South to make school mandatory. Baker, *Color Line*, 52–54.

57. Muhammad, *Condemnation*, 93–94.

58. Muhammad, *Condemnation*, 97. Also see Blackmon, *Slavery by Another Name*, 237–238.

59. Litwack, *Trouble in Mind*, 60.

60. See Litwack, *Trouble in Mind*, 91.

61. Baker, *Color Line*, 84–85.

62. Baker, *Color Line*, 114–117.

63. Mary White Ovington, *Half a Man: The Status of the Negro in New York* (New York: Hill and Wang, 1969), 22, 30–31; Du Bois, *Black North*, 13, 26–27.

64. Du Bois, *Philadelphia Negro*, 312–315.

65. Du Bois, *Philadelphia Negro*, 96.

66. Du Bois, *Philadelphia Negro*, 311–315.

67. Du Bois, *Black North*, 11, 18.

68. Blackmon, *Slavery by Another Name*, 245.

69. Muhammad, *Condemnation*, 108.

70. Ovington, *Half a Man*, 19.

71. Katzman, *Before the Ghetto*, 168–171.

72. Allan H. Spear, *Black Chicago: The Making of a Negro Ghetto* (Chicago: University of Chicago Press, 1967), 44.

73. Guichard Parris and Lester Brooks, *Blacks in the City: A History of the National Urban League* (Boston: Little, Brown, and Company, 1971), 6.

74. Muhammad, *Condemnation*, 106–107.

75. David M. Katzman, *Before the Ghetto: Black Detroit in the Nineteenth Century* (Urbana: University of Illinois Press, 1973), 156.

76. Parris and Brooks, *Blacks in the City*, 19, reported in the *New York Age*, May 14, 1908.

77. Slessarev, *Betrayal*, 7.

78. See Joe William Trotter Jr., *River Jordan: African American Life in the Ohio Valley* (University Press of Kentucky, 1998), 65.

79. Scheiner, *Negro Mecca*, 54–55.

80. See Trotter, *River Jordan*, 65

81. In Northern and Southern cities, black women outnumbered men. John Cummings and Joseph Hill, *Negro Population, 1790–1915,* Bureau of Census (New York: Kraus Reprint Company, 1969), 156.

82. Zieger, *Jobs,* 55.

Chapter 3

1. C. Vann Woodward, Origins of the New South, 1877–1913 (Baton Rouge: Louisiana State University Press, 1951), 379–385. Also see Monroe Lee Billington, The American South (New York: Charles Scribner's Sons, 1971), 232; I. A. Newby, The South: A History (New York: Holt, Rinehart, and Winston, 1978), 368.

2. Douglas A. Blackmon, *Slavery by Another Name: The Re-enslavement of Black People in America from the Civil War to World War II* (New York: Doubleday, 2008), 358–359; found in *Plantation Farming in the United States* (Washington, DC: Government Printing Office, 1916), 36–37.

3. I. A. Newby, *The South,* 333–334.

4. Monroe Lee Billington, *The American South* (New York: Charles Scribner's Sons, 1971), 233–234, 373.

5. James R. Grossman, *Land of Hope: Chicago, Black Southerners, and the Great Migration* (Chicago: University of Chicago Press), 247.

6. Bullock, *History of the South,* 123.

7. Bullock, *History of the South,* 116. Also see W. J. Cash, *The Mind of the South* (New York: Vintage Books, 1941), 223.

8. Kimberley Johnson, *Reforming Jim Crow: Southern Politics and State in the Age Before Brown* (New York: Oxford University Press, 2010), 31.

9. Bullock, *Negro Education in the South,* 138–139.

10. Ibid.

11. Bullock, *Negro Education in the South,* 127. Also see Grossman, *Land of Hope,* 52.

12. Bullock, *Negro Education in the South,* 129–130.

13. See Bullock, *Negro Education in the South,* 135–136. Also see Johnson, *Reforming Jim Crow,* 126–127.

14. Grossman, *Land of Hope,* 250–251.

15. See Grossman, *Land of Hope,* 248–251, 257.

16. Nancy J. Weiss, *The National Urban: 1910–1940* (New York: Oxford University Press, 1974), 33.

17. As late as 1940, the United States Office of Education found that the more education an African American received, the greater the dissatisfaction with the job. See Grossman, *Land of Hope,* 258.

18. Peter M. Bergman, *The Chronological History of the Negro in America* (New York: Harper and Row, 1969), 359.

19. Bergman, *Chronicle History,* 366, 367, 373.

20. See Bullock, *Negro Education in the South,* 150.

21. Woodward, *Origins of the New South,* 407–408.

22. See Gunnar Myrdal, *An American Dilemma* (New York: McGraw-Hill Book Company, 198), 234–235.

23. Leon F. Litwack, *Trouble in Mind: Black Southerners in the Age of Jim Crow* (New York: Alfred A. Knopf, 1998), 208.

24. Litwack, *Trouble in Mind,* 206.

25. Litwack, *Trouble in Mind,* 209; quoted from Johnson, *Highways and Byways of the South,* 346.

26. Litwack, *Trouble in Mind,* 218–219.

27. See Litwack, *Trouble in Mind,* 253; Blackmon, *Slavery by Another Name,* 355–366.

28. See Florette Henri, *Black Migration: Movement North, 1900–1920* (Garden City, New York: Anchor Books, 1996), 43–46. Also see Litwack, *Trouble in Mind*, 306.

29. Aiken, *Cotton Plantation*, 64, 70, 71, 79, 80.

30. See Grossman, *Land of Hope*, 14–15, 28–30.

31. James R. Grossman, "A Chance to Make Good: 1900–1929," in *To Make Our World Anew: A History of African Americans From 1880* II, eds. Robin D. G. Kelley and Earl Lewis (New York: Oxford University Press), 107–108.

32. Henri, *Black Migration*, 52–53.

33. Grossman, "A Chance to Make Good," in *To Make Our World Anew*, 108.

34. Emmett J. Scott, *American Negro in the World War* (New York: Arno Press, 1969), 393.

35. Henri, *Black Migration*, 69.

36. Henri, *Black Migration*, 54.

37. Grossman, "A Chance to Make Good," in *To Make Our World Anew*, 108, 117–118.

38. Henri, *Black Migration*, 93–94.

39. See Ray Stannard Baker, "The Negro Goes North," *World's Work* 34 (July 1917), 319. Also see Grossman, *Land of Hope*, 131.

40. Henri, *Black Migration*, 54–57; Grossman, *Land of Hope*, 188–190. Also see Zieger, *For Jobs and Freedom*, 73–74.

41. Ovington, *Half a Man*, 54–55.

42. Grossman, *Land of Hope*, 128.

43. Seth M. Scheiner, *Negro Mecca: A History of the Negro in New York City, 1865–1920* (New York: New York University Press, 1965), 71–73. See Robert H. Zieger, *For Jobs and Freedom: Race and Labor in America Since 1865* (Louisville: University of Kentucky Press, 2007), 38, 57–58, 69, 83. Also see David

Levering Lewis, *W. E. B. Du Bois: Biography of a Race* (New York: Henry Holt and Company, 1993), 321–322.

44. Scheiner, *Negro Mecca*, 73–74.

45. Parris and Brooks, *Blacks in the City*, 135. Also see Weiss, *National Urban League*, 67–69.

46. Louis R. Harlan, *Booker T. Washington: The Wizard of Tuskegee, 1901–1915* (New York: Oxford University Press, 1983), 202–204.

47. Henri, *Black Migration*, 186. Also see Scheiner, *Negro Mecca*, 90–91.

48. See Khalil Gibran Muhammad, *The Condemnation of Blackness: Race, Crime, and the Making of Modern Urban America* (Cambridge, Massachusetts: Harvard University Press, 2010), 126.

49. Muhammad, *Condemnation*, 127.

50. See Henri, *Black Migration*, 98–99.

51 Henri, *Black Migration*, 96–97.

52. See Grossman, *Land of Hope*, 146–153.

53. Henri, *Black Migration*, 96–97.

54. Grossman, *Land of Hope*, 134–135, 140.

55. Grossman, *Land of Hope*, 138.

56. Grossman, "A Chance to Make Good," in *To Make Our World Anew*, 112–113.

57. See Henri, *Black Migration*, 102–103. Also see Grossman, *Land of Hope*, 168–169.

58. Weiss, *National Urban League*, 106. Also see Scheiner, *Negro Mecca*, 114–118. See Gunnar Myrdal, *An American Dilemma*, Vol. II (New York: McGraw-Hill Book Company, 1962), 557–974. Also see William L. Van Deburg, *Hoodlums: Black Villains and Social Bandits in American Life* (Chicago: University of Chicago Press, 2004), 125.

59. Scheiner, *Black Mecca*, 114–15. Also see Henri, *Black Migration*, 123–124.

60. Henri, *Black Migration*, 92, 94.

61. Henri, *Black Migration*, 74.

62. See Ziegler, *For Jobs and Freedom*, 71.

63. Henri, *Black Migration*, 80, 82, and 85.

64. Henri, *Black Migration*, 82, found in Baker, "Gathering Clouds . . .," *Worlds Work* (June 1916). Also see Grossman, *Land of Hope*, 169.

65. Vanessa Northington Gamble, "There Wasn't a Lot of Comfort in Those Days: African Americans, Public Health, and the 1918 Influenza Epidemic," *Public Health* 125, no.4 (Rep. July 1, 2010): 517.

66. Allan Spear, *Black Chicago: The Making of a Negro Ghetto 1890–1920* (Chicago: University of Chicago Press, 1967), 11, 19, 24–26. Also see Henri, *Black Migration*, 84–85.

67. Henri, *Black Migration*, 86.

68. Henri, *Black Migration*, 91.

69. John Hope Franklin, *From Slavery to Freedom* (New York: Alfred A. Knopf, 1967), 480.

70. Ibid.

71. Spear, *Black Ghetto*, 12. Also see Tuttle, *Race Riot*, 66

72. Spear, *Black Ghetto*, 202.

73. See Tuttle, *Race Riot*, 108–112, 141–142.

74. See Tuttle, *Race Riot*, 92–94, 106, 209. Also see Spear, *Black Chicago*, 214; Chicago Commission on Race Relations, *The Negro in Chicago: A Study of a Race Relations and a Race Riot* (Chicago: University of Chicago Press, 1922), 13, 17, 341–342.

75. Cameron McWhirter, *Red Summer: The Summer of 1919 and the Awakening of Black America* (New York: Henry Holt and Company, 2011), 94.

76. Grossman, *Land of Hope*, 34.

77. H. Viscount Nelson, *Black Leadership's Response to the Great Depression in Philadelphia* (Lewiston, Maryland: The Edwin Mellen Press, 2006), 26–29. Also see Grossman, "A Chance to Make Good," in *To Make Our World Anew*, 115

Chapter 4

1. Of more than four million gainfully employed blacks in the South, 1.9 million labored in low-paying jobs in agriculture, and slightly more than one million worked in lightly regarded positions in domestic and personal services. Charles E. Hall, *Negroes in the United States*, 1920–1932 (New York: Arno Press and the New York Times, 1969), 5 and 291.

2. I. A. Newby, *The South: A History* (New York: Holt, Rinehart, and Winston, 1978), 382–383.

3. Nathan B. Young, "Alabama—Like Miriam," (March 1925), 21; William Pickens, "Arkansas—A Study in Suppression" (January 1923), 34–36; E. Franklin Frazier, "Georgia: Or the Struggle Against Impudent Inferiority" (June 1924), 99–100; found in Tom Lutz and Susanna Ashton, eds., *These "Colored" United States: African American Essays from the 1920s* (New Brunswick, NJ: Rutgers University Press, 1996).

4. See Newby, *The South*, 385.

5. "The Lynching Industry," *The Crisis* 19, no. 4 (February 1920): 183–185. Also see Philip Dray, *At the Hands of People Unknown: The Lynching of Black America* (New York: The Modern Library, 2002), 239–244.

6. See *The Crisis* 29, nos. 1, 5 (May 1920).

7. Douglas A. Blackmon, *Slavery by Another Name: The Re-Enslavement of Black Americans From the Civil War to World War II* (New York: Doubleday, 2008), 375.

8. See "Lynchings: By Year and Race," Tuskegee Archives, law2.umkc.edu/faculty/projects/ftrials/ship/lynchingyear.html. Only one lynching occurred in a Northern state. See Peter M. Bergman, *The Chronological History of the Negro in America* (New York: Harper and Row, 1969), 397, 401.

9. Bergman, *Chronological History*, 433.

10. Philip S. Foner and Ronald L. Lewis, eds., "The Era of Post War Prosperity and the Great Depression, 1920–1936," *The Black Worker: A Documentary History from Colonial Times to the Present,* Vol. VI (Philadelphia: Temple University Press, 1981), 4–5.

11. Louis M. Kyriakoudes, *The Social Origins of the Urban South: Race, Gender, and Migration in Nashville and Middle Tennessee 1890–1930* (Chapel Hill: The University of North Carolina Press, 2003), 117–123.

12. Kyriakoudes, *Social Origins*, 82–83.

13. Kyriakoudes, *Social Origins*, 137–139.

14. "The Flood, the Red Cross and the National Guard," *The Crisis* 35 (1928): 80–81.

15. Ibid.

16. "The Flood, the Red Cross and the National Guard," *The Crisis* 35 (1928): 41–43, 64.

17. Kenneth T. Jackson,_*The Ku Klux Klan in the City: 1915–1930* (New York: Oxford University Press, 1967), 15.

18. Jackson, *Klan in the City*, 128–129, 233–234. Presumably, Klansmen residing in nearby Lansing, Michigan, murdered Malcolm Little's (Malcolm X's) father. Alex Haley, *The Autobiography of Malcolm X* (New York: Ballantine Books, 1964), 12–13. Also see Lionel F. Artis, "The Negro in Indiana, or the Struggle Against Dixie Come North," in *"Colored" United States*, 126.

19. Newby, *The South*, 408

20. Pickens, "Arkansas," in *"Colored" United States*, 34–38. Also see Newby, *The South*, 406–407.

21. *Philadelphia Tribune*, May 3, 1919.

22. Although Italians, Irish, and Jews headed crime syndicates, common views and parlance indicated that blacks were a criminal race despite having no criminals comparable to Al Capone. Muhammad, *Condemnation of Blackness*, 226–227.

23. Muhammad, *Condemnation of Blackness*, 228–229.

24. Muhammad, *Condemnation of Blackness*, 233–234, 245–246.

25. Muhammad, *Condemnation of Blackness*, 230–231.

26. Artis, "Negro in Indiana," found in Lutz and Ashton, *"Colored" United States*, 124.

27. Clinton F. Richardson, "Texas—Lone Star State, April, 1924," in *"Colored" United States*, 257–258

28. See Myrdal, *American Dilemma*, 196.

29. Forrester B. Washington, "Negro Survey of Pennsylvania" (a report prepared by the Commonwealth of Pennsylvania, Harrisburg: Department of Welfare, 1927), 4.

30. See *American Dilemma*, 576–577.

31. See August Meier and Elliott Rudwick, *From Plantation to Ghetto* (New York: Hill and Wang, 1970), 225.

32. Foner and Lewis, *Black Worker*, Vol. VI, 34.

33. See Meier and Rudwick, *Plantation to Ghetto*, 231. Also see Foner and Lewis, *Black Worker*, Vol. VI, 15–16.

34. In 1923 the NAACP prevailed in the *Moore v. Dempsey* case and saved twelve blacks from death sentences mandated by a Southern court. The following year the NAACP successfully defended Dr. Ossian Street, a dentist residing in Detroit who defended his home against a white mob, killing one of the rioters.

35. Guichard Parris and Lester Brooks, *Blacks in the City: A History of the National Urban League* (Boston: Little Brown and Company, 1971), 166–167, 177, 180–183.

36. See Nancy J. Weiss, *The National Urban League: 1910–1940* (New York: Oxford University Press, 1974), 144–145.

37. Weiss, *The National Urban League*, 142–143.

38. See Weiss, *The National Urban League*, 145. Also see Parris and Brooks, *Blacks in the City*, 186–187.

39. See Myrdal, *American Dilemma*, 602–603.

40. *Philadelphia Tribune*, February 8, 1919.

41. Lorraine Chambers, "If She Were Not Dark," *Black Opals* I, no. 2: 4.

42. Meier and Rudwick, *Plantation to Ghetto*, 226–229; Edmund David Cronin, *Black Moses: the Story of Marcus Garvey*_(Madison: University of Wisconsin Press, 1968), 47–47, 69–70.

43. Franklin, *Slavery to Freedom*, 503; Sterling Brown, *Negro Poetry and Drama and the Negro in American Fiction* (New York: Atheneum, 1969), 65.

44. Sterling Brown, *Negro Poetry and Drama and the Negro in American Fiction* (New York: Atheneum, 1969), 71–72.

45. See Alain Locke, ed., *The New Negro* (New York: Atheneum, 1969), x–xi.

46. Artis, "Indiana," in *"Colored" United States*, 127.

47. George W. Lee, "Tennessee—Its Educational Progress," in *"Colored" United States*, 251.

48. Artis, "Indiana," in *"Colored" United States* (March 1926) 128.

49. Lee, "Tennessee," in "*Colored" United States*, 250; J. Milton Sampson, "Virginia," in "*Colored" United States* (July 1923), 271.

50. Roy Wilkins, "Minnesota: Seat of Satisfaction," in *"Colored" United States* (May 1924), 170

51. Bergman, *Chronological History*, 444.

52. Parris and Brooks, *Blacks in the City*, 204; Nancy Weiss, *The National Urban League*, 238.

53. Thomas J. Sugrue, *Sweet Land of Liberty: The Forgotten Struggle for Civil Rights in the North* (New York: Random House, 2008), 12.

54. Johnson, *Reforming Jim Crow*, 121–122.

Chapter 5

1. Guichard Parris and Lester Brooks, *Blacks in the City: A History of the National Urban League* (Boston: Little, Brown, and Company, 1971), 204.

2. Nancy J. Weiss, *The National Urban League: 1910–1940* (New York: Oxford University Press), 238.

3. B. A. Botkin, ed., *Lay My Burden Down: A Folk History of Slavery* (Chicago: University of Chicago Press, 1968), 61.

4. Botkin, *Lay My Burden Down*, 65.

5. Botkin, *Lay My Burden Down*, 147–148.

6. See St. Clair Drake and Horace R. Cayton, *Black Metropolis: A Study of Life in a Northern City*, Vol. I (New York: Harper and Row, Publishers, 1945), 84–85, 128.

7. Philip S. Foner and Ronald L. Lewis, eds., *The Black Worker: The Era of Post-War Prosperity and the Great Depression 1920–1936*, Vol. VI (Philadelphia: Temple University Press, 1981), 306–308.

8. Douglas A. Blackmon, *Slavery by Another Name: The Re-Enslavement of Black Americans from the Civil War to World War II* (New York: Doubleday, 2008), 375–376; Charles S. Aiken, *The Cotton Plantation South: Since the Civil War* (Baltimore Johns Hopkins Press, 998), 133.

9. Raymond Wolters, *Negroes and the Great Depression: The Problem of Economic Recovery* (Westport, Connecticut: Greenwood Publishing Corporation, 1970), 7–8. Also see Blackmon, *Slavery by Another Name*, 376.

10. David R. Goldfield, *Black, White, and Southern: Race Relations and Southern Culture, 1940 to the Present* (Baton Rouge: Louisiana State University Press, 1990), 25.

11. Wolters, *Negroes and the Great Depression*, 3–7, 26–30.

12. See Nicholas Lemann, *The Promised Land: the Great Migration and How It Changed America* (New York: Alfred A Knopf, 1991), 8.

13. Wolters, *Negroes and the Great Depression*, 11–16.

14. Aiken, *Cotton Plantation*, 132.

15. Wolters, *Negroes and the Great Depression*, 8–9; Charles S. Johnson, *Growing Up in the Black Belt: Negro Youth in the Rural South* (New York: Schocken Books, 1941), 8–9.

16. Aiken, *Cotton Plantation*, 123.

17. See Wolters, *Negroes and the Great Depression*, 21–34.

18. Helene Slessarev, *Betrayal of the Urban Poor* (Philadelphia: Temple University Press, 1997), 8.

19. Aiken, *Cotton Plantation*, 120–121.

20. Johnson, *Black Belt*, 53, 55–57.

21. Johnson, *Black Belt*, 54.

22. See Johnson, *Black Belt*, 47–49.

23. Johnson, *Black Belt*, 58–60.

24. Johnson, *Black Belt*, 60–63.

25. David R. Goldfield, *Black, White, and Southern, Race Relations and Southern Culture, 1940 to the Present* (Baton Rouge, Louisiana State University Press, 1990), 56.

26. Johnson, *Black Belt*, 22.

27. H. Viscount Nelson, *Black Leadership's Response to the Great Depression in Philadelphia* (Lewiston, New York: The Edwin Mellen Press, 2006), 33, 38.

28. Wolters, *Negroes and the Great Depression*, 91. Also see Trotter, "From Raw Deal to a New Deal," in *To Make Our World Anew*, ed. Robin D G Kelley, 131–132.

29. Trotter, "From Raw Deal to a New Deal," in *To Make Our World Anew*, ed. Robin D G Kelley, 134.

30. Thomas J. Sugrue, *Sweet Land of Liberty: The Forgotten Struggle for Civil Rights in the North* (New York: Random House, 2008), 35. Also see Michael Goldfield, "Race and the CIO: The Possibilities for Racial Egalitarianism During the 1930s and 1940s," ILWCH, (Fall, 1993), 1, 27.

31. Quoted from the January 1930 edition of *The American Federalist,* found in Elmer Anderson Carter, "A Challenge to the AFL." See Foner and Lewis, *Black Worker,* 335.

32. See T. Arnold Hill, "Open Letter to Mr. William Green, President American Federation of Labor," *Opportunity* (February 1930): 56–57.

33. Carter, "Challenge to AFL"; Forner and Lewis, *Black Worker,* 336; Helene Slessarov, *The Betrayal of the Urban Poor* (Philadelphia: Temple University Press, 1997). 8–9.

34. Carter, "Challenge to AFL." Foner and Lewis, *Black Worker,* 337. Also see *The Crisis,* 43 (September, 1936), 273.

35. P.J. White Jr., "An Open Letter to Mr. William Green of the AF of L," *Opportunity* (November 1934), 350.

36. See "The AFL," *The Crisis* (December, 1933), 292.

37. See Lorraine Chambers, "If She Were Not Dark," *Black Opals* I, no. 2 (1927): 4; H. Viscount Nelson, "Race and Class Consciousness of Philadelphia Negroes with Special Emphasis Between the Years Between 1927 and 1940" (Ph.D Dissertation, University of Pennsylvania, 1969), 16. Josh A. Sides, "Working Away: African American Migration and the Community in Los Angeles From the Great Depression to 1954" (PhD Dissertation, UCLA, 1999), 40–42.

38. Johnson, *Black Belt,* 242.

39. See Johnson, *Black Belt,* 258, 266, 272–273.

40. E. Franklin Frazier, *Negro Youth at the Crossways* (New York: Schoken Books, 1940), 97–98.

41. Johnson, *Black Belt,* 9, 15, 20–22, 97–98.

42. Johnson, *Black Belt,* 94.

43. Johnson, *Black Belt*, 75–76.

44. See Fox Butterfield, *All God's Children: The Bosket Family and the American Tradition of Violence* (New York: Alfred A. Knopf), 71–85.

45. Harry S. Ashmore, *The Negro and the Schools* (Chapel Hill: The University of North Carolina Press, 1954), 26–27.

46. *Philadelphia Tribune*, October 22, 1936.

47. (Annual Report of the Board of Public Education, Philadelphia, Pennsylvania, 1930), 1019. Also see "A Report re Employment Department and Class Work" (YWCA Correspondence, Temple University Archives, October 31, 1931).

48. Aside from the National Urban League that instituted job training for unskilled African Americans, evening schools appeared to have little, if any, roles in helping blacks acquire jobs. Black leadership's efforts in regard to education were geared to help the black middle class. See H. Viscount Nelson, *Black Leadership Responds to the Great Depression in Philadelphia* (Edwin Mellen Press, 2003), chapter 5.

49. Frazier, *Negro Youth*, 91–102.

50. Johnson, *Growing Up in the Black Belt*, 84.

51. Johnson, *Black Belt*, 90–91.

52. Johnson, *Black Belt*, 99.

53. Johnson, *Reforming Jim Crow*, 137–138.

54. IQ tests have been proven biased according to culture, class, and facility with language. See Patricia Sexton, *Education and Income* (New York: Viking Press, 1961), 40. Also see Louis L. Knowles and Kenneth Prewitt, eds., *Institutional Racism in America* (Englewood Cliffs, NJ: Prentice-Hall, Inc., 1969), 35–37.

55. Anandi Mani, Sendhil Mullainathan, Eldar Shafir, Jiaying Zhao, "Poverty Impedes Cognitive Function," *Science* 341, no. 6149 (August 39, 2013): 976–980.

56. Knowles and Prewitt, *Institutional Racism*, 37–40.

57. Goldfield, *Black, White, and Southern*, 57.

58. Mani et al., "Poverty Impedes Cognitive Function," *Science*, passim.

59. Nelson, *Black Leadership*, 56, 86; *Philadelphia Tribune*, May 14, 1930. See also Sides, "Working Away," 42–46.

60. Kenneth W. Goines and Raymond A. Mohl, eds., *The New African American Urban History* (Thousand Oaks, CA: Sage Publications, 1996); Kenneth L. Kusmar, "African Americans in the City Since World War II: From the Industrial to the Postindustrial Era," 332.

61. See H. Viscount "Berky" Nelson, *The Rise and Fall of Modern Black Leadership: Chronicle of a Twentieth-Century Tragedy* (Latham, Maryland: University Press of America, 2003), chapter 5.

62. Although a previous book written by this author focuses on class myopia projected by black leaders in Philadelphia during the 1930s, similar findings held true for African American leaders operating within most major cities of the United States. See Nelson, *Black Leadership's Response to the Great Depression in Philadelphia*, passim.

63. Karen Ferguson, *Black Politics and the New Deal in Atlanta* (Chapel Hill: University of North Carolina Press), 8–9, 96–101.

64. Ferguson, *Black Politics and the New Deal in Atlanta*, 13, chapters 7 and 8.

65. Nelson, *Black Leadership's Response to the Great Depression*, 55–56.

66. *Philadelphia Tribune*, December 28, 1933 and March 5, 1936; *Philadelphia Independent*, September 23, 1936.

67. For a general overview of life in a black ward during the 1930s, see Nelson, *Black Leadership's Response to the Great Depression*, chapter 3. Also see Warren et al., *Color and Human Nature*, 20.

68. Peter M. Bergman, *The Chronological History of the Negro in America* (New York: Harper and Row, 1969), 457.

69. Myrdal, *American Dilemma*, 750, 807, 814.

70. Haywood Patterson, the last Scottsboro Boy, was eventually freed in 1950. See Dan T. Carter, *Scottsboro: A Tragedy of the American South* (New

York: Oxford University Press, 1971), 274-333 passim. Also see Bergman, *Chronological History*, 454.

71. See Angelo Herndon, *Let Me Live* (New York: Random House, Inc., 1937), 190, 193, 293, 296–298.

72. For information regarding "The Call for [a] National Negro Congress" and John P. Davis, "Let Us build a National Negro Congress," go to the Urban Archives, Temple University, Philadelphia.

73. See "Call for [a] National Negro Congress" in the Temple University Archives. Also see Bergman, *Chronological History*, 472.

74. See program for Philadelphia Convention of the National Negro Congress, Urban Archives, Temple University.

75. Wilson Record, *The Negro and the Communist Party* (New York: Atheneum, 1971), 195–196. Also see Herbert Garfinkle, *When Negroes March* (New York: Atheneum, 1969), 31, 47; Sugrue, *Sweet Land of Liberty*, 39.

76. When the CPUSA deserted African Americans to support the Soviet Union's peace pact with Germany in 1939, the relationship between blacks and communism essentially ended. See Gunnar Myrdal, *An American Dilemma*, Vol. II (New York: McGraw-Hill Book Company, 1964), 750, 807, 814, 817–818.

Chapter 6

1. Leon Dixon, Gerald Hynes, and Carolyn Gaines Nelson, "A Black Perspective of American History: Part Sixteen: World War II." Also see James N. Gregory, *The Southern Diaspora : How the Great Migration of Black and White Southerners Transformed America* (Chapel Hill: University of North Carolina Press, 2005), 15. Also see Kenneth W. Goings and Raymond A. Mohl, Kusmer, *The New African American Urban History* (Thousand Oaks, CA: Sage Publications, 1996), 323.

2. Gunnar Myrdal, *An American Dilemma* (New York: McGraw-Hill Book Company, 1964), 253.

3. Charles S. Aiken, *The Cotton Plantation South Since the Civil War* (Baltimore: The Johns Hopkins University Press, 1998), 101–105.

4. Aiken, *Cotton Plantation*, 130. Also see US Census.

5. Myrdal, *American Dilemma*, 410–411.

6. Buchanan, *Black Americans in World War II*, 29–30. Also see Gregory, *The Southern Diaspora*, 93.

7. A. Russell Buchanan, *Black Americans in World War II* (Santa Barbara, California: Clio Books, 1977), 29–30, found in Robert C Weaver, *Negro Labor: A National Problem* (New York: Harcourt Brace, 1946), 45. Also see Thomas J. Sugrue, *Sweet Land of Liberty: The Forgotten Struggle for Civil Rights in the North* (New York: Random House, 2008), 44.

8. Herbert Garfinkle, *When Negroes March* (New York: Atheneum, 1969), 17–19.

9. Myrdal, *American Dilemma*, 412.

10. Bernard Sternsher, ed., *The Negro in Depression and War: Prelude to Revolution*, found in Richard M. Dalfiume, "The Forgotten Years of the Negro Revolution" (Chicago: Quadrangle Books, 1969), 308. Also see Myrdal, *American Dilemma*, fn 3, ccvi. Sugrue, *Sweet Land of Liberty*, 60.

11. Parris and Brooks, *Blacks in the City*, 296.

12. See Josh A. Sides, "Working Away: African-American Migration and the Community in Los Angeles from the Great Depression to 1954" (PhD Dissertation, UCLA, 1999), 80–81.

13. Garfinkle, *When Negroes March*, 23. Also see Sternsher, "Forgotten Years," in *Negroes in Depression and War*, 300.

14. Charles W. Sasser, *Patton's Panthers: The African-American 761st Tank Battalion in World War II* (New York: Pocket Books), 1. Also see Garfinkle, *When Negroes March*, 23, 27.

15. Sugrue, *Sweet Land of Liberty*, 76.

16. Herbert Hill, "Race, Ethnicity, and Organized Labor: Opposition to Affirmative Action," *New Policies*, 2 (Winter 1987), 32–33. Herbert Hill and

James E. Jones Jr., eds., "Black Workers, Organized Labor, and Title VII of the 1964 Civil Rights Act: Legislative History and Litigation Record," in *Race in America: The Struggle for Equality* (Madison: University of Wisconsin Press, 1993), 266. And for evidence of limitations placed on black unionists in the South, see Robert J. Norrell, "Caste in Steel: Jim Crow Careers in Birmingham, Alabama," *The Journal of American History* 73, no. 3 (December 1986), 669–685.

17. Myrdal, *An American Dilemma,* 199–200.

18. Jacqueline Jones, *The Dispossessed: America's Underclasses from the Civil War to the Present* (Basic Books, 1992), 224.

19. W. Lloyd Warner, Buford W. Junker, and Walter A. Adams, *Color and Human Nature: Negro Personality Development in a Northern City* (Washington, DC: American Council on Education, 1941), 23.

20. See Grossman, *Land of Hope,* 146. Also see St. Clair Drake and Horace R. Cayton, *Black Metropolis,* 600.

21. See Sides, "Working Away," 85–87, 95; Committee for Congested Production Areas, *Observations on the Sample Census in the Congested Production Areas,* k Series CA-2 (1944), no. 1–10; St. Clair Drake and Horace Cayton, *Black Metropolis: A Study of Negro Life in a Northern City,* Vol. II (New York: Harper and Row, 1962), 602; Nicholas Lemann, *The Promised Land* (New York: Alfred A. Knopf, 1991), chapters 1 and 2.

22. Robert C. Weaver, *The Negro Ghetto* (New York: Harcourt, Brace, and Company, 1948), 83–84; Sides, "Working Away," 80.

23. Robert C. Weaver, *Negro Ghetto,* 82.

24. Sides, "Working Away," 113.

25. Quoted from "Little Tokyo Committee" (Box 104 NAUL Papers); Sides, "Working Away," 115.

26. Weaver, *Negro Ghetto,* 86–94.

27. Weaver, *Negro Ghetto,* 104.

28. Weaver, *Negro Ghetto*, 351. See Myrdal, *American Dilemma*, 377–379. Also see St. Clair Drake and Horace Cayton, *Black Metropolis: Study of Negro Life in a Northern City*, Vol. I (New York: Harper and Row, 1945), 204.

29. Sides, "Working Away," 106, quoted from Dorothy W. Baruch, "Sleep Comes Hard," *The Nation* (January 27, 1945), 95–96. [YES]

30. Sides, "Working Away," 108.

31. Sides, "Working Away," 122–124, 250. Also see Karl E. and Alma F. Tauber, *Negroes in Cities: Residential Segregation and Neighborhood Change* (Chicago: Aldine Publishing, 1965), 22.

32. Weaver, *Negro Ghetto*, 154, 167.

33. See Weaver, *Negro Ghetto*, 211; Myrdal, *American Dilemma* II, 1010.

34. Parris and Brooks, *Blacks in the City*, 206.

35. James R. Grossman, *Land of Hope: Chicago, Black Southerners, and the Great Migration* (Chicago: University of Chicago Press, 1989), 246–251.

36. See Grossman, *Land of Hope*, 151–152.

37. Erol Ricketts, "The Underclass: Causes and Responses," in George C. Galster and Edward W. Hill, eds., *The Metropolis in Black and White: Place, Power, and Polarization* (New Brunswick: Rutgers University Press, 1992), 219–220.

38. See Gregory, *The Southern Diaspora*, 227, 298.

39. Blum, *V Was for Victory*, 202.

40. See Blum, *V Was for Victory*, 203–204; Buchanan, *Black Americans in World War II*, 50–53. Also see Robert C. Weaver, *The Negro Ghetto* (New York: Russell and Russell, 1948), 91–92.

41. Buchanan, *Black Americans in World War II*, 55–56.

42. Buchanan, *Black Americans in World War II*, 55.

43. Peter M. Bergman, *The Chronological History of the Negro in America* (New York: Harper and Row Publishers, 1969), 500–501. Also see Blum, *V Was for Victory*, 202–206.

44. Parris and Brooks, *Blacks in the City*, 300.

45. See Blum, *V Was for Victory*, 191.

46. Sides, "Working Away," 108, quoted from Elmo William Hoolbrook to Governor Earl Warren, May 11, 1947, Folder 3640, 3677, Earl Warren Papers. For similar findings in Chicago, see Drake and Cayton, *Black Metropolis*, 608–611.

47. Sides, "Working Away," 109–112.

48. Buchanan, *Black Americans in World War II*, 71–72.

49. Gerald Astor, *The Right to Fight: A History of African Americans in the Military* (Cambridge, Mass.: De Capo Press, 1998), 67–168. Also see Buchanan, *Black Americans in World War II*, 72.

50. Myrdal, *American Dilemma*, 419.

51. Parris and Brooks, *Blacks in the City*, 302.

52. Buchanan, *Black Americans in World War II*, 126–127.

53. Herbert Hill, *Black Labor and the American Legal System: Race, Work, and the Law* (Madison: The University of Wisconsin Press, 1985), 374.

54. See Gregory, *The Southern Diaspora*, 92–93.

55. See Gregory, *Southern Diaspora*, 264–265.

56. Gerald Horne, *Communist Front: The Civil Rights Congress, 1946–1956* (Teaneck: Farleigh Dickinson Press, 1988), 15; George Lewis, *The White South and the Red Menace: Segregationalists, Anticommunism, and Massive Resistance, 1945–1965* (Gainesville: University of Florida Press), 55, 144–115; Jeff Woods, *Black Struggle Red Scare: Segregation and Anti-Communism in the South, 1948–1968* (Baton Rouge: Louisiana State University Press, 2004), 9; Manny Marable, *Race, Reform, and Rebellion* (Jackson: University of Mississippi Press, 1991), 21–24.

57. Record, *Negro and the Communist Party*, 272–273, 286.

58. See Sides, "Working_Away, 202.

59. *The Crisis*, March 1949, 72. Also see Wilson Record, *The Negro and the Communist Party* (New York: Atheneum, 1971), 254–262.

60. Sides, "Working Away," 235.

61. Sidney M. Peck, "The Economic Situation of Negro Labor," in *The Negro and the American Labor Movement*, ed. Julius Jacobson (Anchor Books, 1968), 213.

62. Manning Marable, *How Capitalism Underdeveloped Black America: Problems in Race, Political Economy, and Society* (Boston: South End Press, 1983), 28.

63. Sides, "Working Away," 225–226. Marable, *How Capitalism Underdeveloped Black America*, 85.

64. Sugrue, *Sweet Land of Liberty*, 92.

65. David W. Springer et al., *Introduction and Overview of Juvenile Delinquency and Juvenile Justice* (Jones and Bartlett Publishers, Circa 2008–2009), 7.

66. Report of the executive director, October, 1946, YWCA, TUA.

67. Report of the executive director, January, 1947, YWCA, TUA.

68. Buchanan, *Black Americans in World War II*, 128–129.

69. Richard Bardolph, ed., *The Civil Rights Record: Black Americans and the Law, 1849–1970* (New York: Thomas Y. Crowell Company, 1970), 247–248.

70. Sides, "Working Away," 245–246.

71. Leonard Broom and Norval D. Glenn, "The Occupations and Income of Black Americans," in *Blacks in the United States*, eds. Norval D. Glenn and Charles M. Bonjean (San Francisco: Chandler Publishing Company, 1969), 31. Also see Gregory, *The Southern Diaspora*, 92–93. Sucre, *Sweet Land of Liberty*, 94.

72. Between 1944 and 1963, 114 fair employment bills were sent to Congress with none being enacted. Sugrue, *Sweet Land of Liberty*, 94.

73. Hill, *Black Labor,* 379. Also see Sugrue, *Sweet Land of Liberty*, 122.

74. Sugrue, *Sweet Land of Liberty*, 121–122.

75. Bergman, *Negro in America*, 516, 517, 521.

Chapter 7

1. In fact, 1953 marked the last year of relatively low black unemployment. Helene Slessarev, *The Betrayal of the Urban Poor* (Philadelphia: Temple University Press, 1997), 4.

2. Sugrue, *Sweet Land of Liberty*, 52–53, 202–204.

3. Sidney M. Peck, "The Economic Situation of Negro Labor," in *The Negro and the American Labor Movement*, ed. Julius Jacobson (New York: Anchor Books, 1968), 212, 230, 237–238.

4. Jeanne Lowe, "The End of the Line: Race and Poverty in Cities," in *American Urban History: An Interpretive Reader with Commentaries*, ed. Alexander B. Callow Jr. (New York: Oxford University Press, 1969), 526. Also see Blackmon, *Slavery by Another Name*, 381.

5. See Lowe, "End of the Line," in *American Urban History*, 526. Also see Lisa Levenstein, *A Movement Without Marches: African American Women and the Politics of Poverty in Postwar Philadelphia* (Chapel Hill: University of North Carolina Press, 2009), 15.

6. Carl T. Rowan, *South of Freedom* (New York: Alfred A. Knopf, 1952), 257, 259.

7. See Leonard Blumberg, "Migration: A Pilot Study of Recent Negro Migrants into Philadelphia," Temple Urban Archives, Box 3 (Urban League of Philadelphia, 1958), 1, 11–13.

8. See Levenstein, *Movement Without Marches*, 11.

9. Minutes of the Committee Meeting of the Vocational Service Department, 1/146, Box 9, TUA (Urban League October 25, 1956).

10. See Majorie E. Duckrey to Mr. Carter, Box 4, Urban Archives 1/54, TUA (Armstrong Association, June 11, 1957). Also see "A Look at the Vocational Services Department, URB, 1/149, Box 9, TUA, 1–10.

11. Robert H. Zieger, *For Jobs and Freedom: Race and Labor in America Since 1865* (Lexington: University of Kentucky Press, 2007), 164–168.

12. Sumner M. Rosen, "The CIO Era, 1935–55," found in Jacobson, *Negro and the American Labor Movement,* 190.

13. Rosen, "CIO Era," found in Jacobson, *Negro and the American Labor Movement,* 194.

14. See Quillian, "Decline of Male Employment," 244.

15. Executive Director's Report (YWCA, TUA, November–December 1947).

16. Milton Washington, "Meeting the Needs of South Philadelphia, 1957," (YMCA, Temple Urban Archives). Board of Managers correspondence; Milton H. Washington, "Meeting the Needs of South Philadelphia: A New Challenge for the Christian Street YMCA" (Board of Managers, Christian Street YMCA [hereafter YMCA], TUA, 1957).

17. Committee of Management Minutes (YWCA, TUA, May 14, 1958).

18. H. Viscount Nelson, "Philadelphia's Thirtieth Ward, 1940–1960," *Pennsylvania Heritage Magazine* V, no. 2 (Spring 1979): passim.

19. See Board of Managers Meeting (October 7, 1956) and Summary Report of Board Meetings, Board of Managers (YMCA, TUA, 1956).

20. Washington, "Meeting the Needs of South Philadelphia."

21. Executive Committee Minutes (June 27, 1946) and Executive Committee (YWCA, TUA, 1947).

22. See Jane Jacobs, *The Death and Life of Great American Cities* (New York: Vintage Books, 1961), 273–277.

23. Levenstein, *Movement Without Marches,* 7.

24. Found in David Canton's study of Raymond Pace Alexander in "Bewildered White Democrat to Raymond Pace Alexander" (RPA papers, Box 35, Folder

4, May 8, 1957); No name to Alexander, n.d. (RPA papers, Box 35, Folder 5); White Girl to Alexander (Box 35, Folder 4, University of Pennsylvania Archives, August 2, 1957).

25. Unmarried women with children were perceived as being promiscuous, irresponsible, and unlikely to pay rent. See Levenstein, *Movement Without Marches*, 98–99.

26. See Levenstein, *Movement Without Marches*, 112–119.

27. Rowan, *South of Freedom*, 64.

28. See Levenstein, *Movement Without Marches*, 91.

29. Rowan, *South of Freedom*, 69.

30. Louis N. Knowles and Kenneth Prewitt, eds., *Institutional Racism in America* (Englewood Cliffs, New Jersey: Prentice-Hall Inc., 1969), 27.

31. Rowan, *South of Freedom*, 71.

32. Rowan, *South of Freedom*, 74. Also see Delores Acevedo-Garcia, "Residential Segregation and the Epidemiology of Infectious Diseases," *Social Science and Medicine* 451, Issue 8 (October 2000): 1143–1161.

33. See Rowan, *South of Freedom*, 72–74.

34. Raymond Wolters, *The Burden of Brown: Thirty Years of School Desegregation* (Knoxville: University of Tennessee Press, 1983), 41.

35. Rowan, *South of Freedom*, 76–77.

36. Wolters, *Burden of Brown*, 9. Also see Kimberley Johnson, *Reforming Jim Crow: Southern Politics and State in the Age Before Brown* (New York: Oxford University Press, 2010), 143.

37. Besides Washington, DC, and Topeka, Kansas, other sites included New Castle County, Delaware; Prince Edward County, Virginia; and Clarendon County, South Carolina. See Charles J. Ogletree Jr., *All Deliberate Speed: Reflections on the First Half Century of Brown v. Board of Education* (New York: W. W. Norton and Company, 2004), 6; Wolters, *Burden of Brown*, 3–8.

38. George W. Groh, *The Black Migration: The Journey to Urban America* (New York: Weybright and Talley, 1972), 26–27; 31–32.

39. Wolters, *Burden of Brown*, 15.

40. Wolters, *Burden of Brown*, 13.

41. Wolters, *Burden of Brown*, 12–14.

42. See Glenn C. Atkyns, "Trends in the Retention of Married and Pregnant Students in American Public Schools," *Psychology of Education* 41, 1 (1968): 57–65.

43. Harry S. Ashmore, *The Negro and the Schools* (Chapel Hill: The University of North Carolina Press, 1954), 77–78.

44. Levinstein, *Movement Without Marches*, 142–143.

45. "Report of the Visiting Committee on the Evaluation of the Benjamin Franklin High School" (prepared under the direction on The Commission on Secondary Schools of the Middle States Association of Schools and Colleges, Philadelphia, PA, April 23–26, 1951), 2–4. NAACP, 5–7.

46. Levenstein, *Movement Without Marches*, 122.

47. Ibid.

48. Levenstein, *Movement Without Marches*, 124–125, 132.

49. *Youth in the Ghetto: A Study of the Consequences of Powerlessness and a Blueprint for Change* (a report, Harlem Youth Opportunities Unlimited, Inc., December 1963), 7.

50. Youth in the Ghetto, 195.

51. *Youth in the Ghetto*, 195–200. All for additional understanding of problems associated with Harlem youth during the 1950s, see Claude Brown, *Manchild in the Promised Land* (New York: Simon and Schuster, 1965), passim. Also see Claude Brown obituary, *New York Times*, February 6, 2002. And for an even grimmer picture of life in Harlem, see Fox Butterfield, *All God's Children: The Bosket Family and the American Tradition of Violence* (New York: Alfred A. Knopf, 1995), 77–85, 91–92; Eric Schneider, *Vampires, Dragons, and Egyptian*

Kings: Youth Gangs in Postwar New York (Princeton: Princeton University Press, 1999), 107–113; Levenstein, *Movement Without Marches*, 136–137.

52. *Youth in the Ghetto*, 198–200.

53. *Youth in the Ghetto*, 199.

54. *Youth in the Ghetto*, 201–204.

55. See Garth L. Mangum and Stephan Seninger, *Coming of Age in the Ghetto: A Dilemma of Youth Unemployment* (Baltimore: The Johns Hopkins University Press, 1978), 26 and chapter IX.

56. Nicholas Lemann, *The Promised Land: The Great Migration and How It Changed America* (New York, 1991), 118.

57. Blackmon, *Slavery by Another Name*, 390.

58. Sugrue, *Sweet Land of Liberty*, 214.

59. Ibid.

Chapter 8

1. Thomas J. Sugrue, *Sweet Land of Liberty: The Forgotten Struggle for Civil Rights in the North* (New York: Random House, 2008), 255.

2. See Taylor Branch, *At Canaan's Edge: America in the King Years 1965–1968* (New York: Simon and Schuster, 2006), 232–233. Also see Thomas J. Sugrue, *Sweet Land of Liberty*, 256–257.

3. Sugrue, *Sweet Land of Liberty*, 258, 307.

4. Sidney M. Peck, "The Economic Situation of Negro Labor," found in Julius Jacobson, *The Negro and the American Labor Movement* (Garden City, New York: Double Day and Company, 1968), 216–217.

5. Peck, "Economic Situation of Negro Labor," 215–216.

6. *Report of the National Advisory Commission on Civil Disorders* (New York: The New York Times Company, 1968), 229. Hereafter this source will be documented as the Kerner Commission Report.

7. See Robert Dallek, *Flawed Giant: Lyndon Johnson and His Times, 1961–1973* (New York: Oxford University Press, 1998), 211–212 and 216–219.

8. See Sidney Peck, "The Economic Situation of Negro Labor," in *The Negro and the American Labor Movement*, ed. Julius Jacobson (Garden City, New York: Anchor Books, 1968), 212–214.

9. Peck, "Economic Situation of Negro Labor," 212–213.

10. See Taylor Branch, *Pillar of Fire: America in the King Years 1963–65* (New York: Simon and Schuster, 1998), 291.

11. Sugrue, *Sweet Land of Liberty*, 356–357.

12. Sugrue, *Sweet Land of Liberty*, 357.

13. Sugrue, *Sweet Land of Liberty*, 366–367.

14. *Kerner Commission Report*, 251–257. Also see Kenneth Clark, *Dark Ghetto: Dilemmas of Social Power* (New York: Harper and Row, Publishers, 1965), 34–35. Also see Douglas S. Massey, "The New Geography of Inequality in America," in *Race, Poverty, and Domestic Policy*, ed. Julius Jacobson (New Haven: Yale University Press, 2004), 74–180; Alphonso Pinkney, *Black Americans* (Englewood Cliffs, New Jersey: Prentice-Hall, 1975), 86–87.

15. Sugrue; *Sweet Land of Liberty*, 470.

16. See Jacobson and Peck, "Economic Situation of Negro Labor," 214–216.

17. Jacobson and Peck, "Economic Situation of Negro Labor," 216, quoted from S. M. Willhelm and E.H. Powell, "Who Needs the Negro?" *Trans-Action* (October 1964): 3.

18. Jacobson and Peck, "Economic Situation of Negro Labor," 217.

19. Jacobson and Peck, "Economic Situation of Negro Labor, 217. Also see Douglas G. Glasgow, *The Black Underclass: Poverty, Unemployment, and Entrapment of Ghetto Youth* (San Francisco: Jossey-Bass Publishers, 1980), 5.

20. Jacobson and Peck, "Economic Situation of the Negro," 218.

21. See Jacobson and Peck, "Economic Situation of Negro Labor," 224–225.

22. *Kerner Commission Report*, 274–277.

23. *Kerner Commission Report*, 177.

24. See Glasgow, *Black Underclass*, 32.

25. *Kerner Commission Report*, 276–277.

26. See Silverstein and Krate, *Children of Dark Ghetto*, 8–9.

27. Peter M. Bergman, *The Chronological History of the Negro in America* (New York: Harper and Row, 1969), 584–585.

28. Sugrue, *Sweet Land of Liberty*, 329–336.

29. Glasgow, *Black Underclass*, 37–38, 40–41.

30. Stewart E. Tolnay and Suzanne C. Eichenlaub, "Inequality in the West: Racial and Ethnic Variation in Occupational Status and Returns to Education, 1940–2000," *Social Science History* 31, no. 4 (Winter 2007), 487–488. Also see Lincoln Quillian, "The decline of male employment in low-income black neighborhoods, 1950–1990," *Social Science Research* 32 (2003), 225–226, 237.

31. See Quillian, "Decline of Male Employment, 244–245.

32. Glasgow, *Black Underclass*, 47–48.

33. See Glasgow, *Black Underclass*, viii–ix. Also see *Kerner Commission Report*, 284–285.

34. Glasgow, *Black Underclass*, 45.

35. Sugrue, *Sweet Land of Liberty*, 347.

36. See Glasgow, *Black Underclass*, 10–12, 24, 43.

37. *Kerner Commission Report*, 252.

38. Daniel Patrick Moynihan, "The Negro Family: The Case for National Action" (Office of Policy Planning and Research, United States Department of Labor, March 1965), 218–219.

39. Levenstein, *Movement Without Marching*, 5–7.

40. See Alexander, *New Jim Crow*, 45.

41. See *Kerner Commission Report*, 257.

42. *Kerner Commission Report*, 257–258.

43. Correspondingly, employed men revealed a greater tendency to remain with their wives. See *Kerner Commission Report*, 260–261.

44. See Barry Silverstein and Ronald Krate, *Children of the Dark Ghetto*_(New York: Praeger Publishers, 1975), 7. Also see Louis K. Knowles and Kenneth Prewitt, eds., *Institutional Racism in America* (Englewood Cliffs, New Jersey: Prentice-Hall, Inc., 1968), 31.

45. Silverstein and Krate, *Children of Dark Ghetto*, 15–16.

46. Silverstein and Krate, *Children of Dark Ghetto*, 23–27.

47. Lee Rainwater, *Behind Ghetto Walls* (Chicago: Aldine Atherton, Inc., 1970), 218–222. Silverstein and Krate, *Children of Dark Ghetto*, 17–19.

48. Silverstein and Krate, *Children of the Dark Ghetto*, 28, 30–31.

49. Ibid.

50. See *Kerner Commission Report*, 261–262.

51. Knowles and Prewitt, *Institutional Racism in America*, 42–43.

52. See *Kerner Commission Report*, 269.

53. *Kerner Commission Report*, 269–270.

54. *Kerner Commission Report*, 269–273.

55. Draft, "Narcotics and Dangerous Drugs," nn. (Daniel Patrick Moynihan Files, Action Memos, WHCF; SMOF, Box 58, Nixon Library, April 14, 1969), hereafter Nixon Files.

56. *Kerner Commission Report*, 267–268.

57. *Kerner Commission Report*, 268.

58. Alexander, *New Jim Crow*, 40–43.

59. Peck, "Economic Situation of Negro Labor," 225.

60. See Silverstein and Krate, *Children of Dark Ghetto*, 35, 172–173.

61. Silverstein and Krate, *Children of Dark Ghetto*, 36.

62. Rainwater, *Behind Ghetto Walls*, 281–284. Also see Silverman and Krate, *Children of Dark Ghetto*, 113, 246.

63. Jacobson, Peck, "Economic Situation of Negro Labor," 215.

Chapter 9

1. Patterson, "The Urban Underclass and Poverty Paradox," in *The Urban Underclass*, eds. Christopher Jencks and Paul E. Patterson (Washington, DC: The Brookings Institute, 1991), 7.

2. Thomas J. Sugrue, *Sweet Land of Liberty: The Forgotten Struggle for Civil Rights in the North* (New York: Random House, 2008), 518.

3. Half the black women employed full time earned meager wages, leaving a family of four in poverty. Joel F. Handler and Yeheskel Hasenfield, *Black Welfare: Ignore Poverty and Inequality* (New York: Cambridge University Press, 2007), 34–35; Jason De Parle, *American Dream: Three Women, Ten Kids, and a National Drive to End Welfare* (New York: Viking Press, 2004), 93.

4. Helene Slessarev, *Betrayal of the Urban Poor* (Philadelphia: Temple University Press, 1997), 52–55.

5. See Nicholas Lemann, *The Promised Land: the Great Migration and How It Changed America* (New York: Alfred A. Knopf, 1991), 288–291.

6. John G. Cawelti, "That's What I like About the South: Changing Images of the South in the 1970s," in *The Lost Decade: America in the Seventies,* ed. Elsebeth Hurup (Aarthus, Denmark: Aarhus University Press, 1996), 16–17.

7. Hurup and Cawelti, *The Lost Decade,* 12.

8. See Bruce J. Schulman, *The Seventies: The Great Shift in American Culture, Society, and Politics* (New York: De Capo Press, 2001), 3, 8.

9. W. E. B. Du Bois, *The Philadelphia Negro* (New York: Schocken Books, 1967), 385–397.

10. William Julius Wilson, *When Work Disappears* (New York: Alfred A. Knopf, 1996), 194.

11. Slessarev, *Betrayal,* 54–55.

12. See William W. Goldsmith and Edward J. Blakely, *Separate Societies: Poverty and Inequality in U.S. Cities* (Philadelphia: Temple University Press, 1992), 8–10.

13. Handler and Hasenfeld, *Blame Welfare,* 35. Also see Goldsmith and Blakely, *Separate Societies,* 10.

14. See Jeff Chang, *Can't Stop Won't Stop: A History of the Hip-Hop Generation* (New York: St. Martin's Press, 2005), 14.

15. Lemann, *Promised Land,* 201.

16. H. Viscount "Berky" Nelson, *The Rise and Fall of Modern Black Leadership: Chronicle of a Twentieth-Century Tragedy* (Lanham, Maryland: University Press of America, 2003), 234–236.

17. Sugrue, *Sweet Land of Liberty,* 500–501, 504–505.

18. Lemann, *Promised Land,* 282–283.

19. Lemann, *Promised Land,* 282–283 and Jenks and Peterson, *Urban Underclass,* 35.

20. Dan T. Carter, *From George Wallace to Newt Gingrich: Race in the Counter Revolution, 1963–1994* (Baton Rouge: Louisiana State University Press, 1999), 31–35.

21. See Michelle Alexander, *The New Jim Crow: Mass Incarceration in the Age of Colorblindness* (New York: The New Press, 2012), 46–47.

22. Schulman, *The Seventies*, 24–27.

23. See NAACP Annual Reports 1971 (p. 46), 1972 (p. 60), 1973 (p. 51), and 1974 (pp. 45–50). Also see NAACP Annual Reports 1970–1973 (p. 83). [FINE]

24. Schulman, *The Seventies*, 55.

25. See request of Robert J. Brown to the White House, "This is perhaps a subject the 5:00 o'clock group might want to disclose" (April 16, 1969). Also see Attorney General (John Mitchell) to Honorable Robert H. Finch (April 18, 1969); Moynihan concurs with Brown (Box 58, April 21, 1969). William J. King et al., "Perspectives and Recommendations by the Inter-City Seminar on Training the Hardcore" (Box 62, Folder 1, Civil Rights Employment-Environment, Nixon Library Files, March 4, 1969), 1–7, 31–32. Also see Richard M. Nixon's speech on the presidency (*New York Times*, September 20, 1968), in which he declared the federal government would leave job-training efforts to the states. See Bradley H. Patterson Jr., Executive Director, The National Advisory Council On Economic Opportunity, "Decentralization To the Neighborhoods—Conceptual Analysis" (Box 62, Folder 6, Civil Rights—Employment, Nixon Library Files, November 15, 1968).

26. In Pittsburgh, Pennsylvania, efforts to train blacks for construction jobs failed because of political differences between unions, black leaders, and the construction industry. Michael Stern, "Effort to Train Blacks For Construction Jobs Falters in Pittsburgh," *Wall Street Journal* (found in Folder 11, Box 62, Civil Rights Employment, Nixon Library Files, July 24, 1969).

27. New York City, for example, realized a 20 percent increase in technical industries between 1976 and 1980. See Clemet Cottingham, ed., *Race, Poverty, and the Urban Underclass* (Lexington, Mass.: Lexington Books, D. C. Heath and Company), 4–5.

28. C. Michael Henry, *Race, Poverty, and Domestic Policy* (New Haven: Yale University Press, 204), 181–182. Also see Sugrue, *Sweet Land of Liberty*, 486–487.

29. See Sugrue, *Sweet Land of Liberty*, 491. Also see Schulman, *The Seventies*, 57–62.

30. Schulman, *The Seventies*, 76–81.

31. Cottingham, *Race, Poverty, and the Urban Underclass*, 2–4.

32. Douglas S. Massey, "The New Geography of Inequality in Urban America," in *Race, Poverty, and Domestic Policy*, ed. C. Michael Henry (New Haven" Yale University Press, 2004), 180.

33. Inez Smith Reid, "The Environment: An Issue That Minorities and the Poor No Longer Can Ignore," in *Race, Poverty, and the Urban Underclass*, ed. Clement Cottingham (Lexington, Mass: Lexington Books, 1982), 83–104.

34. Schulman, *The Seventies*, 196–197.

35. Lemann, *Promised Land*, 285.

36. Wilson, *Work*, 161.

37. See David W. Bartelt, "Housing the Underclass," in *The "Underclass" Debate: Views From History*, ed. Michael B. Katz (Princeton, New Jersey; Princeton University Press, 1993), 139.

38. As early as 1969, Housing and Urban director George Romney proposed that funds should be earmarked for jobs that could help the urban poor. See Romney, Memorandum for the President (James Coleman Evaluating Equality of Educational Opportunity, Box 79, WCHF-SMDF, Nixon Library Files, August 5, 1969).

39. Future HUD secretary Romney stated that even people in the ghetto wanted less help from the federal government and would rather resolve problems themselves. See George Romney to Dr. Paul McCracken, "Opening Statement by Governor George Romney to the Senate Committee on Banking and Currency" (White House Central Files, Interior Department, Box 79, January 22, 1969). Also see "The Recent Increase in Welfare

Caseloads" (Folder 7, Box 58, Series IV, Council for Urban Affairs, Nixon Library Files), passim.

40. Garth L. Mangum and Stephen F. Seninger, *Coming of Age in the Ghetto: A Dilemma of Youth Unemployment* (Baltimore: The Johns Hopkins University Press, 1978), 1–4.

41. Schulman, *The Seventies,* 26.

42. Crime Reports, First Police District (City Archives, Philadelphia, Pennsylvania, 1933). Letter from James C. Herron, Chief Inspector, Staff Services Bureau, Philadelphia Police Department to H. V. Nelson (July 26, 1978).

43. See David W. Bartelt, "Housing the Underclass," in *The "Underclass" Debate: Views from History,* ed. Michael B. Katz (Princeton, New Jersey: Princeton University Press, 1993), 119.

44. These numbers represent roughly half the New York City average and 40 percent of the nationwide average. See Chang, *Can't Stop Won't Stop,* 13.

45. Ibid.

46. Joe Conason and Jack Newfield, "The Men Who Are Burning New York," *Village Voice* (June 2, 1980): 1, 15–19; Jack Newfield, "A Budget for Bankers and Arsonists," *Village Voice* (June 2, 1980): 13. Found in Chang, *Can't Stop Won't Stop,* 14.

47. Lee Rainwater, *Behind Ghetto Walls: Black Families in a Federal Slum* (Chicago: Aldine Publishing Company, 1970), 252–253.

48. Cottingham, *Race, Poverty and the Urban Underclass,* 6–7. This statistic is contested by Jenks, *Urban Underclass,* 84–86, 95.

49. Cottingham, *Race, Poverty, and the Urban Underclass,* 7.

50. Ibid.

51. Mangum and Seninger, *Coming of Age in the Ghetto,* 65.

52. In 1959, 8 percent of prime-age black males—as opposed to 3 percent whites—failed to find work. By the end of the decade the numbers

increased to 16 percent blacks versus 5 percent whites respectively. Jenks and Patterson, "Urban Underclass," 45, 52.

53. Mangum and Seninger, *Coming of Age in the Ghetto*, 69–70.

54. De Parle, *American Dream*, 93; Mangum and Seninger, *Coming of Age in the Ghetto*, 67–69.

55. William L. Van Deburg, *Hoodlums: Black Villains and Social Bandits in American Life* (Chicago: University of Chicago Press, 2004), 117. Also see Mangum and Seninger, *Coming of Age in the Ghetto*, 67–69

56. Rainwater, *Behind Ghetto Walls*, 221–222.

57. Sharon Lamb, *The Secret Life of Girls* (New York: the Free Press, 2002), 120–122. Also see Rainwater, *Behind Ghetto Walls*, 202–206.

58. Robert I. Lerman and Theodora J. Ooms, eds., *Young Unwed Fathers*. Also see Elijah Anderson, "Sex Codes and Family Life Among Poor Inner City Youths," in *Young Unwed Fathers*, eds. Robert I. Lerman and Theodora J. Ooms (Philadelphia: Temple University Press, 1993), 38, 77–78, 85.

59. Anderson, "Sex and Family," in *Young Unwed Fathers*, 90–91.

60. Others like Charles Silberman placed more blame on failed educators and prejudice than students. See Charles E. Silberman, *Crisis in the Classroom: The Remaking of American Education* (New York: Random House, 19701), 86–87. Also see Mangum and Seninger, *Coming of Age in the Ghetto*, 75–76.

61. For case study evidence, see Lemann, *Promised Land*, 298–299.

62. John Horton, "Time and Cool People," in *Soul*, ed. Lee Rainwater (Transaction, Inc., 1970), 31–50.

63. See Johnson, "Sex Codes," *Young Unwed Fathers*, 94–95; Philip M. Glenson and Glen G. Cain, "Earnings of Black and White Youth," *Race, Poverty, and Domestic Policy*, 461. Also see Richard Majors and Janet Billson, *Cool Pose*, 76–80.

64. Majors and Billson, *Cool Pose*, 73, 76–80.

65. Majors and Billson, *Cool Pose*, 72–73.

66. Majors and Billson, *Cool Pose,* 73.

67. Majors and Billson, *Cool Pose,* 86–89.

68. Majors and Billson, *Cool Pose,* 79–82.

69. Majors and Billson, *Cool Pose,* 42–43, 46–47.

70. William L. Van Deburg, *Hoodlums: Black Villains and Social Bandits in American Life* (Chicago: University of Chicago Press, 2004), xvii–xix, 177–184, 188–190.

71. See Tricia Rose, *Black Noise: Rap Music and Black Culture in Contemporary America* (Hanover, New Hampshire: Wesleyan University Press and University Press of New England, 1994), 26–27.

72. Rose, *Black Noise,* 22–25.

73. Rose, *Black Noise,* 60.

74. Hip-hop culture comprised rap music, dance, and graffiti. See Chang, *Can't Stop, Won't Stop,* 248–250. Also see Robin D. G. Kelley, *Yo' Mama's Disfunktional* (Boston: Beacon Press, 1997), 37, 60–63.

75. Rose, *Black Noise,* 35–36, 38.

76. See Daniel Oliver Tucker, "Graffiti, Art, and Crime," edu/Berkeley.edu/Studentpages/cflores/historygraffiti.html. Also see Rose, *Black Noise,* 41–47.

77. Rose, *Black Noise,* 47–50

78. Lemann, *Promised Land,* 218–219.

79. Deburg, Hoodlums, 186; Schulman, *The Seventies,* 26.

Chapter 10

1. See Robert B. Carleson Files, "Removing the Non-Needy," circa July 1982, 09581-09583, Ronald Reagan Library, hereafter RL. Also see Donald P. Graves to William E. Dannemeyer, July 23, 1980; Dannemeyer to Graves, September 16, 1980; Richard R. Woodmanse to President Reagan, April 6, 1981; and Orrin G. Hatch to President, July 22, 1981 (HV 012, Human Rights, Employment, 04999, RL).

2. Black unemployment increased dramatically during the Reagan administration. Moreover, four in ten black families were headed by women. See Charles Hirschman, "Minorities in the Labor Market: Cyclical Patterns and Secular Trends in Joblessness," in *Divided Opportunities,* eds. Gary D. Sandefur and Marta Tienda, 65–70. Also see James P. Smith, "Poverty and the Family," *Divided Opportunities,* 147.

3. Hirschman, *Minorities,* 78.

4. Although the Reagan administration introduced the enterprise zone concept to create jobs in the depressed inner cities and to revitalize low-income black neighborhoods, it clearly sought to reduce programs designed to benefit the poor generally, and black women and children in particular. Helene Slessarev, *The Betrayal of the Urban Poor* (Philadelphia: Temple University Press, 2007), 11, 57. See the Administration Plan for Enterprise Zones (January 19, 1982). Also see Ted Shafer, "Putting a Stop to Poverty and Decay" (a reprint "From Saint Louis Commerce," Robert B. Carleson files 09581-09583, RL, November 1984).

5. See Joel A. Devine and James D. Wright, *The Greatest of Evils: Urban Poverty and the American Underclass* (New York: A. de Gruyter, 1993) 88–89. Jason De Parle, *American Dream: Three Women, Ten Kids, and a National Drive to End Welfare* (New York: Viking Press, 2004), 39.

6. Ken Auletta, *The Underclass* (New York, Vintage, 1983), iv.

7. Urban League Papers, Schomburg, *Wall Street Journal,* August 8, 1980.

8. Of more than 150 national officers nationwide, only Clarence Pendleton endorsed Reagan for president. See Mark Grossman, *The Civil Rights Movement* (Santa Barbara, California: ABC-CLIO, Inc., 1993), 159.

9. William Julius Wilson, *When Work Disappears: The World of the New Urban Poor* (New York: Alfred A. Knopf, 1996), 55.

10. See William W. Goldsmith and Edward J. Blakely, *Separate Societies: Poverty and Inequality in U.S. Cities* (Philadelphia: Temple University Press, 1992), 16.

11. Goldsmith and Blakely, *Separate Societies*, 145.

12. Anthony Asadullah Samad, *50Years After Brown: The State of Black Equality in America, African Americans Continuing Pursuit of 14th Amendment Rights* (Los Angeles: Kabili Press, 2005), 356.

13. Federal Equal Employment Opportunity Programs, nd. (HV 012, Equal Employment, 088899 [1]-089844 [2], RL, circa July 1982), 4.

14. Slessarev, *Betrayal*, 11, 60–61.

15. Black leaders disliked Reagan primarily because of the administration's anti-affirmative action stance. Representative Gus Hawkins of California, Vernon Jordan of the Urban League, and Eleanor Norton, former head of EEOC, spoke out against Reagan policies. See Memorandum for Don Shasteen from Warren Montgomery, OFCCP Hearing, July 16, 1981, HV 012, Human Rights Employment, June 18, 1988, RL. Also see Wilson, *When Work Disappears*, 159.

16. Robin D.G. Kelley, *Yo' Mama's Disfunktional: Fighting the Cultural Wars in Urban America* (Boston: Beacon Press, 1977), 94, 100–101.

17. See Mission Statement, "Minimum Wage Coalition to Save Jobs" (June 13, 1988) and Senate Republican Policy Committee, "Talking Points on The Minimum Wage" (Congressional Reports, Bolton Papers OA 18689, RL June 29, 1988). Also see Wilson, *When Work Disappears*, 175–176.

18. Frank Levy, *Dollars and Dreams* (New York: W.W. Norton, 1988); Lawrence Mishel and Jacqueline Simon, *The State of Working America* (Washington, DC, Economic Policy Institute 1988, found in Devine and Wright), 96. Also see William A. Johnson Jr., of the Rochester Urban League to The Honorable Ronald Reagan (HV 012, Equal Employment 650000-093299, subject File, WHORM, RL, November 12, 1981).

19. See Devine and Wright, *Greatest of Evils*, 118.

20. See Devine and Wright, *Greatest of Evils,* 118–119.

21. Devine and Wright, *Greatest of Evils,* 38–39.

22. See Devine and Wright, *Greatest of Evils,* 143–148. Also see Slessarev, *Betrayal,* 11.

23. Judith Cummings, *New York Times,* found in Clarence M. Pendleton, Melvin L. Bradley Files, OA 13336, RL.

24. Ibid.

25. See Memorandum For: Principal Staff, Regional Administrators from Leonard Burchman, Assistant to the Secretary For Public Affairs; Subject: The Anatomy of a Hatchet Job, April 7, 1983, *Impact Journal* (HMD Employee's Evaluation of Secretary Pierce, November/December 1983, FG 023, 13000-14099, WHORM Subject File, RL).

26. *Impact Journal,* November/December 1983.

27. H. Viscount "Berky" Nelson, *The Rise and Fall of Modern Black Leadership: Chronicle of a Twentieth-Century Tragedy* (Lanham, Maryland: University Press of America, 2003), 252–253. Also see Slessarev, *Betrayal,* 17–20.

28. Nelson, *Rise and Fall of Modern Black Leadership,* 254–255.

29. See Wilson, *When Work Disappears,* 186–187.

30. Wilson, *When Work Disappears,* 26–27.

31. Wilson, *When Work Disappears,* 154; Goldsmith and Blakely, *Separate Societies,* 110.

32. David W. Bartelt, "Housing the Underclass," in *The Underclass Debate View from History,* ed. Michael B. Katz (Princeton: Princeton University Press, 1993), 124.

33. Katz, *Underclass Debate,* 154.

34. Goldsmith and Blakely, *Separate Societies,* 111.

35. See Wilson, *When Work Disappears,* 47–48. Also see Devine and Wright, *Greatest Evils,* 77–78.

36. Thomas J. Sugrue, *Sweet Land of Liberty: The Forgotten Struggle for Civil Rights in the North* (New York: Random House, 2008), 520.

37. Katz, *Underclass Debate*, 133.

38. Goldsmith and Blakely, *Separate Societies*, 119. Also see Wilson, *When Work Disappears*, 48.

39. Wilson, *When Work Disappears*, 41–42.

40. Goldsmith and Blakely, *Separate Societies*, 134.

41. Lost jobs totaled in the hundreds of thousands. See William Julius Wilson, *The Truly Disadvantaged: The Inner City, the Underclass, and Public Policy* (Chicago: The University of Chicago Press, 1987), 40, 43. Also see Richard B. Freeman, "Employment of Disadvantaged Young Men," in *The Urban Underclass*, eds. C. Jencks and P. Peterson, 119.

42. Wilson, *When Work Disappears*, 32.

43. Goldsmith and Blakely, *Separate Societies*, 135.

44. Wilson, *When Work Disappears*, 118–119, 137–138.

45. Wilson, *When Work Disappears*, 131.

46. Wilson, *When Work Disappears*, 139. Also see Joleen Kirschenman and Kathryn, M. Neckerman, "We'd Love to Hire Them But . . . The Meaning of Race for Employers," in *Urban Underclass*, eds. C. Jencks and P. Peterson, 203–231.

47. Wilson, *When Work Disappears*, 123.

48. Wilson, *When Work Disappears*, 124–125.

49. Wilson, *When Work Disappears*, 127–129.

50. Wilson, *When Work Disappears*, 136.

51. Wilson, *When Work Disappears*, 140–141.

52. See Wilson, *When Work Disappears*, 44.

53. Devine and Wright, *Greatest of Evils,* 35.

54. See Devine and Wright, *Greatest of Evils,* 36.

55. Wilson, *When Work Disappears,* 132–135. Also See Goldsmith and Blakely, *Separate Societies,* 114.

56. Wilson, *When Work Disappears,* 14.

57. Wilson, *When Work Disappears,* 15.

58. Wilson, *When Work Disappears,* 185.

59. Define and Wright, *Greatest of Evils,* 124–125.

60. See Devine and Wright, *Greatest of Evils,* 126.

61. Jeff Chang, *Can't Stop Won't Stop* (New York: St. Martin's Press, 2005), 207–209. Also see Wilson, *When Work Disappears,* 62–63.

62. Alexander, *New Jim Crow,* 48–54.

63. Wilson, *When Work Disappears,* 48–49.

64. See Wilson, *When Work Disappears,* 63–64.

65. Devine and Wright, *Greatest of Evils,* 132–140, 174–175.

66. Devine and Wright, *Greatest of Evils,* 39–41.

67. Wilson, *Truly Disadvantaged,* 21.

68. Wilson, *Truly Disadvantaged,* 22.

69. Wilson, *When Work Disappears,* 22.

70. Wilson, *When Work Disappears,* 143.

71. *New York Times,* July 25, 1981.

72. *New York Times,* June 30, 1986.

73. Wilson, *When Work Disappears,* 193–194.

74. See National Urban League papers, Schomberg Library, *New York Times*, July 25, 1981.

75. Wilson, *When Work Disappears*, 164.

76. Wilson, *When Work Disappears*, 164. Also see Moynihan Report, 170–174.

77. Wilson, *When Work Disappears*, 64.

78. See Devine and Wright, *Greatest of Evils*, 41.

79. Devine and Wright, *Greatest of Evils*, 46.

80. Alford A. Young Jr., *The Minds of Marginalized Black Men: Making Sense of Mobility, Opportunity, and Future Life Chances* (Princeton: Princeton University Press, 2004), 166.

81. Alford Young found that one-third of the men he interviewed held these opinions. See Young, *Marginalized Black Men*, 112–115.

82. Young, *Marginalized Black Men*, 74–75.

83. Young, *Marginalized Black Men*, 82–83.

84. See Young, *Marginalized Black Men*, 76–77.

85. Alex Ogg, *The Hip-Hop Years* (New York: Macmillan Publishers, 1999), 111; Tricia Rose, *Black Noise* (Middleton, Conn.: Wesleyan University Press, 1994), passim.

86. See William L. Van Deburg, *Hoodlums: Black Villains and Social Bandits in American Life* (Chicago: University of Chicago Press, 2004), 196.

87. Chang, *Can't Stop, Won't Stop*, 325–326.

88. Also see Colton Simpson (with Ann Pearlman), *Inside the Crips: Life Inside L.A.'s Most Notorious Gang* (New York: St. Martin's Press, 2005), 57-60, 208-243 passim.

89. Sugrue, *Sweet Land of Liberty*, 520.

90. In 1980 the federal government spent $60 billion per year on urban housing, but by 1986 the administration reduced funding to $36 billion.

91. Devine and Wright, *Greatest of Evils*, 93.

92. Slessarev, *Betrayal*, 12.

93. The Reagan administration argued strenuously against increasing the minimum wage, using the rationalization that this policy would hurt the working poor. Yet at the same time, those among the upper echelon of black families, family income increased significantly. See Statement of Administration Policy, S-837 Minimum Restorative Act, September 19, 1988. Also see Beryl W. Sprinkel to Thomas E. Petri, May 13, 1988. Goldsmith and Blakely, *Separate Societies*, 154–155. Also see Wilson,_*When Work Disappears*, 194–195.

Chapter 11

1. Anuradha Mittal with Joan Powell, "The Last Plantation," *Backgrounder*, Winter (2000): 1–13.

2. See Jason De Parle, *American Dream: Three Women, Ten Kids, and a Nation's Drive to End Welfare* (New York: Viking Press, 2004), 129–137.

3. Helene Slessarev, *The Betrayal of the Urban Poor* (Philadelphia: Temple University Press, 1997), 1–2.

4. Poverty rates for black women specifically increased by 1990. Among black female-headed households, the rate of poverty between 1959 and 1990 comprised 50.6 percent (as opposed to 29.8 percent for whites). Joel A. Divine and James D. Wright, *The Greatest of Evils: Urban Poverty and the American Underclass* (New York: Aldine De Gruyter, 1993), 43 and 83–91. Also see De Parle, *American Dream*, 323–338.

5. See Lillian Breslow Rubin, *Worlds of Pain: Life in the Working-Class Family* (New York: Basic Books, 1976), 164–165. Also see Devine and Wright, *Greatest of Evils*, 148–158.

6. John E. Hansan and Robert Morris, eds., *Welfare Reform, 1996–2000: Is There a Safety Net?* (Westport, Connecticut: 1999), 1 9.

7. See Kevin Phillips, *Wealth and Democracy: A Political History of the American Rich* (New York: Broadway Books, 2002), vii, 383–385.

8. See William Julius Wilson, *When Work Disappears* (New York: Alfred A. Knopf, 1996), 170–172.

9. See Frank Stricker, *Why America Lost the War on Poverty—And How to Win It* (Chapel Hill: The University of North Carolina Press, 2007), 202–203. Also see De Parle, *American Dream,* 94.

10. See Stricker, *Why America Lost the War on Poverty,* 210.

11. See Stricker, *Why America Lost the War on Poverty,* 212–214.

12. Stricker, *Why America Lost the War on Poverty,* 206.

13. Stricker, *Why America Lost the War on Poverty,* 216.

14. See De Parle, *American Dream,* 8–9.

15. See Hansan and Morris, *Welfare Reform,*_9.

16. This phenomenon hardly proved unique and had occurred during the 1960s. See Gabriel Kolko, *Wealth and Power in America: An Analysis of Social Class and Income Distribution* (New York: Praeger Publishers, 1964), ix–xi, 4–7.

17. Slessarev, *Betrayal,* 1.

18. Stricker, *Why America Lost the War,* 193–196.

19. Wilson, *When Work Disappears,* 208.

20. See Wilson, *When Work Disappears,* 210–213. Also see Devine and Wright, *Greatest of Evils,* 158–162; Harvey Kantor and Barbara Brenzel, "Urban Education and the 'Truly Disadvantaged': The Historical Roots of Contemporary Crisis, 1945–1990," *The Underclass Debate: Views From History,* ed. Michael B. Katz (Princeton: Princeton University Press, 1993), 366–369, 380–384, 401–402.

21. Hansen and Morris, *Welfare Reform*, 1–2.

22. Gordon Berlin, "Testimony on the Reauthorization of the Temporary Assistance for Needy Families Program," (mdrc publications, March 2002), 1.

23. Hansen and Morris, *Welfare Reform*, 11.

24. See Phillips, *Wealth and Democracy*, 394.

25. Stricker, *Why America Lost the War on Poverty*, 203.

26. Wilson, *When Work Disappears*, 212–213.

27. Wilson, *When Work Disappears*, 216–217.

28. An established but disturbing trend occurred during the 1990s. Compared to the 1990s when one-third of American babies born outside marriage, in 2012 the number climbed to 41 percent. In 2012, 73 percent of black babies were born out of wedlock opposed to 53 percent Latino and 29 percent white. Although the percentage of out-of-wedlock births for black females declined, 1 percent of all births to unmarried black women increased slightly during the 1990s disproportionably. Far more unmarried African American women had children than Latinos and whites. Daily Mail Reporter, "The Collapse of Family Life: Most Children in US born out of wedlock," MailOnLine, February 18, 2012. Stephanie J. Ventura to Christine A. Bachrach, "Nonmarital Child Bearing in the United States, 1949–1999" (National Vital Statistics Reports, October 18, 2000), 5–6.

29. See De Parle, *American Dream*, 69–70.

30. Lily O. McNair and Cynthia M. Prather, "African American Woman and AIDS: Factors Influencing Risk and Reaction to the HV Disease," *Journal of Black Psychology*, 30, no. 1 (February 2004): 106–108.

31. Thomas J. Sugrue, *Sweet Land of Liberty: The Forgotten Struggle for Civil Rights in the North* (New York: Random House, 2008), 539–540.

32. Devine and Wright, *Greatest of Evils*, 123–124.

33. See Fox Butterfield, *All God's Children: The Bosket Family and the American Tradition of Violence* (New York: Alfred A. Knopf, 1996), 327–329.

34. See Colton Simpson with Ann Pearlman, *Inside the Crips: Life Inside L.A.'s Most Notorious Gang* (New York: St. Martin's Press, 2005), xviii, 186–207.

35. Lou Savelli, Vice President of the East Coast Gang Investigation Association, "National Gang History," 2001.

36. "Diagnostic and Statistical Manual of Mental Disorders," (American Psychiatric Association, Washington, DC, 1994), 645–650.

37. Devine and Wright, *Greatest of Evils*, 129–130.

38. UCLA Psychologists, "Harsh Family Environment May Adversely Affect Brain's Response to Threat" (March 13, 2006).

39. Stricker, *Why America Lost the War on Poverty*, 214–216.

40. Butterfield, *All God's Children*, 283–301.

41. See Janet A. DiPietro, "The Role of Prenatal Maternal Stress in Child Development," Current Directions in Psylogical Science, 3, no. 2 (Baltimore: Johns Hopkins University): 72–73. Also see Jessica McCallin, "Prenuptial depression: why some pregnant women feel despair," *The Guardian*, February 10, 2012. Butterfield, *All God's Children*, 134–135.

42. Butterfield, *All God's Children*, 283–301.

43. Leon Dash, Rosa Lee's Story, *The Washington Post*, September 18–25, 1994.

44. De Parle, *American Dream*, 61, 68–74, 283–284.

45. See Julie A. Phillips, "White, Black, and Latino Homicide Rates: Why the Difference?" *Social Problems* 49, no. 3: 359.

46. Butterfield, *All God's Children*, 325, 327.

47. Paul L. Street, *Racial Oppression in the Global Metropolis: A Living Black Chicago History* (Latham, Maryland: Roman and Littlefield Publishers, Inc., 2007), 267. Loic J. D. Wacquant, "Red Belt, Black Belt: Racial Division, Class Inequality, and the State in the French Urban Periphery and the American Ghetto," in *Urban Poverty and the Underclass*, ed. Loic J. D. Wacquant (Cambridge, Massachusetts,: Blackwell Publishers, Inc., 1996), 249–250.

48. Devine and Wright, *Greatest of Evils*, 63–64.

49. Devine and Wright, *Greatest of Evils*, 63, 72.

50. Blacks also disproportionably consumed more fast food than any other racial or ethnic group. See Shanthy A. Bowman and Bryan T. Vinyard, "Fast Food Consumption of U.S. Adults: Impact on Energy and Nutrient Intakes and Overweight Status," *Journal of the American College of Nutrition* (April 2004): 163–168. Also see Adam Drewnowski and SE. Specter, "Poverty and Obesity: The role of energy density and energy costs," *The American Journal of Clinical Nutrition* 79, no. 1 (January 2004): 6–16; Edith Patiste Harris, "An Assessment of Nutritional Education Needs of Low Income Black Americans By Comparison Food Practices And Diet Related Problems With The Federal Department's Dietary Guidelines" (Howard University, 1984): p.52.

51. See Linda L. Cowling, "California Food Grade: Health and Dietary Issues Affecting African Americans" (September 20, 2006): 2–3.

52. Steven Cummins and Sally Macintyre, "Food Environments and Obesity—Neighborhood or Nation," *International Journal of Epidemiology* 35, no. 1: 100–104.

53. Cowling, "California Food Grade: Health and Dietary Issues," 3–5.

54. Cowling, "California Food Grade: Health and Dietary Issues," 6–9.

55. In 1990 infant mortality rates for blacks, whites, and all races was 18.0, 7.6, and 9.2 respectively. By 1999 corresponding figures were 14.6, 5.8, and 7.1. "Infant Mortality and Low Birth Weight Among Black and White Infants—United States, 1980–2000," *CDC-MMWR Weekly* (July 12, 2000). Also see Thomas A LaVeist, PhD, "Health Disparities and the Minority-Majority," (Johns Hopkins, Bloomberg School of Public Health, 2000, Table 19): 53.

56. Lotie L. Joiner, "The State of African American Health," *The Crisis* 111, Series 6 (November/December 2004): 19.

57. Ibid.

58. Barbranda Lumpkins Walls, "Heart Disease: Number 1 Cause of Death," *Crisis*, 20.

59. Only 24 percent of white people lacked health insurance at the end of the century. Todd Zwillich, "82 Million U.S. Without Health Insurance," WebMD, June 16, 2004.

60. Walls, "Heart Disease," *Crisis*, 20.

61. See Arnessa Howell, "Cancer: A Lurking Adversary, State of African American Health"; Kendra Lee, "Up in Smoke: Blacks and Tobacco Use," 24; and Yanick Rice Lamb, "Obesity: Killing Us a Pound at a Time, 26–27, and Yanick Rice Lamb, "State of African American Health," in *Crisis.*

62. Ervin Dyer, "The New Face of AIDS, Young, Black, and Female," *Crisis*, 29.

63. Dyer, "New Face of AIDS," *Crisis*, 30–31.

64. Ibid.

65. Howard Zinn, "The Clinton Presidency and the Crisis of Democracy," in *The Twentieth Century: A People's History* (May 1998), chapter 23, passim.

66. Jonathan Turley Blog, Mark Espisito, "Republicans Discover Poor People," March 24, 2013. Also Devine and Wright, *Greatest of Evils*, 5–6; Peter Marcuse, "Space and Race in the Post-Fordest City, Enzo Mingione, ed., *Urban Poverty and the Underclass* (Cambridge, Massachusetts: Blainwell Publishers, 1996), 207–211.

67. Jared Bernstein, "Welfare Reform and the Low-Wage Labor Market: Employment, Wages, and Wage Policies," eds. Hansan and Morris, 43–44.

68. Lemann, *Promised Land*, 346.

Epilogue

1. Quoted from Nicholas Lemann, *The Promised Land: The Great Black Migration and How It Changed America* (New York: Alfred A. Knopf, 1991), 219.

2. Jason DeParle, *American Dream: Three Women, Ten Kids, and a Nation's Drive to end Welfare* (New York: Viking Press, 2004), 327.

3. Helene Slessarav, *The Betrayal of the Urban Poor* (Philadelphia: Temple University Press, 1997), 17.

4. Pete Daniel, *Dispossession: Discrimination against African American Farmers in the Age of Civil Rights* (Chapel Hill: The University of North Carolina Press, 2013), 246; Veronica Reed, "Fair Housing Enforcement: Is the Current System Adequate?" in *Residential Apartheid: The American Legacy*, eds. Robert D. Bullard, J. Eugene Grisby III, and Charles Lee (Los Angeles: Center for African American Studies, CAAS Publications, 1994), 222–234. Also see Robert H. Zieger, *For Jobs and Freedom: Race and Labor in America Since 1865* (Lexington: University of Kentucky Press, 2007), 222.

5. Robert B. Carleson papers, the Administration Plan for Enterprise Zones (file #09581-9583, Ronald Reagan Presidential Library, January 15, 1982).

6. Slessarev, *Betrayal*, 17.

7. Randall Kennedy, *Sellout: the Politics of Racial Betrayal*_(New York: Vintage Books, 2008), 67. Also see Paul A. Jargowsky, *Poverty and Place: Ghettos, Barrios, and the American City* (New York: Russell Sage Foundation, 1996), 89.

8. Houston A. Baker, Jr., *Betrayal: How Black Intellectuals Have Abandoned the Ideals of the Civil Rights Era* (New York: Columbia University Press, 2008), 80–84.

9. Information compiled from the RMHC Future Achiever Scholarship Program, 2005–2006 and 2009–2010.

BIBLIOGRAPHY

A NOTE ON SOURCES

The key to the quality of any manuscript depends largely on the availability of pertinent sources. This work is no exception. The Schomburg Library in New York City is an essential stop for scholars engaged in the study of Africans. For anyone studying blacks in Philadelphia, a plethora of information may be found at the Temple University Archives. Information may be found there about the Urban League, the black YMCA and YWCA, the NAACP, and other African American Institutions that provided evidence about African American life in the City of Brotherly Love. The Free Library of Philadelphia (and urban archives from other cities as well) should also be examined by scholars to gain a deeper understanding of impoverished black Americans—a silent, invisible populace that only raises a voice of displeasure by rioting in the streets in response to specific police incidents. Time was also spent perusing the Franklin D. Roosevelt, Richard M. Nixon and Ronald Reagan Presidential Libraries. Issues regarding impoverished African Americans became topics of discussion and occasional action despite the reality that a panacea to eliminate or reduce poverty within black America was never found.

Because most impoverished people fail to record thoughts in diaries, write letters, or leave personal historical records, excerpts obtained from interviews contained in secondary sources has proven essential. Nevertheless, information gleaned from secondary sources that demonstrate how the decisions made by federal, state, and municipal authorities impinged on the lives of disadvantaged African Americans has proven invaluable.

SECONDARY SOURCES

Abi, Omar H. In the Lion's Mouth: Black Populism in the New South, 1886-1900. Jackson: University of Mississippi Press, 2010.

Aiken, Charles S. The Cotton Plantation South: Since the Civil War. Baltimore: Johns Hopkins Press, 1998.

Alexander, Claud. Black Labor White Wealth: The Search for Power and Economic Justice. Bethesda, Maryland: PowerNomics Corporation of America, 1994.

Alexander, Michelle. A New Jim Crow: Mass Incarceration in the Age of Color Blindness. New York: The New Press, 2012.

Ashmore, Harry S. The Negro and the Schools. Chapel Hill: University of North Carolina Press, 1954.

Aster, Gerald. The Right to Fight: A History of African Americans in the Military. Cambridge, Mass.: De Capo Press, 1998.

Auletta, Ken. The Underclass. New York: Vintage Books, 1983.

Baker, Houston A. Jr. Betrayal: How Black Intellectuals Have Abandoned the Ideals of the Civil Rights Era. New York: Columbia University Press, 2008.

Baker, Ray Stannard. Following the Color Line: American Negro Citizenship in the Progressive Era. New York: Harper and Row, 1964.

Bardolph, Richard (ed.). The Civil Rights Record: Black Americans and the Law 1849-1970. New York: Thomas Y. Crowell Company, 1970.

Bergman, Peter M. The Chronological History of the Negro in America. New York: Harper and Row, 1969.

Berlin, Gordon. "Testimony on the Reauthorization of the Temporary Assistance For Needy Families Program. mdrc Publicans, 2002.

Billington, Monroe Lee. The American South. New York: Charles Scribner's Sons, 1971.

Blackmon, Douglas A. Slavery By Another Name: The Re-Enslavement of Black Americans from Civil War to World War II. New York: Doubleday, 2008.

Blum, John Morton. V Was for Victory: Politics and American Culture During World War II. New York: Harcourt, Brace, Jovanovich, 1976.

Botkin, B.A. Lay My Burden Down: A Folk History of Slavery. Chicago: University of Chicago Press, 1968.

Branch, Taylor. At Canaan's Edge: America in the King Years, 1965-1968. New York: Simon and Shuster, 2006.

-----Pillar of Fire: America in the King Years, 1963-1965. New York: Simon and Schuster, 1998.

Brown, Claude. Manchild in the Promised Land. New York: Simon and Schuster, 1965.

Brown, Sterling. Negro Poetry and Drama and the Negro in American Fiction. New York: Atheneum, 1969.

Buchanan, Russell A. Black Americans in World War II. Santa Barbara, CA. Clio Books, 1997.

Bullard, Robert D.; Grigsby, Eugene J. III; and Lee, Charles. Residential Apartheid: The American Legacy. Los Angeles: Center for African American Studies, CAAS Publicans, 1994.

Bullock, Henry Allen. A History of Negro Education in the South: From 1619 to the Present. New York: Praeger Bo0ks, 1970.

Butterfield, Fox. All God's Children: The Bosket Family and the American Tradition of Violence. Alfred A. Knopf, 1995.

Callow, Alexander B. Jr. (ed.). American Urban History: An Interpretative Reader With Commentaries. New York: Oxford University Press, 1969.

Canton, David A. Raymond Pace Alexander; A New Negro Lawyer Fights for Civil Rights in Philadelphia. Oxford; University of Mississippi Press, 2010.

Carter, Dan T. From George to Newt Gingrich: Race in the Counter Revolution, 1963-1994. Baton Rouge: Louisiana State University Press, 1999.

-----Scottsboro: A Tragedy of the American South. New York: Oxford University Press, 1971.

Chang, Jeff. Can't Stop; Won't Stop: A History of the Hip Hop Generation. New York: St. Martin's Press, 2005.

Clark, Kenneth. Dark Ghetto: Dilemmas of Social Power. New York: Harper and Row Publishers, 1965.

Cordusco, Francisco (ed.). Jacob Riis Revisited: Poverty and the Slum in Another Era. Garden City, N.Y.: Anchor Books, 1968.

Cronin, Edmund David. Black Moses: The Story of Marcus Garvey. Madison: University of Wisconsin Press, 1968.

Cottingham, Clement (ed.). Race, Poverty, and the Urban Underclass: Lexington, MA.: Lexington Books, D.C. Heath and Company, 1983.

-----Inez Smith Reid, "The Environment: An Issue that Minorities and the Poor Can No Longer Ignore."

Cummings, John and Hill, Joseph. Negro Population, 1790-1915. New York: Kraus Reprint Company, 1969.

Dallek, Robert. Flawed Giant: Lyndon Johnson and His Times, 1961-1973. New York: Oxford University Press, 1998.

Daniel, Pete. Dispossession: Discrimination Against African American Farmers in the Age of Civil Rights. Chapel Hill: University of North Carolina Press, 2013.

De Parle, Jason. American Dream: Three Women, Ten Kids, and a National Drive to End Welfare. New York: Viking Press, 2004.

Devine, Joel A. and Wright, James D. The Greatest of Evils: American Poverty and the Urban Underclass. New York: Aldine de Gruyter, 1993.

Di Pietro, Janet A. "The Role of Prenatal Mental Development." Current Directions in Psychological Science. Baltimore: Johns Hopkins University Press, 2004.

Drake, St. Clair and Cayton, Horace R. Black Metropolis: A Study of Life in a Northern City Vols. I and II New York: Harper and Row, 1945.

Dray, Philip. At the Hands of Persons Unknown: The Lynching of Black America. New York: The Modern Library, 2002.

Du Bois, W.E.B. The Black North in 1901: A Social Study. New York: Arno Press and the New York Times, 1969.

-----The Philadelphia Negro: A Social Study. New York: Schocken Books, 1967.

-----The Souls of Black Folks. New York Vintage Books, 1990.

Ferguson, Karen. Black Politics and the New Deal in Atlanta. Chapel Hill: University of North Carolina Press, 2002.

Foner, Philip S. and Lewis, Ronald L. (eds.). The Black Worker: A Documentary History From Colonial Times to the Present. Vol. VI. Philadelphia: Temple University Press, 1981.

-----The Black Worker: The Era of Post-War Prosperity and the Great Depression 1920-1936. Vol. VI. Philadelphia: Temple University Press, 1981.

Franklin, John Hope. From Slavery to Freedom. New York: Alfred A. Knopf, 1967.

Frazier, E. Franklin. Negro Youth at the Crossways. New York: Schocken Books, 1940.

Galster, George C. and Hill, Edward W. (eds.). The Metropolis in Black and White: Place, Power, and Polarization. New Brunswick: Rutgers University Press, 1992.

-----Erol Rickets. The Underclass, Causes and Responses.

Garfinkle, Herbert. When Negroes March: The March on Washington Movement. New York: Atheneum, 1969.

Gatewood, Willard. Aristocrats of Color: The Black Elite, 1880-1920. Bloomington: University of Indiana Press, 1993.

Glascow, Douglas G. The Black Underclass: Poverty, Unemployment, and Entrapment of Ghetto Youth. San Francisco: Jossey-Bass Publishers, 1980.

Glenn, Norval D. and Bonjean, Charles (eds.). Blacks in the United States. San Francisco: Chandler Publishing Company, 1969.

-----Leonard Broom and Norval D. Glenn. "The Occupation and Income of Black Americans."

Godshalk, David Fort. Veiled Visions: The 1906 Atlanta Riot and the Reshaping of American Race Relations. Chapel Hill: University of North Carolina Press, 2005.

Goldfield, David R. Black, White, and Southern: Race Relations and Southern Culture, 1940 to the Present. Baton Rouge: Louisiana State University Press, 1990.

Goldsmith, William W. and Blanely, Edward J. Separate Societies: Poverty and Inequities in U.S. Cities. Philadelphia: Temple University Press, 1992.

Goines, Kenneth W. and Mohl, Raymond A. (eds.). The New African Urban History. Thousand Oaks, CA.: Sage Publications, 1996.

-----Kenneth L. Kusmar. "African Americans in the City since World War II: From the Industrial to the Post Industrial Era.

Gregory, James M. The Southern Diaspora: How the Great Migration of Black and White Southerners Transformed America. Chapel Hill: University of North Carolina Press, 2005.

Groh, George W. The Black Migration: The Journey to Urban America. New York: Weybright and Talley, 1972.

Grossman, James R. Land of Hope: Chicago, Black Southerners, and the Great Migration. Chicago: University of Chicago Press, 1991.

Grossman, Mark. The Civil Rights Movement. Santa Barbara, CA.: ABC-CLIO, Inc., 1993.

Haley, Alex. The Autobiography of Malcolm X. New York: Ballantine Books, 1864.

Hall, Charles E. Negroes in the United States 1920-1932. New York: Arno Press and the New York Times, 1969.

Handler, Joel F. and Hasenfield, Yeheskel. Black Welfare: Ignore Poverty and Inequality. New York: Cambridge University Press, 2007.

Hansan, John E. and Morris, Robert (eds.). Welfare Reform, 1996-2000: Is There a Safety Net?. Westport, CN.: Greenwood Press, 1999.

-----Jared Bernstein. "Welfare Reform and the Low-Wage Labor Market: Employment, Wages, and Wage Policies.

Harlan, Louis R. Booker T. Washington: The Wizard of Tuskegee, 1901-1915. New York: Oxford University Press, 1983.

Henri, Florette. Black Migration: Movement North, 1900-1920. Garden City, N.J.: Anchor Books, 1996.

Henry, Michael (ed.). Race, Poverty, and Domestic Policy. New Haven: Yale University Press, 2004.

-----Douglas S. Massey. "The New Geography of Inequality in America."

-----Philip N. Glenson and Glen C. Cain. "Earnings of Black and White Youth."

Herndon, Angelo. Let Me Live. New York: Random House, Inc., 1937.

Hill, Herbert. Black Labor and the American Legal System: Race, Work, and the Law. Madison: University of Wisconsin Press, 1985.

Hill, Herbert and Jones, James E. (eds.). Race in America: The Struggle for Equality. Madison: University of Wisconsin Press, 1993.

-----Herbert Hill. "Black Workers, Organized Labor, and Title VII of the 1964 Civil Rights Act: Legislative History and Litigation Record."

Horne, Gerald. Communist Front: The Civil Rights Congress, 1946-1956. Teaneck, NJ.: Farleigh Dickerson Press, 1988.

Hurup, Elsebeth (ed.). The Lost Decade: America in the Seventies. Aarthus, Denmark: Aarthus University Press, 1996.

-----John G. Cawelti. "That's What I Like About the South: Changing Images of the South in the 1970s."

Jackson, Kenneth. The Ku Klux Klan in the City: 1915-1930. New York: Oxford University Press, 1967.

Jacobs, Jane. The Death and Life of Great American Cities. New York: Vintage Books, 1961.

Jacobson, Julius (ed.). The Negro and the American Labor Movement. Garden City, NY.:Anchor Books, 1968.

-----Sidney M. Peck. "The Economic Situation of Negro Labor."

-----Summer M. Rosen. "The CEO Era, 1935-1955."

Jaynes, Gerald David. Branches Without Roots: Genesis of the Black Working Class in the American South, 1862-1882. New York: Oxford University Press, 1989.

Jencks, Christopher and Patterson, Paul E. (eds.). The Urban Underclass. Washington, D.C.: The Brookings Institute, 1991.

-----Jenks and Patterson. "The Urban Underclass and Poverty Paradox."

-----Richard B. Freeman. "Employment od Disadvantaged Young Men."

-----Joleen Kirschenman and Kathryn M. Neckerman. "We'd Love to Hire Them But...The Meaning of Race for Employers."

Johnson, Charles S. Growing Up in the Black Belt: Negro Youth in the Rural South. New York Schocken Books, 1941.

Johnson, Kimberly. Reforming Jim Crow: Southern Politics and the State in the Age Before Brown. New York: Oxford University Press, 2010.

Jones, Jacqueline. The Dispossessed: America's Underclass From the Civil War to the Present. New York: Basic Books: 1992.

Katz, Michael, Michael B. (ed.). The "Underclass" Debate: Views from History. Princeton: Princeton University Press, 1993.

-----Harvey Kantor and Barbara Brenzel. "Urban Education and the 'Truly' Disadvantaged: The Historical Roots of Contemporary Crisis, 1945-1990."

Katzman, Before the Ghetto: Black Detroit in the Nineteenth Century. Urbana: University of Illinois Press, 1975.

Kelly, D.G. Robin. Yo' Mamma's Dysfunktional: Fighting the Cultural Wars in Urban America. Boston: Beacon Press, 1998.

Kelly, D.G. Robin and Lewis, Earl (eds.). A History of African Americans Since 1880. New York: Oxford University Press, 2000.

-----To Make Our World Anew: A History of African Americans Since 1880. Vol. II. New York: Oxford University Press, 2005.

Kennedy, Randall. Sellout: The Politics of Racial Betrayal. New York: Vintage Books, 2008.

Knowles, Louis L. and Prewitt, Kenneth (eds.). Institutional Racism in America. Englewood, N.J.: PRENTICE-Hall Inc., p. 1969.

Kolko, Gabriel. Wealth and Power in America: An Analysis of Social Class and On Income Distribution. New York: Praeger Publishers, 1964.

Kyriakoudes, Louis M. The Social Origins of the Urban South: Race, Gender, and Migration in Nashville and Middle Tennessee, 1890-1930. Chapel Hill: University of North Carolina Press, 2003.

Lemann, Nicholas. The Promised Land: The Great Migration and How It Changed America. New York: Alfred A. Knopf, 1991.

Lerman, Robert I. and Ooms, Theodore (ed.). Young Unwed Farmers. Philadelphia: Temple University Press, 1993.

-----"Sex Codes and Family Life Among Poor Inner City Youths."

Levenstein, Lisa. A Movement Without Marches: African American Women and the Politics of Poverty in Post-War Philadelphia. Chapel Hill: University of North Carolina Press, 2009.

Lewis, David Levering. W. E. B. Du Bois: Biography of a Race, 1968-1919. New York: Henry Holt and Company, 1993.

Lewis, George. The White South and the Red Menace: Segregationists, Anticommunism, and Massive Resistance, 1945-1965. Gainesville: University of Florida Press, 2004.

Lewis, Michael. The Culture of Inequality. Amherst: The University of Massachusetts, 1978.

Litwak, Leon F. Trouble in Mind: Black Southerners in the Age of Jim Crow. New York: Alfred A. Knopf, 1998.

Locke, Alain (ed.). The New Negro. New York: Atheneum, 1969.

Logan, Rayford W. The Betrayal of the Negro: From Rutherford B. Hayes to Woodrow Wilson. Toronto, Canada: The Macmillan Company, 1969.

Lutz, Tom and Ashton, Susanna (eds.). These "Colored" United States: African American Essays Since the 1920s. New Brunswick, N.J.: Rutgers University Press, 1996.

Mingione, Enzo. Urban Poverty and the Underclass. Cambridge, MA.: Blackwell Publishers, Inc., 1996.

-----Loic J. D. Wacquant. "Red Belt Black Belt: Racial Division, Class Inequality, and the State of the French Urban Periphery and the American Ghetto."

Mingione, Enzo and Marcuse, Peter (eds,). Cambridge MA.: Blackwell Press Publishers, 1996.

-----"Space and Race In the Post-Fordist City."

Majors, Richard and Billson, Janet Mancini. Cool Pose: The Dilemma of Black Manhood in America. Touchstone Books, 1993.

Mangum, Garth C. and Seninger, Stephan. Coming of Age in the Ghetto: A Dilemma of Youth Unemployment. Baltimore: The Johns Hopkins Press, 1978.

Marable, Manny. Race, Reform. And Rebellion. Jackson: University of Mississippi Press, 1991.

Mc Whirter, Cameron. Red Summer: The Summer of 1919 and the wakening of Black America. New York: Henry Holt and Company, 2011.

Meier, August and Rudwick, Elliott. From Plantation to Ghetto. New York: Hill and Wang, 1970.

Mishel, Lawrence and Simon, Jacqueline. The State of Working America. Washington, D. C.: Economic Policy Institute, 1988.

Muhammad, Khalil Gibran. The Condemnation of Blackness: Race, Crime, and the Making of Urban America. Cambridge, MA.: Harvard University Press, 2010.

Mydal, Gunnar. An American Dilemma. Vols. Vols. I and II. New York: McGraw-Hill Book Company, 1964.

Nelson, H. Viscount (Berky). The Rise and Fall of Modern Black Leadership: Chronicle of a Twentieth Century Tragedy. Lanham, MD.; University Press of America, Inc., 2003.

Newby, I. A. The South: A History. New York: Holt, Rinehart, and Winston, 1978.

Ogg, Alex. The Hip Hop Years. New York: Macmillan Publishers, 1999.

Ogletree, Charles J. Jr. All Deliberate Speed: Reflections on the First Half Century of Brown v. Board of Education. New York: W.W. Norton and Company, 2004.

Ovington, Mary White. Half A Man: The Status of the Negro in New York. New York: Hill and Wang, 1969.

Parris, Guichard and Brooks, Lester. Blacks in the City: A History of the National Urban League, 1910-1940. Boston: Little Brown and Company, 1971.

Phillips, Kevin. Wealth and Democracy: A Political History of the American Rich. New York: Broadway Books, 2002.

Pinar, William F. The Gender of Racial Politics and Violence in America: Lynching, Prison, Rape, and the Crisis of Masculinity. New York: Peter Lang, 2001.

Pinckney, Alphonso. Black Americans. Englewood Cliffs, NJ.: Prentice-Hall, 1975.

Powdermaker, Hortense. After Freedom: A Cultural Study of the Deep South. New York: Atheneum, 1968.

Quillian, Lincoln. "The Decline of Male Employment in Low-Income Black Neighborhoods, 1950-1990: Space and Industrial Restoration in an Urban Employment Crisis." Discussion Paper. ERIC, 2002.

Record, Wilson. The Negro and the Communist Party. New York> Atheneum, 1971.

Sasser, Charles W. Patton's Panthers: The Afro-American 761st Tank Battalion in World War II. New York: Pocket Books, 2005.

Rainwater, Lee. Behind Ghetto Walls. Chicago: Aldine Atherton, Inc., 1970.

Rainwater, Lee (ed.) Soul. Cambridge, MA.: Trans-action Books, Aldine, 1970.

Report of the National Advisory Commission on Civil Disorders [AKA Kerner Commission Report]. New York: The New York Times Company, 1968.

Rose, Tricia. Black Noise: Rap Music and Black Culture in Contemporary America. Hanover, NH.: Wesleyan University Press and the University Press of New England, 1994.

Rowan, Carl T. South of Freedom. New York: Alfred A. Knopf, 1952.

Rubin, Lillian Breslow. Worlds of Pain: Life in the Working-Class Family. New York: Basic Books, 1976.

Samad, Anthony Asadullah. 50 Years After Brown: The State of Black Equality in America. Los Angeles: Kabili Press, 2005.

Sandfur, Gary D. and Tienda, Marta (eds.). Divided Loyalties: Minorities, Poverty, and Social Policies. New York: Plenum Press, 1988.

-----Charles Hershman. "Minorities in the Labor Market: Cynical Patterns and Secular Trends in Joblessness."

-----James P. Smith. "Poverty and the Family."

Scheiner, Seth M. Negro Mecca: A History of the Negro in New York, 1865-1920. New York: New York University Press, 1965.

Schnieder, Eric. Vampires, Dragons, and Egyptian Kings: Youth Gangs in Postwar New York. Princeton: Princeton University Press, 1999.

Schulman, Bruce J. The Seventies: The Great Shift in American Culture, Society, and Politics. New York: De Capo Press, 2001.

Span, Christopher M. From Cotton Field to School House: African American Education in Mississippi, 1862-1875. Chapel: University of North Carolina Press, 2009.

Scott, Emmett J. American Negro in the World War. New York: Arno Press and the New York Times, 1969.

Sexton, Patricia Cayo. Education and Income: Inequalities of Opportunity in Our Public Schools. New York: Viking Press, 1961.

Silverstein, Barry and Krate, Ronald. Children of the Dark Ghetto. New York: Praeger Press Publishers, 1975.

Simpson, Colton. Inside the Crips: Life Inside L.A's Most Notorious Gang. New York: St. Martin's Press, 2005.

Slessarev, Helene. The Betrayal of the Urban Poor. Philadelphia: Temple University Press, 1997.

Spear, Allen H. Black Chicago: The Making of a Negro Ghetto, 1890-1920. Chicago: University of Chicago Press, 1967.

Springer, David W. and Roberts, Albert R. Introduction and Overview of Juvenile Justice. Jones and Bartlett Publishers, circa 2008-2009.

Sternsher, Bernard (ed.). The Negro in Depression and War: Prelude to Revolution, 1930-1945. Chicago: Quadrangle Books, 1969.

-----Richard Dalfiume. "The Forgotten Years of the Negro Revolution."

Street, Paul L. Racial Oppression in the Global Metropolis: A Living Black Chicago History. Lanham, MD.: Roman and Littlefield Publishers, Inc., 2007.

Stricker, Frank. Why America Lost the War on Poverty—And How to Win It. Chapel Hill: University of North Carolina Press, 2007.

Sugrue, Thomas. Sweet Land of Liberty: The Forgotten Struggle for Civil Rights in the North. New York: Random House, 2008.

Trotter, Joe William Jr. River Jordan: African American Urban Life in the Ohio Valley. Lexington: University of Kentucky Press, 1998.

Tauber, Karl E. and Alma F. Negroes in Cities: Residential Segregation and Neighborhood Change. Chicago: Aldine Publishing, 1965.

Tuttle, William M. Race Riot: Chicago in the Red Scare of 1919. Urbana-Champagne: University of Illinois Press, 1970.

Van De Burg, William L. Hoodlums: Black Villains and Social Bandits in American Life. Chicago: University of Chicago Press, 2004.

Wade, Richard C. Slavery in the Cities: The South 1820-1860. New York: Oxford University Press, 1964.

Warner, W. Lloyd; Junker, Buford; and Adams, Walter A. Color and Human Nature. Washington, D. C.: The American on Education, 1941.

Washington, Forrester B. Negro Survey of Pennsylvania. Harrisburg: Department of Welfare, 1927.

Weaver, Robert C. Negro Labor: A National Problem. New York: Harcourt Brace, 1946.

-----The Negro Ghetto. New York: Russell and Russell, 1948.

Weiss, Nancy J. The National Urban League: 1910-1940. New York: Oxford University Press, 1974.

Wilkerson, Isabel. The Warmth of Other Suns: The Epic Story of America's Great Migration. New York: Vintage Books, 2010.

Wilson, William Julius. The Truly Disadvantaged: The Inner City, The Underclass, and Public Policy. Chicago: University of Chicago Press, 1987.

-----When Work Disappears: The World of the New Urban Poor. New York: Alfred A. Knopf, 1996.

Wolters, Raymond. Negroes and the Great Depression: The Problem of Economic Recovery. Westport, CN.: Greenwood Publishing Company, 1970.

-----The Burden of Brown: Thirty Years of School Desegregation. Knoxville: University of Tennessee Press, 1983.

Woods, Jeff. Black Struggle Red Scare: Segregation and Anticommunism in the South, 1948-1968. Baton Rouge: Louisiana State University Press, 2004.

Woodson, Carter G. The Mis-Education of the Negro. Trenton, NJ.: Africa World Press, 1998.

Woodward, C. Vann. Origins of the New South, 1877-1913. Baton Rouge: Louisiana State University Press, 1951.

-----The Strange Career of Jim Crow. New York: Oxford University Press, 1966.

Yong, Alfred A. Jr. The Minds of Marginalized Black Men: Making Sense of Mobility, Opportunity, and Future Life Changes. Princeton: Princeton University Press, 2004.

Zieger, Robert H. For Jobs and Freedom: Race and Labor in American Since 1865. Lexington: University of Kentucky Press, 2007.

Zinn, Howard. The Twentieth Century: A People's History. New York: Harper Perennial, 2003.

PRIMARY SOURCES

Journals

A. Cevedo-Garcia, Delores. "Residential Segregation and the Epidemiology of Infectious Disease." Social Science and Medicine, Vol. 451, Issue 8, 1143-1161.

Atkyns, Glenn C. "Trends I the Retention of Married and Pregnant Students in American Public Schools." Psychology of Education, Vol. 41, No. 1, 57-65.

Baker, Ray Stannard. "The Negro Goes North." World's Work, Vol. 34, 1917.

Bowman, Shanthy A. and Vinyard, Bryan T. "Fast Food Consumption of U. S. Adults: Impact on Energy and Nutrient Intakes and Overweight Status." Journal of the American College of Nutrition. April 2004.

Chambers, Lorraine. "If She Were Not Dark." Black Opals, Vol. 1, No. 2.

Conason, Joe and Newfield, Jack.

-----"A Budget for Bakers and Arsonists." Village Voice 1, 15-19.

-----"The Men Are Burning New York."13.

Cowling, Linda L. "California Food Grade: Health and Dietary Issues Affecting African Americans." California Food Guide, September, 2006, 2-3.

Cummins, Steven and Macintyre, Sally. "Food Environments and Obesity—Neighborhood or Nation." International Journal of Epidemiology. Vol. 35, Issue 1, 100-104.

"Dynastic and Statistical Manual of Mental Disorders." American Psychiatric Association, Washington D.C., 1994.

Gamble, Vanessa Northington. "'There Wasn't a Lot of Comfort in Those Days:' African Americans, Public Health, and the 1918 Influenza Epidemic." Public Health, Vol. 125, 2010.

Gibson, Robert A. "The Negro Holocaust: Lynching and Race Riots in the United States, 1880-1950." Yale-New Haven Institute, 2010.

Gidge, Paul A. and Rock, Howard B. "Sweep O Sweep O: African American Chimney Sweeps and Citizenship in the New Nation." William and Mary Quarterly, Vol. 51, No. 3, 507-508.

Hill, Herbert. "Race, Ethnicity, and Organized Labor: Opposition to Affirmative Action." New Policies, 1987, 2.

La Veist, Thomas A. "Health Disparities and the Minority-Majority." Johns Hopkins, Bloomberg School of Public Health, 2000, 53.

Mani, Anandi; Mullainathan, Sendhil; Shafir, Eldar; and Zhao, Jiaying. "Poverty Impedes Cognitive Function." Science, Vol. 341, No. 6149, 976-980.

Mc Callan, Jessica. "Prenuptial depression: why some pregnant women feel despair." The Guardian, February 10, 2012.

McNair, Lily O. and Prather, Cynthia M. "Africa American Women and AIDS: Factors Influencing Risks and Reaction to the HIV Disease." Journal of Black Psychology, Vol. 30, No. 1, 106-108.

Merriam, George S. The Negro and the Nation: A History of American Slavery and Enfranchisement. Charles A. Ellwood book review. The American Journal of Sociology, Vol. XII, 275.

Mittal, Anuradha. "The Last Plantation." Backgrounder, Winter, 2000, 1-13.

Nelson, H. Viscount. "Philadelphia's Thirtieth Ward, 1940-1960." Pennsylvania Heritage Magazine, Vol. V, No.2.

Norrell, Robert J. "Caste in Steel: Jim Crow Careers in Birmingham, Alabama." The Journal of American History. Vol. 73, No. 3.

Phillips, Julie A. "White, Black and Latino Homicide Rates: Why the Difference?" Social Problems, Vol. 49, No3, 359.

Quillian, Lincoln. "The Decline in Male Employment in Low-income Black Neighborhoods, 1950-1990. Social Science Research. Vol. 32, 225-237.

Tolnay, Stewart E. and Eichenlaub, Suzanne C. "Inequality in the West: Racial and Ethnic Variation in Occupational Status and Returns to Education, 1940-2000." Social Science History, Vol. 31, No.4, 487-488.

Work, Monroe N. "Criminality in the South." Annals of the American Academy of Political and Social Sciences. Vol. XLIX, No. 138, 74.

Crisis Magazine

-----"The A. F. of L." Vol. 40, No. 12, 292.

-----"The Flood , the Red Cross, and the National Guard." Vol. 35, No. 2, 41-43.

-----"The Flood, the Red Cross, and the National Guard." Vol. 35, No. 3, 80-81.

-----"The Lynching Industry." Vol. 19, No. 4., 183-185.

-----Joiner, Lotie L. "The State of African American Health." Vol. 111, Series 6, 19.

Arnessa Howell, "Caner: A Lurking Adversary."
Kendra Lee, "Up in Smoke: Blacks and Tobacco Use."
Yanick Rice Lamb, "Obesity: Killing Us a Pound At a Time."
Ervin Dyer, "The New Face of AIDS, Young, Black, and Female."
Walls, Barbranda, Lumpkins. "Heart Disease: Number 1 Cause of Death."

Opportunity Magazine

-----Hill, T. Arnold. "Open Letter to Mr. William Green, President, American Federation of Labor." February, 1930, 56-57.

-----White, P. J. Jr. "An Open Letter to Mr. Green of the A . F. of L." November, 1934, 350.

Newspapers

The New York Times

July 25, 1981
June 30, 1986
February 6, 2002

The Philadelphia Independent

September 23, 1936

The Philadelphia Tribune

February 8, 1919
May 3, 1919
May 14, 1930
December 28, 1933
March 5, 1936
October 22, 1936

Dissertations

Nelson, H. Viscount, "Race and Class Consciousness of Philadelphia Negroes With Special Emphasis Between the Years 1927-1940." University of Pennsylvania, 1969.

Sides, Josh A. "Working Away: African American Migration and the Community in Los Angeles From the Great Depression to 1954." University of California, Los Angeles, 1999.

Miscellaneous

Annual Report of the Board of Public Education. Philadelphia, 1930.

Bloomberg, Leonard. "Migration: A Pilot Study of Recent Negro Migrants to Philadelphia." Urban League of Philadelphia, 1958.

Committee for the Congested Production Areas, Observations on the Sample Census in the Congested Production Areas. 1944, K. Series, CA-2, No. 1-10.

Daily Mail Reporter. "The Collapse of Family Life: Most Children in the U.S. Born Out of Wedlock. MailOnline, February 18, 2012.

Harris, Edith Patiste. "An Assessment of Nutritional Education Needs of Low Income Black Americans By Comparison Food Practices and Diet Related Problems With the Federal Government's Dietary Guidelines." Howard University, 1984, 52.

HARYOU Project. "Youth in the Ghetto: A Study of the Consequences of Powerlessness and a Blueprint for Change." Harlem Youth Opportunities Unlimited, Inc., December, 1963.

Lynchings: By Year and Race. Tuskegee Archives. Law2umkc.edu/Faculty/projects/ftrails/ship/lynchingyear.html.

Moynihan, Daniel Patrick. "The Negro Family: The Case for National Action." U.A. Department of Labor: Office of Policy Planning and Research, March, 1965.

Savelli, Lou. "National Gang History." Vice President of the East Coast Gang Investigation Association.

Tucker, Daniel Oliver. "Graffiti, Art, and Crime." Edu/Berckley.edu/studentpages/cflores/historyofgraffiti.html.

Turley, Jonathan. "Republicans Discover Poor People." March 24, 2013.

Ventura, Stephanie J. to Bachrach, Christine A. "Non Martial Child Bearing in the United States, 1949-1999. National Vital Statistics Reports, October 18, 2000.

UCLA Psychologists. "Harsh Family Environment May Adversely Affect Brain's Response to Threat." March 13, 2006.

Zwillich, Todd. "82 Million in U.S. Without Health Insurance." WdbMD, June 16, 2004.

Index

A

Addams, Jane, 9
ADHD (Attention deficit hyperactivity disorder), 7, 425
AFDC (Aid to Families with Dependent Children), 327, 349, 388, 390
AFL (American Federation of Labor), 67–68, 172–75, 205, 219, 238
AIDS (acquired immune deficiency syndrome), 367, 395, 401, 409–10
Alexander, Michelle, 366
Allen, Henry Justin, 129
America in Black and White (Thernstrom and Thernstrom), 10
American citizenship, 69, 118–19
American dream, 21, 413
American Negro, The (Thomas), 61

B

Baker, Houston A. Jr., 420
Baker, Ray Stannard, 61, 66, 71, 105
black America, 10, 268
Black Belt, 82, 121, 164, 168, 190
black bourgeoisie, 3, 5, 10–11, 64–65, 89, 112, 139–40, 153, 187, 221, 227, 239–40, 242–43, 265, 314–15
black churches, 83, 109–10, 145–46, 387
Black Codes, 26
black conservatives, 349–50
black crime, 61, 63, 138, 212
black criminology, 45, 47
black elite, 10–11, 64, 70, 79, 88
black employment, 111, 132, 202, 281
black enterprisers, 63, 114, 117
black families, 16, 80, 169, 171, 281, 292, 294–95, 298, 326–27, 369
black farmers, 31, 43, 103, 158, 165–66, 404
black females, 17, 82–83, 87, 98, 104–5, 111, 132, 169, 216, 224–25, 243, 259, 292–94, 360, 406
black ghettos, 121, 140–41, 207, 209, 230, 267, 286–87, 301
black indigents, 5, 34, 54, 72–73, 88–89, 122, 134–35, 233, 274, 302–3, 311–13, 318, 322, 351, 414–15
black intellectuals, 77, 155, 171, 192
black laborers, 27, 32–33, 85, 91, 104, 109, 130, 141, 146, 164, 167, 223
black leaders, 58, 76, 108–9, 151, 171–73, 187, 191–92, 195–96, 201, 203, 239, 254, 271, 307, 410–11

black life, 78, 126–27, 153, 155, 168
black males, 34, 131, 142, 273, 285, 292, 305, 313, 333, 360–61, 395
black matriarchy, 142, 292
black migrants, 79, 105–6, 114–15, 117, 136, 144, 147, 210, 212
black mothers, 297, 327, 407
Black North, The (Du Bois), 81
black population, 33, 50, 120, 131, 164, 206, 208, 260, 315, 356, 375, 390
black poverty, 8, 57, 169, 198, 274–76, 353, 364, 379, 415
Black Power, 304
black schools, 41–42, 75, 93, 95, 179, 182, 214, 255
black sharecroppers, 28–29, 31, 166, 169
black slums, 236, 307, 322, 387, 406
black Southerners, 37, 42, 49, 51, 56, 64, 97–99, 120, 135, 197, 199, 207, 256, 268, 409–10
Black Star Line, 150–51
black students, 94, 96, 254–60, 262, 299, 421
black success, 62–63, 419
black teachers, 75, 158, 177, 188
black tenants, 29–30, 100, 122, 133, 166, 198
black unemployment, 203, 224, 274, 296, 306, 393
Booker, Joseph A., 129
Bragg, Shirley, 72

C

Carnegie, Andrew, 84
CETA (Comprehensive Employment and Training Act), 311, 341, 346
Chicago Tribune, 120
CIO (Congress of Industrial Organization), 172, 206, 219, 238–39
Clinton, Bill, 12, 384–88, 390–91, 399, 410–11
Coolidge, Calvin, 126
Cosby, Bill, 4–6, 420
Cox, J. M., 129
CPUSA (Communist Party of the United States of America), 190–91, 196, 221–23, 228, 231
CRC (Civil Rights Congress), 223
culture
    black, 5, 153, 155, 304, 309, 413
    street, 112, 264, 368

D

Delaney, Martin, 29–30
Douglass, Frederick, 11, 54
Du Bois, W. E. B., 10–11, 49, 54, 57, 60–62, 66–67, 76, 79–81, 88–89, 107, 113, 149, 151–52, 310
Dyson, Eric Michel, 4–6, 420

E

ebonics, 13
education
    Negro, 41, 76
    public, 34, 39, 41, 46–47, 76, 93–94, 418
EEOC (Equal Employment Opportunity Commission), 352
Emlen, John, 83